"But what we glimpsed of the 'Eigerwand' looked unfriendly enough, maybe even impossible. Impossible?"

Hans Lauper, *Der Eiger von Norden,* 1932

(above) Posing for their success. The five Swiss climbers after their first winter ascent of the Japanese Direttissima in 1970.

Page 4: Triumph and tragedy in one frame. The view down the Exit Cracks, first climbed by Anderl Heckmair in 1938. Next to the two climbers is the ledge from which Claudio Corti was hauled to safety during a dramatic rescue bid in 1957. Page 5: There was no such rescue in 1935 for Karl Mehringer and Max Sedlmayr. Here, their Munich companions desperately scan the dangerous Wall through a telescope.

EIGER

The Vertical Arena

Edited by Daniel Anker

Contributors
Rainer Amstädter, Daniel Anker, Daniel H. Anker,
Charles Barrington, Marco Bomio,
Walter Däpp, Anderl Heckmair, Roland Heer,
Horst Höfler, Sylvain Jouty, Ueli Kämpf, Peter Krebs,
Arnold Lunn, Yuko Maki, Patrick Moser,
Suke Okazawa, Markus Schwyn, Hannes Stähli, Freddy Widmer

Photographs
Jost von Allmen, Marco Bomio, Robert Bösch,
Bruno Cormier, Ludwig Gramminger,
Kaspar Ochsner, René Robert,
Hannes Stähli, Thomas Ulrich, Ludwig Vörg

Translator
Tim Carruthers

THE
MOUNTAINEERS

A Mountain of History

The Eiger is like no other mountain. It is easy when talking about it to amass superlatives: the most deadly, the most sinister, the one which has provoked the most controversy. The Eiger tends to inspire fear and its reputation is made up of dramas, scandals, and tragedies.

Its fame is not, strictly speaking, that of a mountain: Its first ascent was credited to an almost unknown climber, the most common route of ascent is not particularly beautiful, and the culminating point does not even reach the critical altitude of four thousand meters. Many mountains in the Alps are more deserving of an ascent than the Eiger, beginning with the neighboring Jungfrau. The fact is that the Eiger's fame exists only because of its North Face. There are larger mountain faces, ones at higher altitudes and more difficult ones, but no other face in the Alps presents such a combination of difficulty, difference in height, and altitude.

The Eigerwand possesses another characteristic which is unique in alpinism: Each stage of its main route of ascent has become steeped in history (the Hinterstoisser Traverse, the Swallow's Nest, Death Bivouac, and several others), and all encompass tragic events.

However, other faces have seen similar dramas, other summits have been just as important in alpine history. But the Eigerwand stands out for another reason: Since 1935 one climbs or dies there "live," in full view of the public. Thanks to the telescopes at Kleine Scheidegg, the Eiger is the mountain most popularized through the media and it is not by chance that so many novels and films have chosen it as a setting. The Eigerwand is the only great alpine route that nonclimbers know in detail. These peculiarities explain why we invite you to follow, along with us, the ascent of this redoubtable face, stage by stage, beginning with the first pitches and ending, as should be the case, at the summit. It will sometimes be merely a pretext to explore other aspects of this amazing mountain, beginning with the railway which pierces through to its South East Face, and considering its impact on such domains as literature, the cinema, or politics. Our work frees itself of chronology to such an extent that it evokes the first ascent of the mountain right at the very end. . . .

Thanks to the energy and patience of the man who conceived the idea, the Swiss alpine journalist Daniel Anker, and to the research of his colleagues, this book adds many little-known details and previously unpublished photographs to the history of the Eiger.

Sylvain Jouty

Summit

Mittellegi Ridge

Summit Ice Field

Corti Bivouac

Exit Cracks

Spider

Traverse of the Gods

Ramp Ice Field

Brittle Crack
Brittle Ledges

Waterfall Chimney

Ramp

Third Ice Field

Death Bivouac

Flatiron

Second Ice Field

Ice Hose

First Ice Field

Rote Fluh

Swallow's Nest

Hinterstoisser Traverse

Difficult Crack

Gallery Window

Shattered Pillar

First Pillar

Start

Contents

Entry Pitches

The problem with climbing the North Face of the Eiger is that in addition to getting up 6,000 vertical feet of crumbling limestone and black ice, one must climb over some formidable mythology. The trickiest moves on any climb are the mental ones, the psychological gymnastics that keep terror in check, and the Eiger's grim aura is intimidating enough to rattle anyone's poise....

The history of the mountain resonates with the struggles of such larger-than-life figures as Buhl, Bonatti, Messner, Rébuffat, Terray, Haston, and Harlin, not to mention Eastwood. The names of the landmarks on the face—the Hinterstoisser Traverse, the Ice Hose, the Death Bivouac, the White Spider—are household words among both active and armchair Alpinists from Tokyo to Buenos Aires; the very mention of these places is enough to make any climber's hands turn clammy. The rockfall and avalanches that rain continuously down the Nordwand are legendary. So is the heavy weather: Even when the skies over the rest of Europe are cloudless, violent storms brew over the Eiger, like those dark clouds that hover eternally above Transylvanian castles in vampire movies.

Jon Krakauer, *Eiger Dreams*, 1990.
Eigerwand attempt in 1984.

(facing page) Two heavily laden climbers head up the firn slopes below the foot of the wall to the start of the route. The grey-black wall—with the lighter patch of rock of the Rote Fluh—rises menacingly above them.

Fascination with the Eigerwand

(above) Austrians Heinrich Harrer and Fritz Kasparek and Germans Anderl Heckmair and Ludwig Vörg (left to right) on 24 July 1938 after the first ascent of the North Face of the Eiger.

(facing page) The Wall of Walls rises like a mighty colossus above Kleine Scheidegg, where the tourist industry has regularly set up camp since the eighteenth century.

No mountain in the world has met with quite the same lively popular response as the Eiger, which at 3970 meters is the eleventh highest peak in the Bernese Alps. No single climb has provoked such a furor across such a broad spectrum of public opinion as the first ascent of the Eigerwand, accomplished in 1938 after several brave struggles. Is it not significant that each feature of the classic '38 Route up the North Face has been granted its own name? No other route is so well known in the most intimate detail by so many people who will never climb it themselves. Sylvain Jouty attempts to analyze why this should be, and why the Germans labeled this once-deadly climb as "the last great problem," while the English and Swiss dismissed it as an "imbecile variant."

Never has a mountain face held such importance for so many people: all those who have done it; all those who want to do it; all those who have not yet already done it; all those who will never do it, and know they will never do it, yet still dream about it; all those who dream about it from the comfort of their sofas; all those for whom the Eiger is the showpiece example of Alpine mountaineering that it ought not to be; all those mountain walkers who understand that they are undertaking a gentler form of mountain sport and that the Eiger represents (or represented) a completely different, more extreme form; all those for whom mountaineering is not an adventure but a spectacle that one attends—a beautiful piece of theater moreover, and full of grand emotions. All of these people and more know the Eigerwand. Sometimes they know it so well that they feel they have almost climbed it or they no longer feel the need to climb it.

Yet the great days of the Eiger are now long gone. Nowadays there are too many routes on the North Face for each of them to be of any interest to the public at large. The climbers, too, no longer have the same relationship with the Eiger as they did twenty years ago. For a young, top-notch alpinist, the ascent of the Eiger by the classic Heckmair Route is nothing more than a great climb among many other great climbs. In spite of all this, the Eigerwand continues to fascinate more than any other mountain face.

Anderl Heckmair, Ludwig Vörg, Heinrich Harrer, and Fritz Kasparek

made the first successful ascent of this 1800-meter face over four days, from 21 to 24 July 1938. Prior to this, eight people had lost their lives attempting to climb the Wall, infamous for its stonefall and sudden bouts of dreadful weather, and since then many more have died, either on the climb itself or while descending; all in all, the fatalities total some fifty—a dangerous wall.

The Heckmair Route was, and still is, repeated very frequently, and twenty-two more routes have been added to the Wall without detracting in any way from the dangerous character of the Face or, indeed, from the deep fascination that it holds for climbers.

For the Eiger is, above all, not a summit but a North Face—the Eigerwand.

July 1936. Edi Rainer lies broken and battered on the rocks at the foot of the Wall. His three rope mates did not escape any easier. Since then the talk has been of the Mordwand, the "Wall of Death." The public shudders at the thought and looks on, fascinated.

The best proof of this is the fact that the history of the mountain seems to begin in 1932, with the conquest of its North East Face (the Lauper Route). Not many know that the summit itself was reached in 1858 by the occasional climber Charles Barrington, an Irishman who thereafter seemed to prefer placing bets on racehorses to placing his boots on mountain summits. Similarly, it is not common knowledge that Yuko Maki (the first "real" Japanese Alpinist) climbed the Mittellegi Ridge in 1921.

Maki was later to lead the first successful expedition to Manaslu, in 1956.

The Eiger as an Illustrative Example of the Times

The history of the Eigerwand illustrates fairly well the ambiguity of the relationship between mountaineers and the rest of society. Since 1934, when the first attempts on the North Face were made, the Eiger has acted as a kind of catalyst, bringing to light the nature of these relationships. The same holds true today. Events played out on the stage of the Eiger always have the potential to create uproar and the mountain has certainly not stopped making a name for itself. The community of climbers, apart from differences between various schools of thought, is normally pretty much united. Arguments, generally of a technical nature, are resolved *en famille*. In the case of the Eiger, however, a sort of myopia struck a part of the western climbing world, which took up, sometimes with naïve uninhibitedness, the most stupid accusations of the popular press. Only one other alpine event has had a comparable impact: the dramatic first ascent of the Matterhorn in 1865. In both cases, not only the climbing world was involved, but also the press, the law, and even the state were drawn in. Time and circumstances are in no way alike, but the two events—over and above the equal importance accorded to them in the history of Alpine mountaineering—have served to reveal the ties and tensions that at the same time unite and separate the little world of mountaineering from the rest of society. It was on the Eiger that the situation became clearest. Nationalism, politics, propaganda, money, competition, regimentation, the state—all these elements, about which mountaineering normally wishes to know nothing at all, were mobilized in order to discredit the hard-won first ascent of the North Face of the Eiger. The mountain, that is to say the Wall, is no longer as surrounded by scandal as it was between 1935 and 1938. At that time, mountaineers of every nation, with the help of the press, gave a highly dissonant concert. To give an idea of the heat of the debate, let it suffice to quote Colonel Strutt, president of the Alpine Club: "The North Face of the Eiger remains an obsession for the mentally disturbed of almost every country. The one who makes the first successful attempt will be able to be sure he has accomplished the most imbecile variant since the beginnings of alpinism."

The Eiger as a Stage

Since then the "imbecile variant" on the North Face of the Eiger has enjoyed great success, as we well know. But it is easy to be ironical. It would be better to try to understand. First of all, why this scandal on the Eiger and not elsewhere? After all, many other routes and other mountains in the Alps have known equally tragic episodes; many equally difficult climbs were made during the same period and were climbed without such attendant publicity. One could try to explain the "success" of the Eiger by its physical characteristics, its great height, or its specific difficulties. Is it not said locally that it is "the highest wall in the Alps" (which is, however, not true)? But that might perhaps merely allow one to understand the interest of the mountaineer, not that of the general public. No, the truth is a different one: The Eiger is a theater.

There is a stage (the North Face), the actors (rescue teams and climbers), an auditorium (Kleine Scheidegg) from where the public gazes at the action through telescopes, and even wings, stage exits, and entrances (the Normal Route, the Mittellegi Ridge, and especially the two openings at the very heart of the Wall, the windows of the Jungfrau Railway). So much for the locations themselves. But as in any real theater, the spectacle only acquires great significance in proportion to the way the media reports and exaggerates it to the public at large. Indeed, there is perhaps no other mountain, and even more likely no other mountain face, in

the world which has been the object of so many articles in so many publications. The bibliography of the Eiger, and in particular of the North Face, comprises more than six closely printed pages and includes no fewer than thirty-four literary works (novels, etc.).

Right from the start, the Eiger had a role to play. But even before climbers became aware of the existence of the Eigerwand, the area—or to be more

exact Kleine Scheidegg—had already been transformed into a theater. Kleine Scheidegg itself had always been an outstanding place for the popularization of the mountains, from the first tourist trip in 1771, when it was crossed on foot by the Englishman Norton Nichols, the philosopher and later Bernese provincial governor Karl Viktor von Bonstetten, and the Bernese parish priest Jakob Samuel Wyttenbach, author of the first tourist guide to the Bernese Oberland (1777). In the course of the nineteenth century it gradually became an obligatory stop on the "Tour de Suisse" that a large number of the great men of the time undertook. So much so that in 1884, avalanches were started for the spectators—for a set price and with the aid of a cannon! The trip quickly became a classic, but seemed still to have lost nothing of its fearful appeal; here is what one traveler noted in 1882:

In the Hotel Bellevue at Kleine Scheidegg the walls are hung with the framed portraits of the first ascentionists. For many decades the hotel was the focal point of events on the Face. Climbers, journalists, and tourists came and went in a continuous stream, binoculars in their hands.

(right) Without the press, the North Face and its climbers would play no more than a supporting role. But because it is so easy to reserve a comfortable seat for the Alpine performances on the Eiger, the publicity bandwagon starts rolling. The more hellish the struggle, the greater the crowds around the telescopes, and the more famous the climbers—whether they want to be or not. "We were pressed back against the wall by the mob, and the drumming beat of the questions was worse than that of the stonefall on the Eiger," wrote Czech alpinist Radovan Kuchař in 1961 about the reception he received from the journalists.

(below) In the argot of 1970s Swiss schoolchildren "You got a kiosk on the Eigerwand?" meant roughly "Are you crazy?" The 1961 cartoon took this loaded question as its theme.

"I was several times a hair's breadth away from falling into the most fearsome precipices." It is during the same period that the painter Maximilien de Meuron committed to canvas those fearsome precipices of the North Wall, in his picture "le Grand Eiger" (1825).

The most important stage of this "prehistory" of the Eiger was the construction, at the beginning of the century, of the Jungfrau Railway. Thanks to this, Kleine Scheidegg became easily accessible. Moreover, the railway continued into a tunnel bored into the very mass of the Eiger and equipped with openings hacked out of the rock of the North Face. This moved mountaineer Walter Larden to comment in 1910: "Not only Alpinists, but also travelers of good taste, will certainly find that this railway is a profanation of nature: rather like a merry-go-round in Westminster Abbey." He could not foresee, however, the "circus" that would later be performed on and around the Eiger . . . .

The Eiger as a Spectacle

In the strict sense of the word, a theater is nothing more than the provision of the favorable mechanism required for a performance. Each ascent is thus a performance, to a greater or lesser extent; it would be naïve to deny this. The climber always derives a certain pleasure from recounting his exploits (hence the superabundance of alpine literature). This phenomenon is, to a certain extent, part of the internal economics of the mountaineer. On the Eiger, however, the phenomenon has a completely different scale and meaning, not least because the performance has a great effect on the rest of society. Here, for the first time, every ascent, every attempt, every drama which unfolds on the Eigerwand has been able to be followed "live" by a very wide public. Is this not the reason why television companies, with all their attendant technol-

ogy, descend on the Eiger in order to deliver to their millions of armchair viewers some of the fear and fascination of a North Face ascent? And the public feels itself so involved in the ascent as to produce effects that would be unthinkable elsewhere. These conditions can even deeply influence the nature of the ascent, without the climbers always being aware of it. If each route is normally a personal and incommunicable adventure, here on the Eiger it becomes something else: The portrayal of the ascent has more importance than the ascent itself. Herein lies the ambiguity of this singular Face: The climbers believe they are climbing a mountain which is more prestigious, more difficult, or more interesting than any other, while in reality, climbing on the Eiger changes its very nature and becomes a spectacle. The climber thus exposes himself, like any actor, to the critics.

The Eiger in the Limelight

The consequences of Eiger climbs having the characteristics of a stage performance can be seen first and foremost in the incomparable fame of the Wall. One might object that this Face is the only one that has enjoyed such a dramatic history. Apart from the

fact that this objection is not true (consider, for example, Nanga Parbat, a mountain in which no one shows any interest, other than the climbers), it also fails to recognize that history only exists when it is retold and that the dissemination of history is dependent upon the power of the media that broadcast it.

As a result of its function as a stage, no other mountain in the world has known so many theatrical brushes with the law so early in its history. Let us recall that, in 1959, the Eigerwand was the object of a libel action: Two Swiss Alpinists took proceedings against two other climbers for defamation of character, these latter having expressed doubts about the veracity of the formers' ascent of the Face. Heckmair, in fact, was appointed an expert witness by the court. Or, can one imagine any other high alpine face to which access might be forbidden by a government? That is, however, exactly what happened on the Eiger. A ban issued in July 1936 by the Conseil d'Etat of Bern was lifted again in November, of course, after climbers had opposed it and some lawyers had cast doubts on its legality. All were in agreement in thinking that such a measure would have been absolutely useless in denying climbers access to the Face. If there is a single mountain that illustrates as clearly as does the Eiger and its North Face the inherent dichotomy that exists in the relationship between mountaineering and the rest of society, it is this unique theatrical device that is the prime example. This vertical stage relegated to the background what is normally the very essence of mountaineering—the ascent itself—and at the same time dragged the secondary effects of the performance into the limelight, distorting them to an absurd level.

The Eiger Divides Nations

It was this theater that was the reason why the manifest lack of understanding shown before the Second World War by the western mountaineering world toward German mountaineers crystalized on the Eigerwand. The German climber became the symbol of a

(left) A snowboarder catches big air, alpine-style. For him the big black Wall behind is simply a backdrop for his all-important board artistry.

(following pages) The cows are not bothered about the climbers. But the latter can hear the bells of the former from up on the Face. So near and yet so far.

barbaric, decadent, "Nazified," or, in a word, reprehensible, kind of Alpinism.

These criticisms came above all from England and from Switzerland, which believed it their duty to defend the "holy traditions" of mountaineering, but they were also taken up in France, albeit in a slightly weaker and more moderate tone. Without doubt, the seizing of power in Germany and the Anschluss of Austria by the Nazis contributed to this attitude. A different concept of Alpinism with fairly disreputable political motivations was attributed to the Germans. But, strangely enough, the Italian climbers—they too compromised by an equally detestable regime—received far less criticism, even though their concept of Alpinism was similar in many respects to that of the Austro-Germans. Perhaps the old cultural opposition between Latin and Germanic cultures nourished the debate. Whatever the case may be, harsh words were spoken. Significantly, it is in a work of fiction which appeared during the Second World War (*Mount Analogue* by René Daumal) that one finds the best description of the perverted concept of mountaineering attributed to the prewar German climbers. "He belonged to a school of alpinism that one could—*grosso modo*—call 'the German school.' One could sum up the

method of this school in this way: One attacks the sheerest face of the mountain by the most rotten and crumbling couloir, the one most bombarded by falling stones, and one goes straight up towards the summit without looking left or right for more convenient detours. In general, one kills oneself, but one fine day, a national team arrives alive at the top."

OVO
TATSACHEN-
BERICHT No. 38

Interview mit einem Bezwinger der Eigernordwand.

Nachdem uns gesagt wurde, dass die Bezwinger der Eigernordwand Ovomaltine mitgenommen hatten, haben wir Kasparek interviewt. Er äussert sich wörtlich:

„Ich verwende Ovomaltine schon seit einigen Jahren. Ich bevorzuge sie vor allen Nahrungsmitteln, schon deshalb, weil sie äusserst leicht verdaulich ist und infolgedessen bei grossen Vorhaben nicht im geringsten belastet.

Es spricht wohl am stärksten für den grossen Wert der Ovomaltine, wenn ich erkläre, dass ich und mein Kamerad Harrer zur Bezwingung der Eigernordwand mit 13 kg. Proviant ausrückten und 10 kg. davon wieder ins Tal zurückbrachten. Von Ovomaltine ist uns allerdings kein Stäubchen übrig geblieben. Auch Ovo Sport hat sich bewährt und wurde besonders von meinem Kameraden Harrer gerne genommen."

Abschliessend bemerkt er, dass ohne Ovomaltine derartige alpinistische Hochleistungen kaum durchführbar wären.

Für ein bequemes Leben ist jede Nahrung ausreichend. Wo aber am Schreibtisch, in der Werkstatt, im Sport, Höchstleistungen erzielt werden sollen, da ist nur Ovomaltine gut genug.

In Büchsen zu Fr. 2.— und
Fr. 3.60 überall erhältlich.   Dr. A. WANDER A.G., BERN

A. 457

The Eiger Induces People to Lie

Certain climbers were accused of coming to the Eiger to obtain an Olympic medal, others of having the sole aim of being decorated by the Führer, or following an order "from on high." Finally, they were even accused of technical incompetence. As for Sedlmayr and Mehringer, people even went as far as saying that they only attempted the ascent in order to gain a role in a film! In fact, I believe that no serious Alpinist would be able to contest the exceptional performance of these two men when, in 1935, they breached the steep cliffs of the Face by forcing a direct line to a point some 700 meters below the summit, where they were caught out in bad weather and froze to death.

The real problem is not whether the accusations are based on fact; rather, it is the misconceptions of the contemporary development of Alpine mountaineering held by those who made those allegations. Whatever the foundations on which they rest their case, these accusations are merely the further development of a single idea, then accepted by a great part of the western mountaineering milieu: namely, that German Alpinists "are not normal"; that what they do is not Alpinism and therefore should not be measured in Alpine mountaineering terms. It was obviously much easier to excommunicate these climbers than to attempt to understand them. True and honest criticism has no need to be slanderous. It would, of course, be naïve to believe that the climbers' motives were not also tinged with the wish for fame or social advancement. It remains to explain where such a lack of understanding comes from.

The Eiger Causes Climbers to Become Enemies

Let us first of all establish how much Alpine mountaineering tradition differs between the Eastern and Western Alps. Up until the First World War the British climbers had been at the forefront of Alpine exploration. They were from the upper middle classes or were aristocrats—in any case, cultivated people, educated, humanists, and without money problems. They formed the intellectual elite of Great Britain. Leslie Stephen (1832–1904), for example, long-time president of the Alpine Club and first ascentionist of many Alpine summits, was a renowned critic and the father of Virginia Woolf. John Tyndall (1820–1893), mountaineer and research glaciologist, was a great scholar. This material and intellectual richness showed through in their concept of mountaineering: For them it was a matter of a very pleasant activity, certainly, but one which hardly justified the sacrifice of a life, or of a career. After the First World War, the English mountaineers still lived in this tradition: Aware of the role that their elders had played in climbing, they did not realize that the torch had passed to others. For them, the conquest of the Alps had

(right) In 1957 Claudio Corti intended to make the first Italian ascent of the North Face with his partner Stefano Longhi; after falling on the summit wall he was rescued and is seen here being looked after by rescue specialist Erich Friedli. His partner's body remained on the Face—for two further years.

(below right) Chris Bonington uses a rock piton to investigate the contents of a tin at a bivouac on the first British ascent in 1962; he "sold" the first attempt, made four weeks previously, to the *Daily Mail*.

been completed; it was time to turn toward other horizons, above all, toward the Himalayas. According to them, it was there that the future of mountaineering lay, not in the opening up of "the most imbecile variants" in the Alps. Moreover, nothing encouraged them to practice acrobatic climbing on the Continent; they had at home enough rocky walls to keep them happy in this area. The mountains were something else. Alpine mountaineering having reached its peak, "the Golden Age" of the conquest was over. The classic climbs were still of interest; the rest could only be decadence. The Austro-German climbers were breaking the mold, were "perverting the honorable traditions of Alpinism." In this matter, it is symptomatic to see the difference in treatment in the pages of the *Alpine Journal* between the ascent of the North East Face of the Eiger in 1932 ("a superb expedition") and that of the Eigerwand a few years later. There was a further reason for this irreconcilability on the part of the British: With a few notable exceptions, the German climbers had thus far concentrated their efforts in the Eastern Alps. The British suffered an acute attack of paranoia when they saw that German and Aus-

trian teams had set up camp at the foot of the Eiger—right in the heart of "their" mountains.

The Eiger Helps Climbers Achieve Recognition

The German climbers lived Alpinism in a very different way from the British. A certain exaltation of danger, of death, of the risks inherent in mountaineering, as well as a sort of morbid aestheticism, formed part of the German alpinist's tradition. The British tended more toward positivism, seeing Alpinism as a reasonable activity. The German climbers had rather the opposite tendency and considered the mountain as a total, all-encompassing experience. The work of the influential Austrian mountaineer and author Eugen Guido Lammer bears witness to this tendency. Climbing without a guide was certainly commonplace and accepted, and had been heavily influenced moreover by great names in mountaineering: Hermann von Barth, Georg Winkler, Paul Preuss, to name three of the most famous.

These differing states of mind were without doubt nourished and maintained by something much more important: The climbers in Germany did not necessarily come from the same place in the social order as in Great Britain. This is, of course, a generalization, yet the differences are obvious. The accounts of German climbs were full of

money problems, journeys by bicycle or on foot, and little material details. The German climbers were often students, sometimes laborers or, as one might say nowadays "marginals," but almost always penniless. And these men, who put so much into mountaineering, sometimes sacrificing all normal life, invested much more in the mountain than the English, for whom climbing was simply one pleasure among many. It was only natural that the Germans should have sought a certain social recognition, which the English had no need of because they had already achieved it.

Being poor, the only playground for the Germans' activities was the nearby Alps, and that is why those who attacked the last unclimbed walls of the Western Alps had no concept of going against tradition. On the contrary, they felt that they were following in the

course of history. In 1937, Vörg expressed it thus: "We young alpinists are aware that we can only contribute to the exploration of the Alps by resolving the so-called last great problems." And it is in the distance between these two expressions—"last great problem" and "imbecile variant"—that one can find the source of the polemic surrounding the Eiger.

We can be sure that if the then president of the Alpine Club, Colonel Strutt, had judged the Eigerwand to be one of the last problems of the Alps, he would not have considered the first men to make the ascent as mentally deranged! There is an oft-quoted example for this. The German attempts on Nanga Parbat were, during the same period, every bit as deadly as those on the Eiger, yet the *Alpine Journal* maintained a serious tone in its accounts of them. The reason is that Nanga Parbat

The Wall, set at an average angle of 64 degrees, is in shade; the sun only reaches a part of the Exit Cracks and the summit snowfield. On the right is the West Flank, almost free of snow, between the South Ridge and the West Ridges. View from the summit: The sharp arête of the Mittellegi Ridge (left top); below, the North East Face and its formations of ice.

was considered by the British as an interesting mountaineering problem.

The Eiger Is No Lunatic Asylum

If every climber possessed of a measure of bravery was labeled as mentally ill, the best pages in the history of Alpine mountaineering would have been written by lunatics and the majority of first ascents accomplished by madmen. The German climbers were

Suddenly, German and Austrian climbers who had previously been pushed to the sidelines of society were caught in the glare of the spotlights, signing autographs and attending public speaking engagements.

22

accused of going to the foot of the Eiger "on orders." In the case of Kurz and Hinterstoisser, in 1936, the opposite was true. As soldiers on holiday leave the two men were already up on the Face when the order arrived from their superior (who had got wind of the plan) forbidding them to make their attempt. Similarly, the suspicion that it

was only the 1936 Olympic gold medal for mountaineering that the two climbers were really after is no more serious. Let us note at this point that it was the British who had first been the guilty parties in this respect; the 1924 Prix d'alpinisme awarded by the International Olympic Committee had been bestowed upon General Bruce, who led the third expedition to Everest. Then, in 1932, the gold medal for mountaineering was given to the Schmid brothers (for the first ascent of the North Face of the Matterhorn) and to the Himalayan mountaineer Paul Bauer.

More serious is the accusation of incompetence. In actual fact, almost all the serious contenders for the first ascent were very strong climbers in the Eastern Alps and in no way beginners. But it is nonetheless true that they almost all underestimated the difficulties of the Face under ice and snow. It was less a matter of incompetence than of poor judgment of the specific problems posed by the Eigerwand. All credit was due to Vörg, Heckmair, and Matthias Rebitsch (Rebitsch had made three serious attempts with Vörg in 1937) that they proved to have better judgment.

The Eiger Is (Not) Adorned with a Swastika

Let us move on to the central point. It is true that the first ascent of the Eigerwand was widely exploited by the Nazi regime. The first account of the climb, entitled "Um die Eiger-Nordwand" and compiled by the four protagonists, appeared in 1938 in the NSDAP press, the Nazi party organ. It is, of course written in the "langage" of propaganda. The book ends with a photo with the caption "the finest reward"; in it one sees the four climberheroes being congratulated by Hitler.

All the authoritarian regimes have known how to misuse sport for the purposes of propaganda, and Nazi Germany merely carried on, on a wider scale and more efficiently, a practice that had enjoyed wide currency before that time. In 1936, the Berlin Olympic Games provided the opportunity for a vast production, in the course of which

all anti-Semitic notices in the town were taken down so as not to shock the visitors. Leni Riefenstahl—a former actress and climber, who can be seen at work in Fanck and Pabst's *Die weisse Hölle von Piz Palü*—produced for the occasion, with the backing of vast resources, the films *Fest der Völker* and *Fest der Schönheit,* about which it could be said—depending on one's standpoint—that they represented "the peak of National Socialist cinema" or "the most admirable monument ever raised to the beauty of sporting effort." After the ascent of the Eigerwand, it was the same Leni Riefenstahl (she got to know Heckmair as a mountain guide in 1937) who organized the meeting between Hitler and the four climbers. This use of sport, moreover, is by no means the sole reserve of authoritarian regimes: One only need view the excesses of chauvinism to which football matches lend themselves, here and elsewhere. And whether one wants it to or not, mountaineering itself contributes to the wider image or the prestige of a country, whatever the political circumstances may be. It might be noted here in passing that even today mountaineers are still decorated by heads of state.

But one must recognize that mountaineering, with its warlike vocabulary and its metaphors of conquest, lends itself particularly well to abuse by authoritarian ideology. It would be a mistake to believe that this is limited to the Eiger or even to Nazi Germany. Who would ever dream of reproaching the top Italian Alpinists Raffaele Carlesso and Giusto Gervasutti for having accepted the gold medal for athletic merit from the hand of Mussolini himself in Rome in 1935? Who still remembers that the accounts of first ascents in the Dolomites appeared just as often in *Sport Fascista* as in the Italian Alpine Club's *La Revista Mensile?* And one could quote other examples of the connections between mountaineering and nationalist propaganda.

It can never be a question of defending, by means of mountaineering, even the smallest aspect of Nazi barbarism. It has been proven that some climbers were indeed Nazis: the Austrian partnership of Harrer and Kasparek, or Willi Angerer and Edi Rainer, two of the four victims of the tragedy of 1936, effectively adhered to this ideology. But a blanket condemnation is wrong, since to accuse all those who have ever attempted the ascent of the Eigerwand of doing so to defend a cause would mean one was of the opinion that political conviction can be expressed through the act of climbing—namely, by the choice of a type of ascent, in the belief that this somehow mirrors an ideology. Accordingly, an attempt on the Eigerwand would be of more value politically than the ascent of the North Face of the Matterhorn. At the time, numerous criticisms were implicitly based on this idea, at least subliminally. In fact, without ever acting, the climber is political by very reason of his noninvolvement. A nonpolitical stance is nothing more than the passive acceptance of the dominant opinion. It is very probable that such was the political position of most of the climbers of the period. Rather than an active involvement, theirs was the kind of indifference that can justify anything.

The Eiger Does Not Stand Apart from Society

Mountaineering lives on in the dangerous and fictional assumption that the summits are neutral terrain. The attitude is fictional, since climbing has never

(left) "The wind whipped the free end of the rope" was the original caption for this photograph, which shows Hias Rebitsch—by no means a daredevil Alpinist—abseiling down the Shattered Pillar; in 1937 he and Ludwig Vörg became the first men to effect a successful retreat from the Face.

Heinrich Harrer's rucksack, in which he carried a swastika banner to the summit on his 1938 ascent of the North Face. Harrer's Nazi past only came to light in 1997—the White Spider was suddenly tinged with unpleasant brown marks.

In 1936 suspicion was leveled at two Eigerwand climbers, saying that they had only set foot on the route in order to win the gold medal for alpinism at the Berlin Olympics. In 1968 it became possible to purchase a gold commemorative medal bearing the inscriptions "First Ascent of the North Face of the Eiger 1938" and "Kasparek—Harrer—Vörg—Heckmair." The largest medal (60 mm in diameter and weighing 105 g) cost 992 Swiss francs, the smallest (20 mm, 3.5 g) cost 36 francs.

done anything other than gradually socializing a territory by taking a slice of terra incognita (which the mountains once were) and making it a social place with all the forces of society at work. Nowadays, with the Alps a politically highly contentious territory, this tendency is more obvious than ever—consider, for example, the Alpine Convention or the attempt in Switzerland to construct two new Alpine through routes. Ultimately, we must get away from the notion of the mountains as a pure, ideal world free of any kind of conflict, that the most vacuous metaphors (those of the high places) seek to convey. The greatest mistake any climber can fall victim to is the belief that he can use the mountains to escape the sociopolitical system in which he lives. This is the lesson that today's climbers can learn from the "Golden Age" of Alpine conquest.

The Eiger Occupies an Exceptional Position

In the nineteenth century, there were no last great problems; this idea first appeared only after the First World War. For some time, climbers had had the feeling that the conquest of the Alps was nearing its end. Had one not reached the "limit of what is humanly possible," embodied in the sixth grade on the scale of difficulty then so widely disparaged? Notions such as "impossible" are contemporaneous, as is the feeling of having exhausted the possibilities on the field of play. This led to a certain eagerness and to increased competition among climbers. One of the clearest examples of this "last great problem" state of mind is the sentence written by Jaques Lagarde shortly after the first ascent of the North Face of the Matterhorn in 1931: "With just a few exceptions the conquest of the Alps has now reached its conclusion." One of these exceptions was the Eigerwand! Other faces, just as difficult and just as high, were conquered during the same period, yet these were not counted among the last great problems. That is

the case, for example, for the North East Face of the Dent Blanche in the Valais Alps, or the North West Face of the Ailefroide in the Dauphine. What was it then that these faces lacked? Without doubt, the fact that several attempts had failed. A face conquered without further ado on the first attempt could not represent a real problem. No doubt they also lacked the necessary publicity, without which there could be no fame, not even within the limited circles of the mountaineer.

The Eiger Lives on Myth and Legend

In the stock exchange of mountaineering values, the Eigerwand has held out longer than its colleagues, the Walker Spur on the Grandes Jorasses and the Matterhorn North Face. As in myths, the reputation of an ascent is nourished both by real facts and imaginary elements. The tragic history of the Eiger, the numerous deaths, the real dangers of the Wall, have protected it against too rapid a devaluation. At the same time certain elements were exaggerated, thus amplifying the myth. This means that the reputation and the prestige of an ascent have little to do with a rational appreciation of the difficulties and the real problems. It used to be said, for example, that retreat from the Eigerwand was impossible, yet Vörg and Rebitsch disproved the point in 1937 and Schlunegger and Krähenbühl did the same ten years later.

It would be a mistake to assume that the Eiger is ever climbed for the real, objective difficulties alone. The climber cannot pass by such historic places as the Hinterstoisser Traverse, the Swallow's Nest, the Flatiron, Death Bivouac, and the Traverse of the Gods—to name only five of twenty-five such features—without recalling the events that took place there: Yesterday's history defines today's ascent. Each ascent is, of course, first and foremost a personal adventure, but it only translates into action because the desire to climb a particular route has previously manifested itself. The desire of a climber to climb a route always comes from an historical account, a story which is allied to the myth. It is not crucial whether or not the facts surrounding the myth are correct; what is important is the close connection with a certain type of mountaineering. In the case of the Eiger, this is evidently an heroic type of Alpinism—warlike, aggravated, a type of climbing to which we are all sensitive, even if we really feel that nowadays it is quite different. The history of the Eigerwand is in some small way our myth—created for us, the climbers—the somber, disturbing myth of heroic Alpinism. It is for this reason that it encapsulates so wonderfully well an entire and irrevocably concluded period of mountaineering history, one which today's climber is no longer capable of considering without nostalgia.

I, for my part, wish merely to establish from this history of the Eiger that the protagonists were—by virtue of their concept of mountaineering—innovative mountaineers. I refuse to denigrate their achievements for reasons that have nothing to do with mountaineering.

With this, a new problem arises. Mountaineering is always dangerous—everyone knows this. But there are different degrees. Is there a limit, beyond which the risk is no longer justifiable? If no one had been prepared to take on these risks, then the Eigerwand would perhaps still be unclimbed . . . .

The Eiger Fascinates in a Different Way

If the history of the Eiger is fascinating and full of secrets, it is also due to another, less obvious reason. The North Face of the Eiger was, for a while, the only route in the whole world about which the classical debate of mountaineering has not managed to resolve itself. The beauty of climbing, the pleasure of the act of climbing, the joy of being successful—none of these words meant a thing on the Eiger, and could not be used in discussions about it. In the many accounts of this climb, the

Ludwig Vörg laden with flowers on his arrival in 1938 at Sonthofen, where he was employed as a trainer at the SS Ordenburg. The Nazis capitalized ruthlessly on the victory of the German–Austrian team; the climbers themselves hardly objected. Vörg's left arm is bandaged; he injured it during the first ascent.

remaining impression is admittedly very strong, but rather worrisome and enigmatic: Just what was it that the climbers were hoping to find on that Wall?

Fascination with the Eiger . . . attraction and repulsion. This fascination, as with every extreme feeling, has the face of Janus, passing without warning from the positive to the negative. It is an impression that is gained from many accounts of the climb. Never has any other route better highlighted this reversibility, or rather this indecision, about the pleasure experienced by the climber. The Eigerwand is an ultimate mountaineering experience and one where the climber moves furthest away from the reasonable. And in this sense, therefore, an exemplary route.

Sylvain Jouty (born 1949) was editor-in-chief of the Paris-published *Alpinisme & Randonnée* magazine from 1981 to 1998. He is also a writer and edited a series of mountaineering books, *Retour a la montagne,* published by Editions Hoëbeke (Paris). His book *L'odeur de l'altitude* won the first prize in the Salon du Livre de Montagne de Passy in 1999. In 1978, he wrote the keynote preface for the second French edition of Anderl Heckmair's *Les trois derniers problemes des Alpes* (Editions Slatkine, Geneva), entitled "Fascination de l'Eigerwand"; it is this text, in revised form, which is reprinted here.

First Pillar

The rock was smooth, compact limestone, forming a succession of short walls and ledges. At first the lowness of the walls made the going quite easy, but it was clear that higher up, where the ledges grew narrower and the walls longer, we would come up against some delicate ground ....

Presently we found the first signs of human passage in the form of a torn hat and some old rags. Had they belonged to those who had given their lives for the useless conquest of this world of stone? The sadness that could be evoked by such cast-offs was unutterable. It was as if a sinister irony of Fate was at work, for beside these traces of men who had died reasserting their humanity in a world where the machine had become master we found numerous bits of scrap iron from the construction of the Jungfrau Railway.

Lionel Terray, *Les Conquérants de l'inutile (Conquistadors of the Useless)*, 1961.
Eigerwand in 1947.

(facing page) Ruth Baldinger and Thomas Ulrich break trail up the deep snow of the first few pitches. The First Pillar is visible in profile above them. In the background, the Wetterhorn and Mittelhorn, basking in the winter sun.

No Tracks on the Eiger

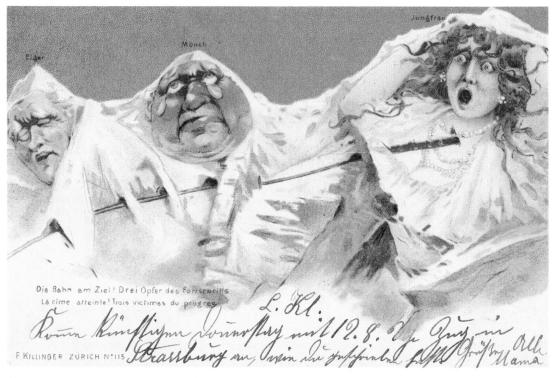

Die Bahn am Ziel! Drei Opfer des Fortschritts
Là cime atteinte! Trois victimes du progrès

F KILLINGER ZÜRICH N°115

(above) The postcard depicts the Eiger, Mönch, and Jungfrau, horrified at the tunnel about to be bored through their innards. The Jungfrau Railway was to run right up to the summit of the Jungfrau; in 1903 there were also plans to construct an additional funicular from Eismeer Station direct to the summit of the Eiger, as the map (facing page) shows.

The Jungfrau Railway is world famous. Yet it is a little-known fact that at the end of the nineteenth century there had been three attempts to construct a railway line on the Eiger. All of them failed, for different reasons. Historian Patrick Moser rolls back the years and tells the story of the Eiger railway that was never built.

September 24, 1894, was a decisive date in the history of the Eiger, although it is mentioned in none of the history books. On this day, after extensive discussion, the shareholders of the Wengernalp Railway Company voted by a margin of 1342 to 1058 to reject a proposal presented by their board of directors to take over the concession for a projected railway line on the Eiger.

In the spirit of railway fever that gripped the end of the nineteenth century, the Eiger—like its companions the Mönch and the Jungfrau—was to get its own railway line. In February 1892, two managers of the Bernese Oberland Railway, Emil Strub and Hans Studer, filed a formal application with the Swiss government for a concession to build a rack railway and cable car to run from Kleine Scheidegg via Eigergletscher to

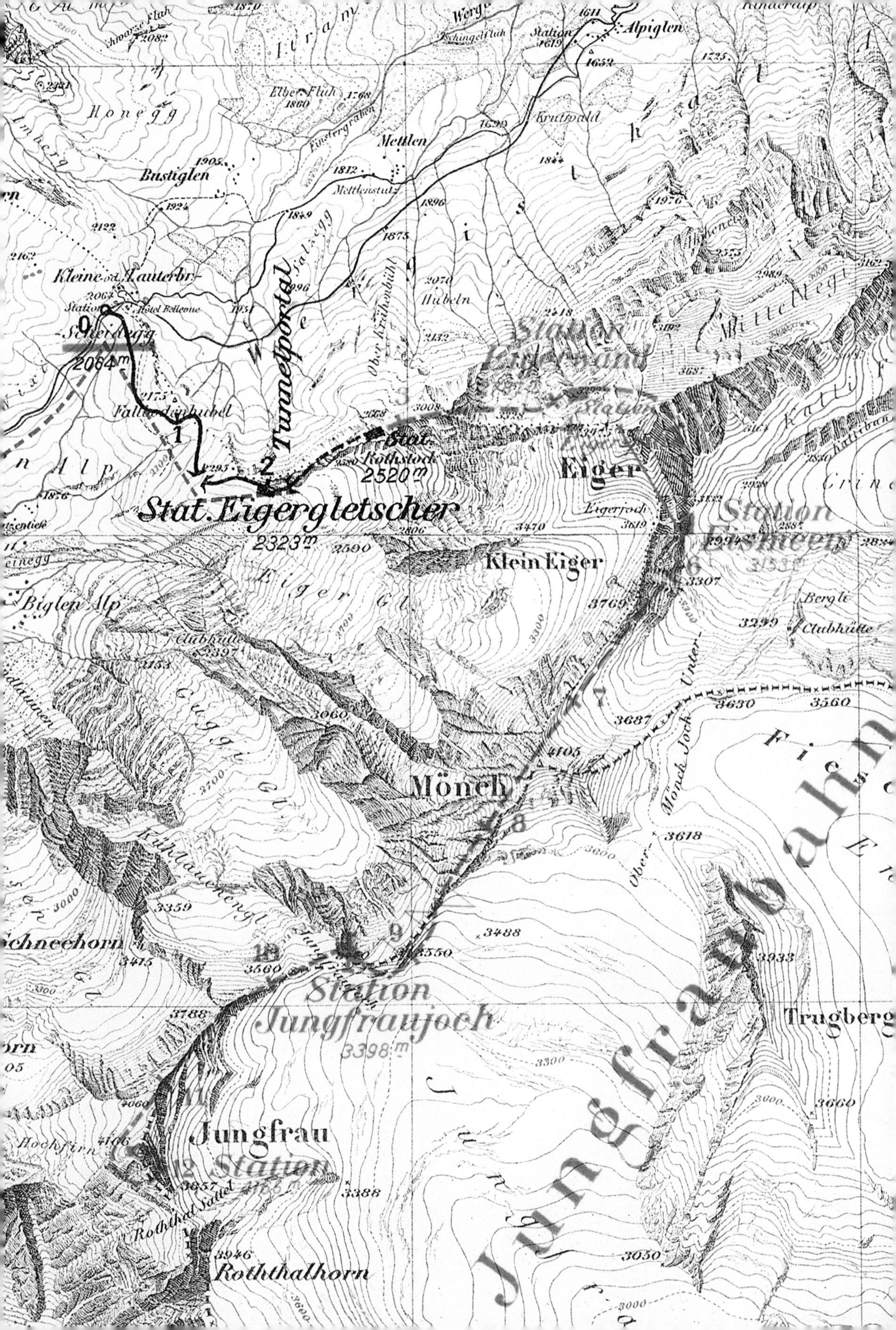

Alpiglen
Station
Honegg
Bustiglen
Mettlen
Kleine-od. Lauterbr.
Station
Hotel Bellevue
Scheidegg
2064m
Tunnelportal
Fallbodenhubel
Stat. Rothstock
2520m
Stat. Eigergletscher
2323m
Station Eigerwand
Eiger
Eigerjoch
Station Eismeer
Klein Eiger
Bergli
Clubhütte
Mönch
Mönch Joch
Trugberg
Schneehorn
Station Jungfraujoch
3398m
Jungfrau
Station
Roththal Sattel
Roththalhorn
Jungfraubahn

(right) The intention of Wilhelm Feldmann and the Jungfrau Railway Company to construct a tourist cable car from the Eismeer Station via the Eigerjoch to the summit of the Eiger never got further than the drawing board.

(facing page) Wilhelm Feldmann planned the Wetterhorn Lift, whose first section opened on 27 July 1908—the first tourist cable car in the world. The extension up to the top of the Wetterhorn was never built, and the lift itself shut down in 1915 and was dismantled and scrapped in 1934.

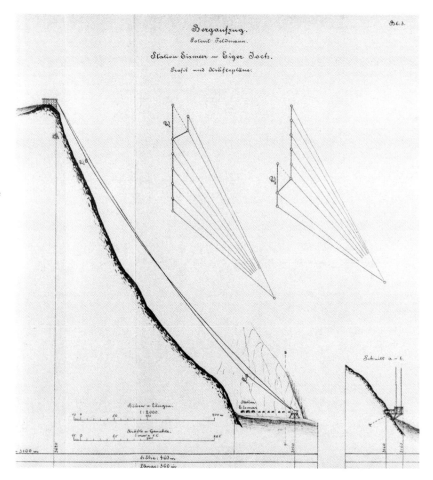

the summit of the Eiger. They did so even though at that time the engineer Maurice Köchlin had already been granted permission by federal authorities to build a line from Stechelberg up to the top of the Jungfrau. (Köchlin's plan eventually failed when he was unable to obtain funds.)

Strub and Studer pointed out that, unlike Köchlin's project, the Wengernalp line to Kleine Scheidegg would be materially helped by the construction of the Eiger railway. In their opinion, the Eiger was less prone to fog than the Jungfrau and more suited for building a summit station because a larger site was available. Strub and Studer received the concession they applied for from the Swiss councils without any major problems, although all parties involved must

have been well aware that, from the point of view of return on investments, it was possible to implement plans for either the Eiger or the Jungfrau railway but not both.

No long after, Zürich industrialist Adolf Guyer-Zeller hit upon a plan that was to present the public with a further project for a railway line on the Jungfrau. Emil Strub and Hans Studer feared for their Eiger railway, since they had still not found any investors. They protested to the Federal Council that Guyer-Zeller had planned his line between Kleine Scheidegg and Eigergletscher to run along the same route as the prospective Eiger railway. At the same time, Strub and Studer attempted to sell their concession to the Wengernalp Railway and presented

BERGBAHN **MÜRREN** FUNICULAIRE
1650 M.ú.M.
SUISSE · BERNER-OBERLAND · SWITZERLAND

The cable car from Mürren to the Allmendhubel began operating in 1912. From the top, cows and people both had a splendid view across to the Eiger (left) and Mönch. Poster by Ernst Hodel, 1925.

annual general meeting the shareholders were convinced that a Jungfrau rail link held the promise of a greater return on their investments than a railway on the Eiger. Meanwhile, Strub and Studer still had no investors. It was now a simple matter for Guyer-Zeller to convince them finally to abandon their plans for an Eiger railway. In return, they received a standstill payment of 15,000 Swiss Francs. Furthermore, Strub was later to be engaged in planning the construction of the Jungfrau Station and became the first director of the Jungfrau Railway Company.

In the early part of 1899, after the death of Guyer-Zeller, the Jungfrau Railway Company found itself in financial difficulties for the first time, and both national and foreign newspapers announced that the Eiger railway project was back on the agenda once more, since a line to the summit of the Eiger would be cheaper to build than the Jungfrau railway. Although these reports were largely the product of creative journalistic license, the rumor was not entirely without foundation. At the time the Jungfrau railway tunnel had been pushed as far as the provisional station at Rotstock, which was situated between Eigergletscher and today's Eigerwand Station.

Outmaneuvering the Competition

Four years later, after the opening of the Eigerwand Station, the Jungfrau Railway Company submitted an application to the federal authorities for a concession to build a branch line from the planned Eismeer Station to the Eiger. They then purchased shares in the Bergaufzug Feldmann AG lift company, which had already constructed the Wetterhorn lift. With these two maneuvers they effectively stifled any potential competitive projects. However, the Federal Council would only agree to sanction plans for a joint venture with Feldmann to construct an aerial funicular from Eismeer via the Eigerjoch to the summit of the Eiger on the understanding that the Jungfrau railway went no farther than Eismeer Station. In other

their detailed plans to the Lauterbrunnen District Council, thereby putting the pressure on Guyer-Zeller.

Guyer-Zeller Pays Handsomely for Standstill Agreement

Guyer-Zeller saw the danger, however. He realized that he would be unable to bring about his Jungfrau railway plans as soon as construction of the Eiger railway was underway. With the help of his Bern solicitor he prevented the Wengernalp Railway Company once and for all from acquiring the Eiger railway concession. At the

words, in order to obtain the concession for the construction of the cable car the Jungfrau Railway Company would have had to abandon their plans to extend the line as far as the Jungfraujoch. They were not prepared to negotiate on this point.

Plans drafted by a group of Grindelwald townspeople for a funicular railway from the Lower Grindelwald Glacier to Eismeer met with similar failure. The summit of the Eiger remained free from construction work.

The story shows how very closely linked the Eiger and Jungfrau railway projects were. In the end, common reputation swung the vote in favor of the Jungfrau railway. With his unorthodox plans for the line—heading toward the Jungfrau via the Eiger and the Mönch, even though a direct line from Eigergletscher straight up onto the Jungfrau would have been technically possible—Adolf Guyer-Zeller effectively prevented any competitive projects from being presented after the Eiger railway

concession had elapsed. His heirs played the same clever game of business politics. Although the plans worked out by Hans Studer and Emil Strub for the Eiger railway were never realized, traces of this project can still be found today. Strub and Studer had envisaged a rack railway running from Kleine Scheidegg to Eigergletscher. They had also intended to take the electrical power required both for the construction and the running of the line from the "Schwarze Lütschine" at Burglauenen. Today a power station stands at that place; it was built at the turn of the century by the Jungfrau Railway Company and remains the property of the company to this day.

Patrick Moser (born 1966) is a historian and author of the book *Damit wird die Jungfrau zur Demoiselle: Projektierung und Bau der Jungfraubahn* (Chronos Verlag, Zurich), the first comprehensive and scientific account of this railway.

The first Eiger railway of 1892 was to have run as a rack railway from Kleine Scheidegg to the foot of the Eiger, with a cable car from there to the summit. Watercolor by Roland Flück, 1997, 64.5 x 102.5 cm.

Shattered Pillar

"By this time it was 5 A.M. and light. Waterfalls cascaded over us, and in the Hotel Kleine Scheidegg opposite the first lights were going on. The loose debris of stones and old snow on the ledge called for our full concentration, but otherwise the technical difficulties were slight and the routefinding simple, as we already knew this section of the face. We quickly gained the crest of the first pillar above the loose snow and rock, traversed obliquely out to the right, and—still unroped—climbed upward to the right of the cleft spur.

We stopped only briefly when we reached the bottom of the Difficult Crack. We racked up the carabiners and ice and rock pegs on our climbing harnesses, put the many tapes and rope slings around our necks, and tied on with the 50-meter rope. Bivouac equipment, provisions, and spare clothing stayed for the time being in our rucksacks.

A rope was already in place, probably left by the film crew who had been shooting their spy-thriller *The Eiger Sanction,* which made things easier for us.

Reinhold Messner, *Die Grossen Wände (The Big Walls),* 1977.
Eigerwand in 1974.

(facing page) Ueli Bula reads the route description by the light of his head torch. There are various possible lines up the lower, technically easier, but in parts dangerous, section of the North Face; it is possible to go badly off-route, however, especially in the dark. The Shattered Pillar is a convenient waymarker.

Looking for Clues on the Old Eiger Trail

These ladies and gentlemen are on the first section of the safeguarded walkway to the summit of the Rotstock, a mountain that measured 2669 meters at the turn of the nineteenth century. The plaque rightly promises "a splendid panoramic view."

A cable-protected route up the Eigerwand? Once upon a time there was a *via ferrata*—a route of iron—not directly on the North Face itself but a little way beyond its most westerly edge, in the gully near the Rotstock and up the reddish rocky tower above the Eigergletscher Station. At the turn of the nineteenth century, ladies in wide skirts and gentlemen in straw hats would ascend a safeguarded path from the former Rotstock Station up to the sunny viewing terrace on the Rotstock (2663 m) where all around were sheer vertical drops. On 8 September 1997, Daniel Anker set out to follow in their footsteps.

Walter Egger, himself a locomotive driver on the Kleine Scheidegg–Jungfraujoch route, and the president of the Grindelwald Mountain Guides Association, arranged on our behalf for the

train to make an unscheduled stop at the Rotstock Station, unused for around ninety years and only minutes into the journey through the Eiger Tunnel. My guide pushed open the heavy, wooden half doors that led outside.

It was cool and shady on the rubble-strewn ledge at the base of the Eigerwand. Overhead, the rock pinnacles of the West Ridge of the Eiger rose vertically into a strikingly blue sky. Beyond the sheer vertical drop we looked down onto sun-drenched alpine pastures and, in the distance, Kleine Scheidegg.

Artificial Cliff Walkway

"The first tunnel station, albeit still only provisional in nature, is the 'Rothstock' Station, opened on 2 August 1899." This appears on page 5 of the brochure "The Jungfrau Railway, Bernese Oberland (Switzerland)," printed on 18 June 1903, upon the opening of the Eigerwand Station, which is still in operation today. From the brochure, we learn more about the former Rotstock Station: "It is sited at kilometer 2880 at an altitude of 2530 meters above sea level and affords the visitor the opportunity to ascend the artificial cliff walkway to the top of the Rotstock (2669 m). From here rich views may be had: To the North, beyond the Lauberhorn and the many lakes of the interior of the country, one can see to the Jura Mountain Range."

"There are steps here," Walter Egger repeatedly reminds me as we climb the steep crag at whose foot we emerged, scrambling, from the Rotstock Tunnel. There is nothing to be seen of the railings that were here; only once do we discover the remains of an iron post.

Toward the Light

After the first steep step the terrain eases back. We climb up through a scree basin at the bottom of which lie sections of bent aluminum staves. Walter Egger surmises that they might be from filming work. According to the locals, Luis Trenker is said to have filmed parts of his *Sein Bester Freund*—also known under the title "Drama on the Eiger"—on the Rotstock. During work on the film his assistants had allegedly dismantled the railings bounding the path in order to prevent anyone holding on to the old ironmongery by mistake.

We make our way diagonally upward through the rocky amphitheater and on up to the broad saddle between the Rotstock and the West Ridge of the Eiger. We tread the path of least resistance, placing our boots again and again on footholds that are just a little too perfect to be entirely natural, certain that we are walking along the historic old path. Then, shortly before the last scramble up to the saddle, comes a surprise—an ancient ladder, fully 3 meters high, followed by three iron staples anchored with rotting wooden wedges into holes drilled in the rock: the last metal remains of the original Eiger Path. A few more paces and the scenery changes abruptly—sunshine, warmth, and a view across to the mighty, glaciated masses of the Mönch and the Jungfrau. From here we could descend the West Flank to the Eigergletscher Station (2320 m), following the lowest section of the Normal Route. But we set out to climb the Rotstock.

Eiger Trails Past and Present

Again, the chiseled-out steps are there, barely visible, masked by the diagonal structure of the rock, yet immediately obvious as soon as we step on them. If only all the little changes to the mountain made in the name of tourism were as well attuned to its natural features!

We soon step out onto the flat summit plateau of the Rotstock. The view down is at once lovely and fearful. The railing is long since gone and the

bench, where once tourists would rest and dab away the pearly sweat of fear and exertion with silken handkerchiefs, has perhaps been swept by the Föhn storms into the abyss below.

"The view from the Rotstock is both interesting and impressive," wrote the English mountaineer, alpine historian, and Grindelwald resident W. A. B. Coolidge in the *Alpine Journal* of 1894/95. He recommended the climb to mountaineers staying at Kleine Scheidegg as a morning walk to be made on the day of departure. Only a few years after this recommendation the first ill-shod Eiger tourists were to be seen romping up the Rotstock. After the closure of Rotstock Station, however, the Eiger's artificial walkway fell into disuse and oblivion.

There is another trail, opened in 1997 and running from the Eigergletscher Station, beneath the overhanging North Face of the Rotstock, up to the carpet of green below the Eigerwand and then down to the restaurant and the tinkling cowbells of Alpiglen. It is known as the Eiger Trail and is a popular hike.

(above) An iron ladder is still in place on the rediscovered tourist path, just above the former Rostock Station.

Daniel Anker (born 1954), journalist and author *Best Dayhikes in California*, Bruckmann, Munich, 1995), climbed the Eiger via the Mettellegi Ridge and skied down the Northern Eigerjoch.

Gallery Window

Sure enough one ankle was hanging loose and twisted badly. The head cut, though wide, was superficial. The rim of his hard hat had pushed forward and sliced open his face over the cheekbone. Gory but not immobilizing. But what to do? Thoughts of soloing down and alerting a rescue party, but that would have meant a major operation. Racking my brain, I reread my *White Spider* mentally. It clicked: the Gallery Window! This was the waste-shaft from the Eiger-Jungfrau Railway that came out onto the Face below and to the right of the Difficult Crack. We must be very near it. It was the traditional escape for hard-pressed parties escaping from the Face....

After what seemed like ages and a great deal of hard sweating, we collapsed into the tunnel. It was an incredibly strange contrast. The tunnel is a very weird place. Out of the wild, blowing rain of the Nordwand we came into this electrically lit science-fiction cave with eerie, moaning winds. To add to the sense of the ridiculous there was a neon advertisement by the entrance. I could only stand shaking my head in bewilderment. It was almost too much for my mind, which was still grappling with the day's retreat and the accident.

Dougal Haston, *In High Places*, 1972.
Eigerwand attempt in 1962; Eigerwand in 1963.

(facing page) The Grindelwald mountain guide Kurt Egger and German journalist Katia Mössner at the Gallery Window. The occasion: the media conference in summer 1998 for the TV broadcast "Eiger-Nordwand live."

The Queen of the Mountain Railways and Her Dark Side at Eigergletscher

During the construction of the Jungfrau railway the laborers, mostly Italian in origin, drilled for ten years into the Eiger. Seven bore holes were created in the 4-kilometer-long Eiger Tunnel: an opening just beyond the tunnel entrance at Eigergletscher, the provisional Rotstock Station, the breakthrough onto the North Face made by dynamiting, the Gallery Window so well-known in mountaineering circles, a little peephole before the Eigerwand Station, and finally the two stations—Eigerwand and Eismeer—hewn from the rock of the mountain. The tunneling was toilsome, dangerous, sometimes even deadly work, and was almost always poorly paid. And conditions at the workers' barracks at Eigergletscher—cut off from the outside world in winter—violated regulations. Jungfrau Railway histo-rian Patrick Moser sheds light on the daily grind of the tunnel laborers.

Every year around half a million people travel on the Jungfrau Railway. All of them pass by the Eigergletscher Station. Some of them might wonder just how the railway originated, yet only a very few tourists are in fact aware of the important role played by the workers' colony at Eigergletscher during the construction of the Jungfrau Railway in the years between 1896 and 1912. The sole reminders of these hard times are the foundations of the former workers' barracks alongside the railway line.

The construction of the Jungfrau Railway is generally described in literature as the heroic deed of the Zürich industrialist Adolf Guyer-Zeller. He developed the concept in a flash of inspiration, procured the necessary concessions, secured financing, and made all the other preparations. He treated his workers like a father treats his family. Finally, he also made arrangements for the project to be continued after his death. In part we have the Jungfrau Railway Company to thank for this representation of events that has has become legend. The Company placed a bust in honor of Adolf Guyer-Zeller on the Jungfraujoch, yet to this day they have not commemorated the workers and the victims of the construction of the line.

During the construction work, as many as 200 people lived at Eigergletscher, among them 160 Italian laborers. For eight hours' work a day they received a small daily pay packet of between 4,30 and 8 Francs, depending on the work carried out. Although there were performance bonuses, pay was

Jos. Els Kaufmann
Luzern 1898

(below, upper) At the Eigergletscher barracks three laborers had to share one bunk bed.

(below, lower) During the construction of the railway, thirty laborers lost their lives, most of them in explosions, and some in electrical accidents.

docked for provisions, contributions to the company's own sickness benefit scheme, and accident insurance. In extreme cases, these deductions could amount to as much as fifty percent of gross pay. On the opening of the Kleine Scheidegg–Jungfraujoch section of the line in the summer of 1912, a round trip cost 32 Francs, a sum that represented eleven times the net daily pay of a manual laborer (without performance bonus).

"A Disgraceful Pigsty"

The only thing that was free of charge was the accommodation at the barracks, and this was correspondingly parsimonious in its fixtures and fittings. There were no cupboards, tables, or chairs and far too few bed spaces. Three men had to share a bunk; it consisted of straw only and quickly became moldy. On one occasion, after

an inspection of the arrangements, even the Board of the Jungfrau Railway Company was obliged to admit that conditions at Eigergletscher were "disgraceful" and spoke in this context of a "pigsty."

The fact that there was no serious epidemic outbreak at Eigergletscher bordered on the miraculous, the more so since the little community was cut off from the outside world during the winter. If the workers wished to visit a restaurant they had to go all the way down to Wengen; several times, construction workers froze to death en route from Wengen to Eigergletscher. Although the Jungfrau Railway Company did run a hotel at Eigergletscher it was expressly forbidden for the workers to set foot in it; during the winter months it was in any case closed.

Starvation Wages

In the autumn, the Jungfrau Railway Company had to have all the provisions needed until spring transported up to Eigergletscher. The actual menu plans show, however, that the workers' diet can at best be described as insufficient. There was practically only meat, or a meat-based broth, with pasta or rice; potatoes appeared on the menu only on extremely rare occasions. For breakfast, only milky coffee was served—a barely adequate meal for those engaged in heavy manual labor. The lack of variety and the small portions meant that the workers were forced to procure additional food either down in Wengen or at the railway company's own shop at Eigergletscher.

Dynamite and High Voltage

Work on the construction of the Jungfrau Railway was hard. Each shift was of eight hours' duration, and this at a height of between 2300 and 3400 meters above sea level. Further difficulties consisted of the shape of hard layers of quartzite rock, power failure, malfunctioning ventilators, dust, noise, snow and freezing cold, and accidents with explosive charges and high voltage equipment. A total of thirty workers lost their lives during the construction of the

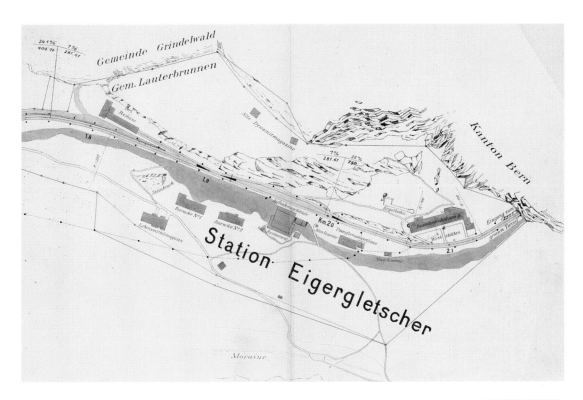

Jungfrau Railway, most of them as a result of accidents with explosives. A further danger was the high voltage. At the turn of the century this was still a new phenomenon and one whose deadly effects were seriously underestimated. In addition to the deaths there were numerous injuries, particularly to the eyes, hands, and fingers. In the biggest explosives accident, in February 1899, six Italian laborers died. The explosion in November 1908, when the entire stock of 30,000 kilograms of dynamite stored in a depot near the Eigerwand Station went up, caused a stir both at home and abroad. The blast could allegedly be heard as far away as the Black Forest, yet on this occasion at least there were no victims to mourn. As luck would have it, an alert engineer had arranged for the dynamite to be stored away from its original place next to the workers' barracks.

It is bewildering that the Jungfrau Railway Company only applied themselves to improving their safety procedures after their insurers applied massive increases to their accident insurance premiums as a result of the

numerous accidents. In fact, the management did not even consider it necessary to employ their own company doctor. The physician responsible had his practice in Wengen and in winter it took him more than five hours from first hearing of an accident to arrive at Eigergletscher. Nowadays it is no longer possible to judge just how many accident victims might have been saved had it been possible to have their wounds treated in time by a qualified doctor.

During the construction of the Jungfrau Railway from 1896 to 1912 as many as 200 people lived at Eigergletscher. In winter the "Eiger Village" could only be reached on foot.

Legitimate Strikers, Not "Rowdy Roughnecks"

(below) The Eigerwand Station with the panoramic portholes in the North Face. Before panes of glass were installed, only a low fence provided security.

Reaction by the laborers to the unreasonable and inequitable conditions was inevitable. Most of them opted for silent protest and simply moved on to another construction site. They were employed as seasonal workers and

(facing page) Working with the high-voltage drilling equipment and ventilators was a risky business (upper). Well-fed construction managers and investors celebrate the inauguration of the Eigerwand Station on 18 June 1903 (lower).

were itinerant; the turnover of workers at the Eigergletscher site was correspondingly high. Nevertheless there were six strikes called during the sixteen-year construction period. The main points of disagreement were insufficient provisions and too-high deductions from their pay packets. On one occasion the workers were able to prevent the appointment of an unpopular supervisor; on another they forced the site manager to depart. They had intervened to attempt to block the introduction of jackhammers, which were to have replaced the conventional drilling rigs.

These hammers had to be clamped between the legs, and the vibrations caused many workers to experience involuntary and repeated ejaculation. Several of them complained of becoming quite wet, while others had to miss shifts through exhaustion.

Although the strikes always revolved around concrete grievances and thus were manifestly devoid of any political agenda, the Board and the directors always chose to believe that the unrest had been planned long in advance. In this context, they spoke of "black sheep," "unruly elements," "roughneck brothers-in-arms" and "rabble-rousers" who had to be cleared out of the way. They were happy when, after unsuccessful strikes, the alleged ringleaders took their leave and a "cleansing"—as they referred to it—of the workforce could be noted.

Despite all the difficulties, the Jungfraujoch was reached in 1912, almost ten years later than Guyer-Zeller had originally planned. The reasons for this delay were not only the inadequate planning and the unexpected obstacles encountered but also the insufficient financing, since during his lifetime Guyer-Zeller had remained unable to win over investors to his project and had thus paid various bills from his own private purse. After his death in the spring of 1899 the scheme had been seriously endangered, and even after the opening of the railway in the summer of 1912 it was to be many years before the Jungfrau Railway was in secure financial circumstances.

Chronology of the Jungfrau Railway

1896 Construction of the Jungfrau Railway begins.
1897 The Eigergletscher site is developed. This is to serve as a base camp for the construction work. A station, restaurant, administration offices, workers' barracks, canteen, and shops are constructed.
1898 Opening of the stretch of line from Kleine Scheidegg (2061 m) to Eigergletscher (2320 m).
1899 Breakthrough and opening of the provisional station at Rotstock (2520 m).
1900 The townspeople of Grindelwald submit an application for a funicular between Grindelwald Gletscher and Ofni.
1903 Breakthrough and opening of the Eigerwand Station (2865 m). The Jungfrau Railway Company submits an application for a funicular to run from Eismeer via the

Eigerjoch to the summit of the Eiger.
1908 Explosion in the dynamite stores at the Eigerwand Station. 30,000 kilograms of dynamite go up in smoke.
1912 Breakthrough and opening of the Jungfraujoch Station (3454 m).
1924 Opening of the luxury hotel, the Berghaus, at the Jungfraujoch.
1930 Opening of the research station at the Jungfraujoch.
1937 Opening of the Sphinx Observatory.
1972 The Berghaus burns down.
1987 Seventy-five-year celebration of the Jungfrau Railway. Opening of the new building, Top of Europe, on the Jungfraujoch.
1996 Opening of the two-story wintergarden around the Sphinx Observatory.

Difficult Crack

Lying in my sleeping bag I listen to the noises coming from the Wall. Dull rumbling and loud creaking bear frightening witness to the Wall's ceaseless activity. My head is full of Eiger stories, which make more interesting reading than many a thriller. In spite of this I finally manage to fall asleep.

It is already late in the day when I peel myself out of my sleeping bag and make coffee. Now I see this gigantic Face close up for the first time. A mighty, concave wall with its cargo of deadly stones and avalanches thundering down relentlessly through its gullies. With a slightly dry throat I gather my belongings together. I am still not seriously intending to set off onto the Wall. No, just to look, to breathe in a bit of good North Wall air.

I climb quickly over fields of firn snow to the real start of the route. Piles of snow still remain in the Wall. Without pausing I climb past the Shattered Pillar to the Difficult Crack, the start of the real difficulties. I'm in good shape and curiosity takes hold of me. I will simply go as far as I can and then abseil down again; bearing in mind this "get-out clause" I put meter after meter of this rock behind me, rock which in parts is nerve-wrackingly brittle.

Frank Jourdan, *Im Lot,* 1995.
Eigerwand in 1983.

(facing page) Several parties at work on the Difficult Crack, the first big test on the Heckmair Route. Far below is the rubble-strewn base of the North Face.

A Country Divided by a Wall

Berbot

Zur Verhütung weiterer Unglücksfälle erläßt hiermit der Staat Bern gestützt auf Art. 118 E./G. zum Z.G.B. und unter Androhung der vorgesehenen Bußen ein Verbot für jede Begehung der Eiger-Nordwand.

Die Polizeiorgane sind angewiesen, für strikte Befolgung dieses Verbotes zu sorgen.

Für die im Gange befindlichen Bergungsarbeiten kann der Regierungsstatthalter von Interlaken Ausnahmen von diesem Verbote bewilligen.

Bern, den 25. Juli 1936.

Für den Staat Bern,
Der Präsident: Seematter.
Der Staatsschreiber: Schneider.

Bewilligt:

Der Gerichtspräsident von Interlaken i. B.:
Allembach.

(above) In July 1936 the State of Bern banned the climbing of the North Wall of the Eiger. It had to rescind its decree on account of legal challenges only four months later.

(facing page) For many Swiss mountaineers the development of the Eigerwand had already been finalized with the climbing of the North East Face in 1932. The Lauper plaque is on the right of the knife edge of the Mittellegi Ridge.

Othmar Gurtner from Lauterbrunnen was against it, and in 1937 wrote: "It is not the government of Bern that decrees this, but the Eiger itself in unambiguous terms. Anyone who does not understand its voice is deaf and should be led away from the dangerous area in the same way as you would lead a blind person away from tram tracks and onto the pavement." Hans Schlunegger from the neighboring village of Wengen was for it and wrote nothing, but acted as a mountain guide and was a top Alpinist. He took part in the tragic rescue attempt of Toni Kurz in 1936 and in 1947 made the first Swiss ascent of Eiger's North Wall. Daniel Anker has collected different points of view in Switzerland about its most famous Wall.

Othmar Gurtner (1895–1958), the son of a hotelier from Lauterbrunnen, was an Alpinist and a journalist with a cutting pen. On 24 July 1936 his full-page article "The Eiger Wall Tragedy" appeared in the Swiss newspaper *Sport* with the following opening: "The July siege in 1936 was a failure. Retreat from the snowy graves of those who went missing in 1935. Three men beaten by the ice. The last died of exhaustion. Six dead on the Eigerwand. One dead on the Schneehorn. Will this frivolity continue? The Eiger has beaten three of the presumptuous ones, and brought the fourth to a death from exhaustion due to hunger, fear and extreme cold. Four mountain guides braved the rockfall for seven hours to save the last remnants of life of the desperate men who, driven compulsively by misguided delusions of recognition, wanted to carry off the mightiest wall of the Alps as a sacrifice to the temple of their new gods." Three days after the death of Toni Kurz in front of the eyes of his rescuers and one day after Gurtner's verdict, the State of Bern issued a ban on all climbing on the North Face "under the threat of the penalties as prescribed by law." However, a special permit was granted to recover the dead.

Verbal sentencing of the Eiger's North Wall climbers, the ban, and rescue and recovery work—which were tricky in every respect—were the three topics that shaped the difficult relationship of Switzerland with its most famous wall between the 1930s and the 1960s. This fame and the commotion that goes with it clearly hampered any chance of improving the atmosphere.

Making Hay Instead of Dying

Certainly many dramas occurred because the North Face climbers did

Hans Lauper on the Faulhorn, Grindelwald, on 21 June 1936. Three days later the first man to climb the North East Face was dead, having succumbed to an insidious illness. The final photo was taken by Dr. Oskar Hug, and Othmar Gurtner wrote the obituary; both were vehement critics of attempts at climbing the North Wall.

not wait for the best conditions. The *Sport* in July 1936 had this to say about a strapping guide from Grindelwald who also eyed the Wall lovingly: "What was this, so to speak, legitimate Eigerwand contender doing last Sunday while the German ropes were carrying out preparations for the assault. He was harvesting crisp hay that was basking in the sunshine and gathering it into a little barn. As long as the Eigerwand is covered in fine snow, making hay is more profitable than heroic suicidal assaults."

This was the stance widely held by leading Alpinists in the years prior to the first ascent of the North Face of the Eiger—unsubstantiated feelings of superiority.

The feeling was that the North Face had already been climbed by "tourists" Hans Lauper and Alfred Zürcher and mountain guides Joseph Knubel and Alexander Graven via the so-called Lauper Route up the North East Wall.

The *Neue Zürcher Zeitung (NZZ)* newspaper in July 1936 had this to say: "Remember 20 August 1932: The Eiger North Wall was masterfully conquered by four of the best Swiss alpinists with a healthy manly joy in the mountain experience and consummate skill."

Suicide and Lovers' Tryst

There are three reasons for the lack of understanding on the Swiss side toward the Eiger North Wall candidates. On a mountain sport level the Swiss did not like the use of pitons, carabiners, and rope as was the norm in Alpinism in the Eastern Alps. Politically, German and Austrian climbers were regarded with suspicion—rightly so with hindsight. And psychologically, comments such as "The Swiss guards can't do anything; we're going to do the Wall," from people like Hans Teufel, who perished on his first attempt at the Schneehorn North Face, did not help to alleviate the situation. Dr. Oskar Hug's verdict in the *NZZ* is exemplary: "The conquering of the Eigerwand is

ninety percent a matter of luck. Advanced technology, fanatical fearlessness in the face of death, resistance, and toughness all take second place. Imponderables, chance, luck, protection from real dangers (avalanches, etc.) are so overwhelming that this climb no longer fits into the category of mountaineering. It is far more a degenerate form of the medieval crusades." And to answer his own question as to whether or not it should be made illegal to attempt the North Face of the Eiger he gave the significant answer: "No. Suicide is not illegal either." There were, however, other opinions. In 1938 the *Sport* printed a down-to-earth speech by the Solthurn politician and former president of the Swiss Alpine Club (SAC) Robert Schöpfer: "Such climbs are preferable to becoming soft or being mollycoddled, preferable to the gallant lovers' tryst or even to a moral decline. It is to be regretted when such climbs take victims, but one must admit that even daredevil climbs have their place in cultural life."

Ban or Rescue

For legal reasons the climbing ban could not be upheld and thus the government rescinded it again in 1936. But with the start of the next climbing season the Council of the State of Bern freed the mountain rescue stations from their duty of rescuing from the Eigerwand. They also demanded that prospective North Wall climbers bring their own rescue services with them. The Munich Mountain Watch, the German Alpine Club's rescue organization, had already tried to help with the rescue of Toni Kurz. However, red tape on the German side (!) meant that they arrived too late and all that remained was for them to recover the body.

Later on the relationship between local and foreign rescue workers caused some friction—as, for example, with the 1957 Corti tragedy with the repercussions for the recovery of Stefano Longhi; his body was hanging as

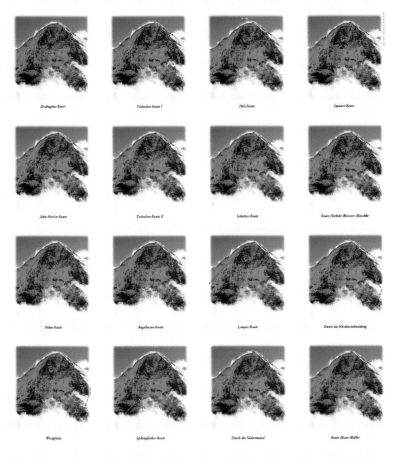

Wenn Sie mehr über die Tschechen-Route und die Japaner-Route wissen als über einen Bull- und einen Bearmarket: Überlassen Sie Ihre Geldangelegenheiten doch einem unserer Spezialisten **UBS Private Banking** *Der Spezialist für Ihr Vermögen* für Private Banking. Mit einem Beratungsmandat oder einem Verwaltungsauftrag haben Sie die Gewissheit, dass Ihr Geld in guten Händen ist. Während Sie Ihre Hände für die Dinge frei haben, die 3000 Meter und mehr über der Bahnhofstrasse liegen.

Wir machen mit.  Schweizerische Bankgesellschaft

A good fifty years after the ban, the private Swiss Banking Corporation uses the controversial Wall in advertising for hard business.

human proof of the "suicidal" Wall above the Traverse of the Gods and as proof of a half-successful rescue attempt. Thus mountain guides and railway officials from Grindelwald were suspected first of not wanting to rescue and second of even having hindered the efforts of voluntary rescuers from many countries (including Switzerland).

SAC was also denounced as the only club involved to have invoiced for the rescue, following which the saying "If a Swiss man eats a nail, a screw comes out" once again did the rounds, above all in the English press.

Victims Above, Victims Below

The payment demands made by the

Two climbers practice with a top rope on artificial holds on a simulated Eigerwand. It was built in October 1995 at the Jungfraujoch during the Swiss Tourist Board's "Winter Sun" campaign—a thankful choice, as many alpinists and tourists have made the journey to Switzerland because of the world-famous North Face.

Swiss during the 1950s and 1960s led, in general, to the criticism that the local rescuers had hardly contributed to the rescues on the Face but always made out an exaggerated bill. Scottish mountain guide, and member of the summit team on the Harlin Direttissima Route in March 1966, Dougal Haston, of all people, stood up for the accused mountain guides in his book *The Eiger.* He pointed out that for them mountaineering was no hobby but a profession and that, for this reason, they were within their rights to demand wages for those days on which, instead of taking clients out climbing, they had been involved in rescuing and recovering injured people who had no guides of their own.

But back to the turbulent year of 1957: Christian Rubi from Wengen, one of the courageous rescuers who had almost saved Toni Kurz and who was president of the Swiss Mountain Guides Association twenty years later, strongly defended his colleagues from the Jungfrau region after the *NZZ* and the SAC had attacked their behavior during the Corti rescue. The more deeply seated reason for Rubi's exaggerated stance was, however, completely different according to Jack Olsen in his book *The Climb up to Hell,* which describes the whole Corti-Longhi affair brilliantly

and excitingly. Rubi, who came from the working classes, had not one good word to say about the middle-class hotelier Fritz von Almen, owner of the hotel at Kleine Scheidegg. Von Almen was on the one hand helper, mentor, and—indirectly—rescuer of the Eigerwand climbers (they were allowed to stay in his hotel for a modest sum, and he watched their ascent with a 72x magnifying telescope). On the other hand he also made considerable profit out of the whole commotion. In a tragedy like that in 1957 his hotel was full of tourists and journalists. In one statement that was circulated Rubi insinuated that the whole rescue operation of Corti and his companions was the result of propaganda from the reporters, photographers, and hotel managers. A Social Democrat, Rubi's verbal attacks cost him his seat in the National Council, the Swiss parliament. One more victim of the North Wall.

The Sylphlike Swiss Versus the Austrian Oxen

Like Christian Rubi, Hans Schlunegger also came from Wengen. They were similarly aware of their responsibility to their profession, their calling, their homeland—"and even to life itself." Max Oechslin, for many decades editor of the SAC magazine *Alpen,* also fitted the mold: "But we do not approve of the fact that the pure mountains we inherited from our fathers are now branded a playground for record breakers." It was only logical that a prominent SAC member should describe the fifth ascent by four men from the Jura as "an idiotic prank." Jean Fuchs, Marcel Hamel, Raymond Monney, and Robert Seiler were pitched against Leo Forstenlechner and Erich Waschak, who had achieved the fourth ascent at the same time in one day: "Compare these delicate boys with the vigorous and powerful Austrians. It is obvious that the robust Viennese men should cope better with the ghastly North Wall."

The Swiss press was even more fiercely critical of Loulou Boulaz, the second ascentionist of the North Face of the Grandes Jorasses, when she attempted the climb with the Geneva Alpinist Pierre Bonnant, getting as far as the Difficult Crack. On 22 July 1937 the Swiss national press office sent a piece entitled "To the Eiger Storm" to all the editors in the country. It read, "The Eiger situation is getting worse. On Wednesday we read in the *Sport* from the pen of Othmar Gurtner, a courageous adversary of this idiotic mountain climbing, the following appeal to the famous Genevan Alpinist and skier Loulou Boulaz, who clearly can find no rest from the fame of being the first female to conquer the Grandes Jorasses: 'Yesterday morning at two o'clock the Bonnant-Boulaz team started up the Eigerwand. They reached the snow ledges beneath the Rote Fluh and as the weather turned they sensibly climbed down, reaching Alpiglen by nightfall. Fortunately the Genevan only has time this week but is determined to climb the Face if the weather is good.' To reproaches, the answer was given: 'We have achieved a lot of other things before.' Not so fast, Miss Boulaz. The Eiger is stronger than you. You are damaging your career and muddying the reputation of the Swiss mountaineers, together with whom you have been honored because of your wonderful and up to now lucky achievements. Hopefully bad weather will rescue you from the destruction that is almost certainly yours if you insist on setting foot on the Eiger intent on forcing the route at all costs. Leave this frivolous playing with death to the misguided ambitions of those who want to put their lives on the line for such a madcap idea. Do not tell us that what you do is no concern of ours. Your actions invite publicity."

In 1937 Loulou Boulaz made an attempt on the Eigerwand with Pierre Bonnant. This was strongly criticized by the Swiss press. The Genevan Alpinist had already proved, with the second ascent of the North Face of Grandes Jorasses with Raymond Lambert—together in this picture outside the Chamonix Station—that she could keep up with the best mountaineers of her time. From 1936 through 1941 Boulaz was a member of the Swiss National Ski Team and in 1937 she won a bronze medal in the slalom.

The First Swiss Summit with a Name

As Rudolf Rubi writes in his monograph about the Eiger, the Eiger is "the first summit in the Swiss Alps to bear a name that can be traced." In a document drafted in Latin about the sale of a plot of land sent from Ita von Wädiswyl to the Provost in Interlaken on 24 July 1252 it says next to the description of territory *"ad montem qui nominature Egere"*—"to the mountain that is named Egere." Fifty years later the name crops up again in a mortgage document written in German. There it says "under Eigere." Rubi writes that the "Mons Egere" owed its early name to the immediately neighboring areas that were both populated and cultivated. "It was a landmark that could not be missed." But what does Eiger mean? There are four explanations.

1. The name "under Eigere" is supposed to go back to the first settlers, in Old High German Agiger and also Aiger; for this reason the mountain above was called Aigers Geissberg and sometimes just Geissberg. Fortunately it did not remain at that. Geissberg (goat mountain), Mönch (monk), and Jungfrau (virgin) do not make good advertising copy.

2. There may be links with the Latin word *acer* and the Greek word *akros* for "sharp or pointed"; hence also the French term *aigu* of the same meaning.

3. The former way of writing "Heiger" could come from the pronunciation of "dr hej Ger"; *hej* means "high" and Ger was a spear of the ancient Germans.

4. Or does the name have something to do with the "ogre"—the man-eating giant of fairy tales? Since the tragic attempts to climb the North Face in the 1930s, the Eiger is commonly given the name "ogre" in French.

Hinterstoisser Traverse

I read the account of an early attempt at a first ascent of the face by four young climbers which became a desperate retreat that ended in disaster. The story of their battle to survive only to die almost within reach of rescue has become legendary. Toni Kurz, the last to die, was left hanging hopelessly in space. I saw a photograph of him hanging, slumped on his rope, with foot-long icicles growing from the points of his crampons, frozen in his last living moment when he whispered "I'm finished" to his rescuers; he died only yards from salvation. The manner of his death was the most poignant, most desperate, and heroic that I had ever read about.

When I finished reading the *White Spider* at fourteen I vowed to myself that I would never become a mountaineer. I would stick to rock climbing. Little did I realize that eleven years later in a peculiar twist of fate I would find myself in a position similar to Toni Kurz's and remember him as I fell into darkness.

Joe Simpson, *This Game of Ghosts,* 1993.

(facing page) Ueli Bühler launches out across the Hinterstoisser Traverse on a new rope in the grey of early morning. Back in 1936, just one of these old fixed ropes would have been enough to allow Andreas Hinterstoisser to retreat and stay alive.

Heroes or Victims?

The Alpenverein Youth Leader Ernst Enzensperger, of Munich, campaigned fiercely to establish youth teams. He believed in the values "which make youth hiking a breeding ground for the manhood which our nation so desperately needs: Simplicity, subordination, and camaraderie . . . . Everything in our times would be pitiful if it were not striving for that one great goal, wrong and unsuccessful if it did not raise itself out of the pitch-black background of German need, if it did not shine into the magnificent red dawn of a new becoming. After the dawn comes the day which the old folk would like to experience and which the young folk need to experience. The new, greater, more masterful, all-encompassing German Fatherland." At the first postwar meeting in 1919 of the German and Austrian Alpenverein (DÖAV), the world's largest mountaineering club with over 250,000 members and over 400 sections, the elitist Munich section Bayerland had already enshrined the care of "the spirit of the Fatherland" as the basic principle of the club. What this meant became obvious in 1924. At the extraordinary general meeting in the German Theater in Munich the Alpenverein decided—with a ninety percent majority—to exclude the Jewish section Donauland; all thirteen Munich sections were in agreement.

"Well in those days it was nearly always the case that on a Sunday somebody fell to his death. The body would be recovered on Monday and the funeral would take place on the Thursday. After the funeral we planned the expedition for the following weekend." Decades after the drama of 1936 on the North Wall Anderl Heckmair remembers the Dienst VI, which incorporated the top people in the Munich mountain rescue service. On that occasion its members were only able to recover the bodies on the Hinterstoissier rope.

Was the death of the German and Austrian mountaineers Andreas Hinterstoisser, Toni Kurz, Willy Angerer, and Edi Rainer a disaster of the mystical dimensions or a tragedy as portrayed in the ideology of heroic Alpinism? Rainer Amstädter uses the example of the failed attempt at the North Wall in 1936 to document the significance of German Alpinism in its multifaceted relationship to culture, politics, and the economy.

Mehringer-Sedlmay

First Bivouac

Lower Snowfield

Second Bivouac

Upper Snowfield

Third Bivouac

Second Bivouac

First Bivouac

Difficult Step

Third Bivouac
Falling Traverse

Reconnaissance
Bivouac

Rescuers

Gallery Window

Hinterstoisser-Kurz
Rainer-Angerer Party

Chronicle of the events of 1935 and 1936 from the newspaper *Sport* on 24 July 1936.

(Extract:)
21 August 1935.
The line climbed by the Mehringer-Sedlmayr rope.... The upper cross shows the area in which both were sighted for the last time after a heavy storm during the night of 24 August 1935. After which both men disappeared.

18 July 1936.
Climb of the two rope teams Hinterstoisser-Kurz and Rainer-Angerer; reconnoiter bivouac 7 July 1936 reached at 8.00 hours. Difficult downwards traverse ("Fallender Quergang") in 2 hours to the lower snowfield. Climb over the Difficult Step in 5 hours to the upper snowfield and diagonally up to the first bivouac. On 19 July set out to traverse the wall and climb to the second bivouac (fog). On July 20 the snowbound group has disappeared and the climb to the upper third of the wall has been abandoned. At 12.00 hours start of the descent from second to first bivouac and at 17.00 hours descent from the upper snowfield to the Difficult Step. The third bivouac is reached at 20.30 hours. On the morning of 21 July descent over the lower snowfield to and attempt to back climb the downward traverse. With the weather closing in descent to band of cliffs. Midday start to abseil. Before 15.00 hours three men claimed by the ice. The sole survivor's cries for help are heard after 15.00 hours by the railway track inspector.

From the Youth Movement to Elitist Alpinism

For two decades countless former officers from the First World War who were Alpenverein functionaries trained their youth to carry out obediently their duties in the all-German fight for reunification. "People of special goodness will force their way through everywhere,"maintained the Viennese Alpinist Fritz Rigele in his article "Der Eishaken" ("The Ice Piton"), which appeared in 1925 in the magazine *Bergsteiger,* the mouthpiece of the "alpine peoples'" agitation, and supported by the DÖAV. "We German mountaineers, however, are hurt by the peoples' need and distressed by their efficiency. Claim them for yourselves in the battle with the mountains. For you will still need battle practice." The invention of the ice piton, the forerunner of the modern ice screws with which climbers today secure themselves on the Eigerwand and elsewhere, is attributed to Rigele. During the first ascent of the North West Face of the Grossen Wiesbachhorns (3570 m) in the Glocknergruppe in 1924, Rigele and Bayerland member Willo Welzenbach, the first to climb many of the north walls in the Bernese Alps, used ice pegs for the first time to overcome the vertical obstacle in the middle of the ice wall.

The use of rock and ice pitons, which was scorned by many British and Swiss Alpinists (though only with them was it first made possible to climb faces such as the Eiger North Wall at all), was justified by the Germans in the interwar years not only in climbing terms but also ideologically: "The wish to reject all artificial aids would also mean having to reject completely the desire to fight and overcome, which inspires the modern mountaineer."

Radical German nationalist teachers, youth leaders, and clubs steered the sporting needs of the youth in their clubs, their joy in achievement, their need for competition, and their search for meaningful tasks in a clearly political direction. Thus it was no surprise that the National Socialist Reichsport leader Hans von Tschammer-Osten endorsed the usefulness of Alpinism as early as 1934. Nor did he want to be deprived four years later of congratulating the first North Wall climbers personally by telegram. And he is also in the famous photograph that shows Heckmair, Vörg, Kasparek, and Harrer with Hitler. (See also page 171).

From Life as a Mountain Vagabond to Success Fanaticism

In those days of increasing political hostility and economic hopelessness, some Alpine protagonists were forced to flee to a life as mountain gypsies. The problems that stemmed from a less than rosy economic climate increased many German and Austrian climbers' positions as outsiders both in climbing circles and socially. According to Viennese Sepp Brunhuber in the *Bergsteiger* magazine in 1940, mountaineering would serve as a "means of compensation for one's own feelings of inferiority, an escape from the tragic experience of a defeat or failure, in alpine activity that promised success and was a vent for one's feelings." In 1938 he undertook the first winter climb of the vertical to overhanging North Wall of the Cima Grande di Lavaredo (Dolomites) with Kasparek as preparation for the Eiger North Wall. Conquering longer, more difficult, and more dangerous walls became a sort of ritual of initiation among elite groups of youth teams and top mountain clubs. "Do or die" was the motto. Heroic Alpinism used the necessary physical closeness of the rope for the stylization of roped teams as "fraternization in life and death." And here once again a link was made with politics in that the camaraderie of the climbing rope was often used as a symbol of united deployment of strength for the greater whole, the national community.

The Last Great Problems of Heroic Alpinism

In the 1930s, the boundaries of possibility were pushed even further when the North Faces of the Matterhorn, the Grandes Jorasses, and the Eiger, so dangerous because of rock- and icefall, avalanches, and storms, were elevated to the position of the "three last great problems" of the Alps. In 1931 the Matterhorn North Wall "fell," as it was said in the jargon of the day. For this reason the Bavarians Franz and Toni Schmid received a special prize for outstanding Alpine achievement of the preceding four years at the 1932 Olympics in Los Angeles. Only Franz was able to receive his gold medal. His brother had fallen to his death at Whitsun in 1932 on the Gross Wiesbachhorn. In the book *Youth on Rock and Ice* there are the pointed sentences: "He is a toughly resolute fighter for whom there is only victory or defeat, but no fraternization with the opposition. Having to abandon plans and retreat is almost an emotional catastrophe for him." After the Germans Martin Meier and Rudolf Peters had climbed the North Face of the Grandes Jorasses for the first time in 1935, only the Eiger North Wall remained to be conquered.

The Tragedy of Toni Kurz and His Companions

It is early summer of 1936 and German mountaineers have already pitched their tents beneath the Wall. Albert Herbst and Hans Teufel from Munich achieve the first ascent of the Schneehorn North Wall while waiting for better conditions on the Eigerwand. Teufel falls to his death in an avalanche during the descent.

The Grindelwald guide representative Gottfried Bohren announces in the local paper, *Echo von Grindelwald,* that mountain guides have been freed from their duty of rescue on the North Wall so that they are not forced into dangerous situations which others have chosen

wilfully. A few days later the exiled Austrians Willy Angerer and Edi Rainer arrive in Grindelwald and make their first exploratory trip onto the Eigerwand. Three weeks before the Olympic games in Berlin, Bavarian mountain soldiers Andreas Hinterstoisser and Toni Kurz, newly registered army mountain guides, arrive from Bad Reichenhall. The news is greeted with interest in Berlin.

Only on 11 July, after pressure from Nazi Germany, Papen, the German Ambassador, forces the signing of an agreement with Austria. The Germans see this as the first step toward annexing Austria. A victory for the two rope teams would have the desired symbolic strength.

On 18 July both teams climb separately, but using the same route, onto the Wall. Thanks to a downward tension traverse, Hinterstoisser reaches continuation of the route above a steep, smooth rock slab beneath the Rote Fluh. At the end of the traverse he attaches the rope. The others follow easily using the fixed rope. After traversing they take the rope in again. Thus their retreat is impossible. You cannot back climb a downward tension

"If only the weather holds" is the hope voiced by Andreas Hinterstoisser in a conversation with Grindelwald photo reporter Hans Jegerlehner, who had spent the final evening before the ascent with him and his roping partner Toni Kurz. Jegerlehner also took the famous photo of the two Eiger North Wall hopefuls. He worked for the renowned *Neue Zürcher Zeitung* and *Basler Nachrichten.* The weather did not hold. But that was only one reason for the disaster.

traverse. Apparently none of the men is thinking of retreat. The Hinterstoisser-Kurz party begin to lead over the First Ice Field. When Angerer and Rainer fall back they drop a rope to the Bavarians in order to bring up Angerer, who has been injured by rockfall. After a first bivouac on the edge of the Second Ice Field the four carry on in spite of Angerer's obvious injury. Over the whole day both ropes only climb 200 meters of the 1800-meter Wall and must bivouac for a second time.

On the third day they slowly reach Death Bivouac where Mehringer and Sedlmayr had frozen to death the previous year. Angerer's injury has slowed progress to such an extent that a joint arrival at the summit no longer seems possible. Alone, Rainer is unable to bring down the injured Angerer so they all begin the descent. In the late evening they bivouac on the upper edge of the First Ice Field for the third time. During the night the weather finally turns: It pours down and the temperature continues to plummet. On day four the rocks on the traverse— the section of the climb that will become known by the name of the first man to climb it—are icy and impassable. Thus the only remaining possibility for the four climbers is to abseil straight down the vertical to overhanging rock sections.

Albert von Allmen, the track inspector of the Jungfrau Railway, sees them

from the Gallery Window. They are 150 meters above him standing on a knob of rock, and he promises he will put the kettle on for them when they reach the Window. However, when he looks up an hour later three of them have already perished in the rockfall and avalanches of fresh snow. Hinterstoisser has fallen all the way to the foot of the Wall. Angerer has hanged himself on his rope while falling. Rainer has frozen to death hanging on his rope. Only Toni Kurz is still alive and crying for help. Von Allmen calls the railway station using the line telephone. In spite of their having been freed from their duty to rescue, four mountain guides make a special expedition up to the Gallery Window. Threatened by rockfall and avalanches, they are unable to climb the treacherous, ice-covered rock up to Toni Kurz. Promising to return the next day, they climb back down to Window at dusk.

Meanwhile, the Mountain Watch in Munich has been notified. Their leader, Ludwig Gramminger, gathers a rescue team from Dienst VI (for the sixth level of difficulty) that comprises the best Munich mountaineers of the 1930s. The following morning an airplane from the German Interior Ministry leaves for Bern with the rescue team on board. On this day, Toni Kurz, who against all expectations has survived the stormy night, dies trying to reach the local guides by abseiling down the overhang that separates them. The *National-Zeitung* newspaper of Basel prints Arnold Glatthard's report on the front page on 23 July 1936:

'"Comrade, just a little further and you've made it!'

But suddenly Kurz stops making progress.

'What's up?'

In answer a weak 'I can't get the knot through the carabiner.' (In order to cover the 50 meters distance two ropes must be tied together).

'Try comrade, you have to do it.'

"If anything happens, the film's in there. You know where it is." Toni Kurz to Jegerlehner, the reporter, about his film from the first attempt at climbing up to the Rote Fluh. Kurz put the film in a spare rucksack which stayed in the tent below. The only other film of the tragic attempted assault was found but could not be developed.

Kurz is still 5 meters from the rescuers.

But it is not meant to be. The German has no strength left in his thickly swollen fingers. He lets his arm fall. A gust of wind turns his body from the vertical to a horizontal position. The guides can't reach him from below, as the unfortunate man is now hanging in midair 4 meters away from the Wall. He no longer hears the repeated calls for him to take courage. The end is rapidly approaching. 'I can't do it!' he calls in an even weaker voice. He then lets both arms fall and collapses completely. The last courageous fighter on the Eiger North Wall has been released from his suffering."

When the mountain guides return to the Gallery Window, eight mountain rescuers from Munich have just arrived. All that remains for them is to recover the bodies. As they, too, are unable to reach Kurz swaying on his rope in the air, they cut through the rope with a knife attached to a long pole. His body plummets to the depths. While rescuers are looking for the bodies of the fallen mountaineers as well as Angerer and Rainer, the body of Max Sedlmayr, who had perished the year before, is also found. On 24 August 1936 Rudolf Peters and Hans Hintermeier, mountain soldiers detailed to look for Kurz's body, find it in a deep crevasse at the foot of the Wall. The search for Hinterstoisser is abandoned in September; the German-Austrian rope of Matthias Rebitsch and Ludwig Vörg find him in 1937 on their first attempt at the Wall.

"Homecoming for a Dead Legionary"

On 5 September 1936 the *Oberländische Volksblatt* of Interlaken prints an announcement from the *Linzer Volksblatt* entitled "Homecoming of a Dead Legionary" to mark the occasion of the burial of Edi Rainer in Salzburg: "The dreams of a young man worthy of regret, have in the Third Reich (to

which he is said to have fled for political reasons) no more been fulfilled than those of many others like him, for only after lengthy service in the legion was he given the job of clerk. Rainer was one of the best climbers in Salzburg, very popular and respected in climbing circles. Thus his political defection was even more regrettable as in him one of the best mountain comrades had gone beyond the bounds."

Rainer was, like his roping partner

"I can't go on" or "I can't do it." Whatever his last words were, they, like the brutal picture of the hanging Toni Kurz, will go down in Alpine history. Both Ludwig Gramminger, member of the Munich rescue team, and Walter Gabi, the photographer from Wengen, pressed the shutter—for personal use and for publication, respectively.

Willy Angerer, a member of the Austrian SA (the paramilitary NS terrorist organization "Sturmabteilung"). After the National Socialists came to power in Germany in 1933 the SA and the SS were responsible for the bombing attacks in Austria. Thus, Hitler's NSDAP forced the annexing of Austria. After a hand grenade attack injuring thirty the NSDAP was banned in Austria. In ever-increasing numbers young men who might have done anything wrong crossed the border. Edi Rainer was taken prisoner, but he managed to escape to Germany during a spell in the hospital. The refugees were grouped

together in Munich as the "Austrian Legion," given military training and positioned on the border as an armed force against Austria. National Socialist terrorist attacks were constantly on the increase. The illegal SS movement was supported by members of the Tyrolean intelligentsia, for example in the teaching body at the University of Innsbruck, whose principal Raimund Klebelsberg had also been president of the DÖAV since 1934. The smuggling of explosives from Munich to the Tyrol and the infiltration of SS assassins was accomplished with the support of different Alpenverein sections by lending use of their mountain huts.

After the failure of the terrorist politics of the radical National Socialists, the agreement reached between the Germans and Austrians on 11 July 1936 resulted in the legalization of the moderate Austrian Nazis and thus in the increase of National Socialist pressure. At the general meeting of the Alpenverein on 27 July 1936 Klebelsberg was already able to support openly and warmly their turn to National Socialism. In his address he also mentioned the "honorable memory of those whose lives were sacrificed on the Eiger."

(preceding pages) Stormy scenes on the main stage and in the wings. The influential British *Alpine Journal* called the first ascent of the North Side of the Eiger of 1932—the Lauper Route on the North East Face (on the left, in shadow)—a great route; by contrast, six years later, the ascent of the true North Face (on the right, in sunlight and wisps of cloud) was dubbed the most imbecile variant since the beginning of Alpinism.

(above) "We don't want to die, we're still young and want to live. We always leave our way down open. We know that it takes luck and we have to count on that." The Eiger warriors and SA members Edi Rainer and Willy Angerer in a newspaper report by Jegerlehner. To Othmar Gurtner, Jegerlehner's greatest rival, Rainer and Angerer said, "If it is possible to do the Wall we'll do it—if not, we'll stay up there."

Confession of Guilt

The reaction to the drama on the Eigerwand, as published in the *National-Zeitung,* ranged from justification and defense through recognition and approval to criticism and judgment for foolhardiness and dicing with death. Amidst those voices that spoke of mock heroism and failed existence was that of Alpine author Gunther Langes, inventor of the giant slalom and the first to climb the Schleierkante of the Cima della Madonna in the Pala group of the Dolomites. He saw a mock heroism being bred in the fight to conquer the last problems. Great was the fault of the ideological climate in which the mountaineering youth had grown up, he wrote in *Bergsteiger*.

He was one of the few to confess to his own involvement in this development: the frivolous misjudgment, the underestimation, and the denial of the objective dangers because of a "superhuman will." Thus a devastating judgment has been passed about the last stages of the development of alpinism, which we tolerated, which we admired and against we put up no fight. It is not those who died on the Eiger Wall who are guilty; no, we are, each one of us who is involved in alpinism."

Rainer Amstädter (born 1951) is a mountain guide, sport climbing trainer at the University Sport Institute in Vienna, sport historian, lecturer at the Institute for Sports Studies at the University of Vienna, consultant for the television channel ORF for the program "Land of Mountains," and correspondent for the Austrian outdoor magazine *Land of Mountains*. His book *Alpinism: Culture, Organization, Politics,* the first comprehensive social, cultural, and ideological history of German and Austrian mountaineering, was published in 1996.

"Rescue and transport down of Toni Kurz's body." Shots from the Eiger North Wall film made by the Munich Mountain Rescue Team, found sixty-two years after the tragedy.

Swallow's Nest

At seven o'clock the traverse is already behind them, but something is on course for them from above; they are hit, not by falling stones but by empty food tins. Incredible, the unexpected dangers you might encounter up here. They notice now that they are not completely alone on the Wall. From the Swallow's Nest two of their predecessors look down on them. They all know each other well. The antagonists in this early morning tin attack are Jenny and Hausheer. They have bivouacked, cooked, and breakfasted here, and are highly surprised to receive the early visitors from below. The two new arrivals, Martin Epp and I, are no less surprised to see Paul and Werner up here. We know that Paul has already completed some moderate climbs, but he has no experience on ice so to speak. Werner, on the other hand, is not supposed to have been on a proper big mountain route at all. The Eigerwand is to be his first. Let's hope there are no accidents.

Paul Etter, *Gipfelwärts*, 1968.
Eigerwand ascent in 1962 and descent in 1963.

(facing page) Fritz Maurer and Max Zehntner take a short break at the Swallow's Nest. On early ascents this was a popular site for a first bivouac.

From the Eiger Cave to the Eiger-Ostegg Hut

(above) The Mittellegi Hut built in 1924: pictured during construction with the first ascentionist of the Mittellegi Ridge, Amatter, in the foreground; and with the supply helicopter and the extension added in 1986 (facing page, upper).

(facing page, lower) The Eiger cave, which was mentioned for the first time in 1828 and rediscovered in 1984.

On the Mönch there are three huts: the Guggi on the north side, the Mönchsjoch on the south side, and the Bergli. On the Jungfrau there are only two of them: Rottal and Silberhorn. And until 1997 the Mittellegi Hut was the only Alpine shelter on the Eiger. Marco Bomio looks back over 170 years of hut construction history on the Eiger.

"Eiger cave? Never heard of it, no idea." That was the usual reaction even from the older mountain guides and mountaineers when in 1984 they were asked by local historian Rudolf Rubi about this bolt-hole at the back of the Eiger that is so steeped in legend. While doing research for the Grindelwald homeland book series *In the Valley of Grindelwald,* Rubi had come across Eiger cave mentions in various tour reports. This first Alpine shelter on the Eiger now seemed to have been forgotten. What other option was there than to set off on the search for the cave "beneath the great Horn of the upper Kalli behind the Eiger," as the position of the Eiger cave was described by Caspar Rohrdorf in 1828? And, indeed, on a cloudless August Sunday in 1984 we were able to rediscover the Eiger cave at about 2600 meters in the lower Challiband, 150 meters south of the 2677-meter point (on the "d" of Unders Challiband on sheet 1229, "Grindelwald," of the 1:25,000-scale Swiss map).

Rohrdorf's Royal Cave

The entrance to the cave is over 10 meters wide and several meters high, but the inside does not represent the classical view of a cave. The floor is on a considerable incline and very uneven so that Caspar Rohrdorf's description of "Royal Cave" seems a little exaggerated. In addition to this, the Grindelwald mountain guides whom he had engaged in order to climb the Jungfrau, and who had chanced upon the cave en route, had to make the sleeping area accessible by making stone steps and leveling it out with stone slabs. On one stone slab letters have been etched or chiseled; for example, an R—possibly even from Rohrdorf—or CA, which, as Rubi suspects, can most probably be traced back to the first Eiger climber Christian Almer. Since our rediscovery the Eiger cave has been used for overnight stops now and again by Alpinists who love to return to the origins of mountaineering. Its regular use had, however, already come to an

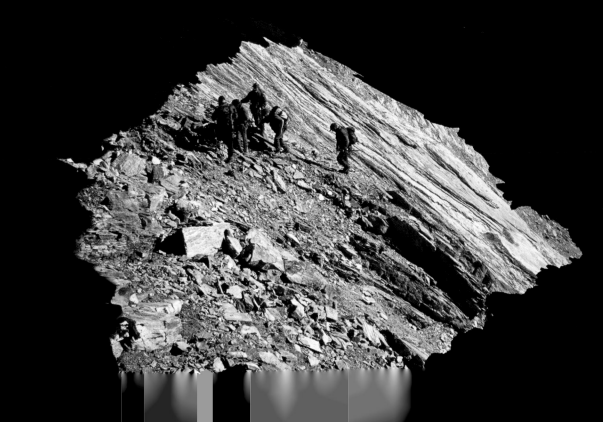

end in 1869 when the Swiss Alps Club's Bergli Hut (3299 m) was built on the other side of the ice lake on the Bergli crags.

The Swallow's Nest of the Mountain Chaplain

In the *Echo of Grindelwald* on 6 August 1904 the Grindelwald mountain chaplain wrote about the origins of this Alpine shelter—the eighth hut of the SAC which was founded in 1863: "The hut was built in the summer of 1869 in

Between 1869 and 1903 the Bergli Hut was rebuilt and extended three times. Since then this shelter, which at one time was the only one on the far side of the Eiger, Mönch, and Jungfrau, has remained the same—a jewel from the pioneering days of Alpinism.

Grindelwald and transported up in the autumn. Guide Christian Bohren had undertaken the transport for 400 Francs. The Swallow's Nest was completed at the beginning of July 1870. It had cost almost 900 Francs, and in addition a few Francs for internal fittings." In 1883 a new, drier Bergli Hut was constructed, and this in turn gave way to a third in 1903. On account of the tourist and mountain house on the Jungfraujoch (1924–1972) and the Mönchsjoch Hut (3650 m), which came into use in 1979, the Bergli Hut lost its significance for Alpine tourists. In addition, it could only be reached by experienced high-level climbers. Anyone in this bracket

who is also not averse to Alpine historical romanticism would find this a uniquely situated shelter in the ice mountains behind the Eiger.

Yuko Maki's Ridge Hut

Only 1.5 kilometers away from the Eiger cave as the crow flies is the equally legendary Mittellegi Hut (3355 m). Its history is, however, not mysterious and is quickly told: Pleased at the successful first ascent of the Ridge on 10 September 1921 and so that subsequent mountaineers need not bivouac unprotected on the isolated ridge like the first climbers, the Japanese Yuko Maki gave the mountaineers 10,000 Francs for the construction of a shelter on the Mittellegi Ridge. It was built in 1924 and only renovated for the first time over sixty years later in 1986. With the renovation the hut was kept in its original condition and the shingle on the roof and the side walls was replaced. In the same year, in order to relieve the problem of space, a few meters east of the Mittellegi Hut an additional shelter in the form of a tubular steel construction was created. Now almost thirty people can be accommodated on the Mittellegi Ridge. However, because in good weather conditions even more mountaineers spend the night in the Mittellegi Hut, and thus the cooking of meals and the payment of overnight taxes by the Alpinists there cause ever-increasing difficulties, since 1995 a warden has been engaged to oversee catering and maintain good order in the Mittellegi Hut.

The Guides' Jubilee Hut

Until 1997 the Mittellegi Hut was the only shelter that was actually situated on the Eiger itself. The Mönchsjoch Hut, which serves as a starting point for the Eiger climb via the Eigerjöcher, lies, of course, at the foot of the South East Ridge. The difficult connecting ridge between the two summits with the southern and northern Eigerjoch was climbed for the first time in 1874 by George Edward Foster, a rich banker from Cambridge, with the guides Hans Baumann and Ulrich Rubi; they did not have enough time to continue to the summit of the Eiger via the south ridge. The first climb of this ridge was accomplished by the same party two years later, when they reached the northern Eigerjoch directly via the heavily crevassed Eiger Glacier.

In 1998 the Grindelwald Mountain Guide Club celebrated its 100th birthday. As a lasting memory of this jubilee the Grindelwald mountain guides built a second hut on the Eiger. This simple mountain shelter with space for twelve people is on the most northeasterly part of the Mittellegi Ridge on the Ostegg at 2320 meters. From the Alpiglen Station of the Wengern Alpine Railway it takes three to four hours to reach the hut on a marked and often isolated path with easy to moderately difficult sections of scrambling (fixed ropes) in two places. It is worth visiting the hut merely because of its unique position high above the Grindelwald Valley. For Alpinists who are not afraid of terrain that is crumbling in parts, the Eiger-Ostegg Hut serves as a starting point for the traverse of the Eigerhörnli to the Mittellegi Hut. This makes for a difficult tour with unusual scenery: At the key point on the feature known as "the Hick," which used to be made less laborious with a fixed rope, bolts have been inserted for belays and protection. The first traverse was made on 6 August 1927 by the Japanese Saburo Matsukata and Samitaro Uramatsu with the Grindelwald guides Emil Steuri and Samuel Brawand. In future it will also be possible to do a complete traverse of the Eiger in two and a half days without taking any bivouac gear. A great present that the Grindelwald Mountain Guides' Association has given itself—and all mountaineers—to celebrate its 100th birthday!

Marco Bomio (born 1954), main occupation senior school teacher, secondary occupation mountain guide and journalist for the specialist alpine press, lives in Grindelwald, in the shadow of the Eiger.

Zur
Mittellegihütte

In 1998 the Grindelwald Mountain Guides' Association erected the Eiger-Ostegg Hut on the most northeasterly part of the Mittellegi Ridge. Thanks to this hut and the Mittellegi Hut, the Eiger can now be climbed from Grindelwald in two and a half days.

Rote Fluh

The Rote Fluh is a wall within a wall. After the first third of the Face this dark, 300-meter precipice can be seen to the right of the First Ice Field. A kind of North Face of the Cima Ovest di Lavaredo stuck in the middle of the Eigerwand, as Hermann Buhl put it seventeen years ago. Those who knew the North Face had often spoken of the Rote Fluh but all thought that it would surely never be climbed, since it was really a route in itself. But the Japan Expert Climbers' Club (JECC) people came, saw, and conquered. From 15 to 30 July, the five little men and the dainty little girl, Michiko, worked on the lower half of the Face as industriously as ants, convinced that at some time they would be raising their flag—covered in signatures and well-wishes—on the summit of the Eiger....

Above the Difficult Crack, the Japanese climbers left the classic route taken on the first ascent and struck out into new territory on the left-hand part of the Rote Fluh: 180 meters high, vertical, with mostly overhanging rock that was frightening even for masters of Grade VI climbing; featureless reddish-yellow rock with only the occasional tiny ledge or thin crack line and otherwise nothing but shadows and the void.

Toni Hiebeler, *Abenteuer Eiger*, 1973.
Japanese Route in 1969.

(facing page) A member of the Swiss team, who made the first winter ascent of the 1969 Japanese Direttissima, jumaring up the fixed ropes on the overhanging Rote Fluh in January 1970.

The Alpine Development of the North Side

A night out on the Eiger-wand. Whoever intends to climb old or new routes on the huge, shadowed Wall has to get used to the idea of spending at least one night out, whether it is a comfortable night in the hammock or an ill-protected one on a sloping ledge.

More than sixty years have passed since the first ascent of the North Face by Anderl Heckmair and companions in July 1938. Since then, twenty-plus routes have been added and there appears to be no end to the developments in sight. Each generation of mountaineers sought out and realized its own objectives on the north side of the mountain in accordance with the standard of equipment available, the climbing techniques being used, and the general or individual mountaineering ethics subscribed to. This fascinating Wall will remain a place of special adventure. Daniel H. Anker, who himself has climbed three new North Wall routes, provides an overview of the developments.

For the best climbers and mountaineers of the 1930s the greatest challenge was a first ascent of the most impressive faces on the three highest and most famous Alpine summits. In the summer of 1931 the brothers Franz and Toni Schmid were the first to climb the North Face of the Matterhorn. The year 1935 saw Rudolf Peters and Martin Meier's success on the Croz Spur of the Grandes Jorasses. What remained was the gloomy precipice of the Eiger. Although the Swiss team of Hans Lauper and Alfred Zürcher—with Valais mountain guides Alexander Graven and Joseph Knubel—had already climbed the steep North East Face on 20 August 1932, the real North Face, even steeper and more intimidating, remained inviolate.

The first serious attempts—by the Germans Karl Mehringer and Max Sedlmayr in 1935 and again in 1936 by a rope of four comprising Andreas Hinterstoisser, Toni Kurz, Willy Angerer, and Edi Rainer—had ended with two tragedies, with all six mountaineers meeting their deaths. The reputation of the infamous Eigerwand was born. The mountain's stubborn refusal to succumb and its fame attracted new aspirants. All hoped to climb the difficult Face and thus achieve the greatest success of their mountaineering careers. To do so, they were prepared if necessary to take great risks. In July 1937 Bertl Gollackner died attempting the Lauper Route high on the Mittellegi Ridge; his partner, Franz Primas, was rescued. On 21 June 1938 two Italians, Bartolo Sandri and Mario Menti, fell to their deaths on the

North Face, from a point level with the Difficult Crack.

Under the Spell of the Heckmair Route

Four weeks later, on 21 July 1938, the Austrians Heinrich Harrer and Fritz Kasparek started out. For the first ascent of the ice-plastered Wall they had only one pair of crampons between them. They realized their mistake on the First Ice Field but the weather was (still) good and they had their German competitors, Anderl Heckmair and Ludwig Vörg, who had begun their definitive attempt on the climb one day later, snapping at their heels. Heckmair was well aware of the fact that on this Face rapid progress can mean the difference between life and death. Yet he still allowed himself to be persuaded to join forces and climb with the slower Austrians. After the bivouac on the upper section of the Ramp the bad weather naturally arrived. In spite of this it was clear to him that the way ahead lay upward; after all, several times before on his winter ascents he had experienced bad conditions on the mountains, and had braved snow-covered rock and ice-cold fingers. Although one or two things did not go exactly according to plan, the rope of four reached the summit on 24 July 1938 and descended happily down the West Flank to continue their lives in the glare of the spotlights.

After the Second World War the greatest challenge was a repeat of the route of the first ascentionists. The great fame of the Eigerwand—founded on the tragic attempts to climb it, the work of the Nazi propaganda machine in lionizing the first ascent, and the difficulties presented both by the climbing and by the weather conditions—attracted climbers of all shapes and sizes. Several inexperienced climbers managed what for them was a very risky route, while others lost their lives on it—all under the eyes of the spectators and reporters manning the telescopes at Kleine Scheidegg and

Alpiglen. Even the real experts among the mountaineering fraternity were unable to resist the lure of the Eiger-wand. The first repeat of the '38 Route went to the Frenchmen Louis Lachenal and Lionel Terray, two of the best Alpinists of the time, from 14 to 16 July 1947. The following ascents all took the route climbed by the first ascent party. Although several teams attempted to force a direct route from the Flatiron to the Spider, this was really just a case of finding a shorter form of the original route. All these attempts failed to overcome the difficulties presented by the wet and icy rocks below the ice field of the Spider.

The Race for the Harlin Direttissima

At the beginning of the 1960s a new generation of young and talented climbers arrived on the scene. They had not experienced the war firsthand, either at the front or protecting their own borders. They came in search of their own objectives. They found their challenges in winter or solo ascents and in opening up new routes in a direct fall line from the summits. These young climbers were not interested in the first-ascent traditions of the prewar generation. They were no longer shy of placing dozens of pitons and using

Posing for posterity: Jörg Lehne, Günther Strobel, Roland Votteler, Dougal Haston, and Siegfried Hupfauer on 25 March 1966. Together they climbed through a terrible snow-storm to complete the Harlin Direttissima, done over one month in expedition style by German and Anglo-American teams and the first new line on the Face since the Heckmair Route.

(right) In the summer of 1969 a Japanese team of five men and one woman overcame the Rote Fluh—180 meters high at this point—using 150 bolts and 20 normal rock pegs, fixed ropes, and ladders. In January 1970 five Swiss climbers repeated this, the second Direct Route on the Eigerwand. This and photo on facing page originate from this ascent.

(facing page) Delicate and exposed climbing on the summit wall.

etriers; artificial climbing from piton to piton became fashionable. Featureless sections of rock were dealt with summarily by placing expansion bolts.

After the first winter ascent of the Heckmair Route in March 1961 by the Germans Toni Kinshofer, Anderl Mannhardt, and Toni Hiebeler and the Austrian Walter Almberger (they climbed first as far as the Gallery Window, returning with the good weather one week later and completing the climb from the Window to the summit) and the first solo ascent on 2 and 3 August 1963 by the Swiss mountain guide Michel Darbellay, many of the top mountaineers of the day concentrated their attention on an Eiger Direttissima. It is significant that the first winter ascent of the Lauper Route by the Swiss rope of Hans Peter Trachsel and Gerd Siedhoff had to wait until 1964 and took place without arousing any great attention.

From 1963 on it was as if there was an outbreak of a contagious disease as Eiger aspirants turned up from everywhere. Experience in the use of fixed ropes and interim camps, gained on expeditions to the eight-thousanders of the Himalayas and big-wall climbing in California's Yosemite Valley, was transferred to the most famous faces in the Alps. It was a time of great change, and not just in mountaineering—everything seemed possible. Technology was developing apace; the first manned space capsule had just orbited the Earth.

In March 1966 the stage was set. Since higher temperatures held the danger of stonefall in a direct fall line from the Spider, the climbs took place in winter. The new route required over a month of work, ascending and descending on fixed ropes, stocking and improving camps and always with one rope doing the lead climbing and fixing a rope for the climbers following to ascend using jumars. A German and an Anglo-American team were each attempting to find a route up the Face just a short distance from each other. Only after John Harlin fell to his death from a damaged fixed rope when climbing back up with additional equipment did the two groups join forces, climbing together through a snowstorm to finish off the route and reach the summit.

Crowds on the North Pillar, Bolts on the Japanese Direct

After the first ascent of the so-called Winter Direttissima, the next new route aspirants were not long coming. There was still room for a Summer Direttissima, and on the left side between the classic Heckmair Route and the Lauper Route a prominent pillar awaited a first ascent. In the summer of 1968 two ropes of four set to work almost simultaneously on the North Pillar. On 28 July the Polish team of Krzysztof Cielecki, Tadeusz Laukajtys, Ryszard Szafirski, and Adam Zysak started up to the west of the Pillar. They climbed parallel to the Harlin Direttissima, doubtless flirting with the idea of a new direct route to the left of the classic Heckmair Route. However, they were repulsed by the 200-meter-high, partially overhanging rock step above the Eigerwand Station, and traversed off left across ledges before climbing straight up to join the North Pillar and finishing up the Lauper Route to gain the summit.

Two days after the Polish ascent, the brothers Reinhold and Günther Messner,

with Toni Hiebeler and Fritz Maschke, attacked the weakest point to the east of the Pillar with their sights firmly set on the North Pillar itself. For this group—and particularly for Reinhold Messner—it was obvious that the line should be logical and climbed with the

Whether caught in powder snow avalanches on the Central Ledges of the Japanese Direttissima (above) or stormbound at base camp on the West Ridge pillar (below), successful North Face ascents are always dependent on the right weather and equipment.

least equipment possible. Three weeks earlier, the Messner brothers had done a new route on the Heiligkreuzkofel in the Dolomites with a very exposed crux section boasting Grade VII difficulty, a level that at the time did not officially exist, not by a long chalk (the maximum was VI+). Their new route on the Eigerwand took a line to the left of the actual arête of the North Pillar.

Almost exactly two years later, from 28 to 31 July 1970, the three Scotsmen Ian McEacheran, Bugs McKeith, and Kenny Spence opened up a very diffi-

cult route up the steep rock pillar of the North Ridge. The first three steep sections of the climb—a total height difference of some 600 meters, involving Grade VI free climbing and very hard aid on normal rock pegs—were equipped with fixed ropes. They then climbed on up the now easier angled pillar, breaking through onto the uppermost section of the Face at the same point as the Lauper Route that came in from the North East Face.

Meanwhile, in mid-July 1969, a group of Japanese—among them a woman—had dared to attempt a summer direct route. In tried and trusted expedition style they had discovered a climbable passage through the Rote Fluh, the steepest part of the entire North Face of the Eiger. Using the predominantly artificial climbing techniques fashionable at the time, many hand-drilled bolts and fixed ropes, they forced a line up this mostly overhanging reddish-yellow wall. In this way, Takio Kato, Yasuo Kato, Susumu Kubo, Hirofumi Amano, Satoru Nigishi, and the woman doctor Michiko Imai gained the Second Ice Field, where they jettisoned their fixed-rope lifeline to the ground. Over some very difficult free climbing terrain, the Japanese continued, heading for the summit, always keeping one camp on the Face to which they returned down fixed ropes each evening until the next could be found and established higher up. After a total of one month, they climbed out onto the summit.

The following winter the Japanese Direttissima received its first winter ascent, by the Bernese Oberland team of Hans Peter Trachsel, Peter Jungen, Otto von Almen, Hans Müller, and Max Dörflinger, all members of the "Bergfalken" extreme climbing club.

The Czech Invasion and Exploratory Forays onto the West Ridge Pillar

For a few years, the Wall had some respite from mountaineers with first-ascent ambitions. Then, in the summer of 1976, the best Czech alpinists were finally allowed to travel through the Iron Curtain to climb in the Alps. Jiří Šmíd, Sylva Kysilková, Petr Plachecký, and Josef Rybička needed no second bidding and straightaway attempted a new line slightly right (west) of the Japanese Route. This very demanding climb traces a line through the right-hand side of the Rote Fluh in its lower part and was the first route on the North Face of the Eiger not to finish at the summit (3970 m) but at 3700 meters on the West Ridge.

Šmíd and Rybička were gripped by Eiger fever. One and a half years later they returned to the North Face with Miroslav Šmíd and Jaroslav Flejberk to climb another new route, this time in winter. They chose the 300-meter-broad, unclimbed section of the Face between the North Pillar on the left and the lower part of the Harlin Direttissima and the Ramp on the right. Using predominantly artificial techniques, they worked their way up the steep wall from 16 January to 27 February 1978.

Up until that time, the rock walls at the outermost right-hand section of the North Face had remained untouched, apart from an exploratory foray by Heckmair who, on his first attempt with Theo Lesch in 1937, had followed the line of least resistance up the wall right of the Geneva Pillar, reaching the West Ridge at a height of some 2800 meters. At the end of the 1970s, a new generation of young Swiss climbers had begun to become interested in the Eiger. It was no longer important to reach the summit by as direct a route as possible, or by another new route. Rather, a vertical to overhanging rock pillar below the West Ridge was to become the focus of their attention, even though in the bigger picture of the northern precipice this appeared as only a small bit part. Although barely twenty years old, Geneva climbers Michel Piola and Gérard Hopfgartner were fascinated by this over 300-meter-high, featureless wall. On the cliffs of the Saléve region near Geneva, they had experimented with the techniques required on the most difficult new routes; futhermore,

With the first route on the West Ridge Pillar in 1979, the Geneva team of Michel Piola and Gérard Hopfgartner ushered in a new era on the North Face. Nowadays, the Geneva Pillar has already achieved classic status as a free climbing route. Kaspar Ochsner has climbed it in both summer (photo) and winter (first ascent in February 1981).

they had begun to climb existing routes free, without the aid of pitons. After several attempts, August 1979 saw their successful first ascent of the Geneva Pillar. The route "Les Portes du chaos" required for the first time free climbing in the lower seventh grade, quite apart from the approach up the initial rocks. It was only at the end of the 1970s that the decision was made to extend the alpine grading system upward, beyond VI+. The name of the route, too, was a sign of the new era, in tune with the imaginative (or otherwise) route names gracing the smaller crags of the *klettergarten* (climber's garden). This first ascent provided the impulse for further new rock routes to be put up on this section of the Wall. In the climbing scene, the talk began to turn to "all free" and sport climbing, as free climbing pitches increasingly began to be protected by bolts.

New Routes in Multipack Format

In the 1980s on the North Face, two distinct trends could be observed. On the one hand there were new routes going up at the highest levels of technical difficulty, mainly climbed by Swiss parties; on the other hand, good alpinists from around the world came here to satisfy their desire to climb a new route on the Eigerwand, ending on the summit if possible. The rock structure on the central part of the Face did still

Eiger man from Eastern Europe. Czech climber Jiří Šmíd was involved in three new routes between 1976 and 1986. The Czech Pillar was also the first climb not to finish on the summit. With over 100 bivouacs to his name, Šmíd was also one of the Eiger bivouac kings. In 1999, he was killed by rock-fall while opening a new route at the Schwarzmönch, the northwestern bastion of the Jungfrau.

offer possibilities, although the gaps between the routes were growing narrower and routes crossing each other became more common.

In August 1981, Swiss free climbing pioneers Hans and Christel Howald, with 8000-meter-peak collector Marcel Rüedi, added a natural new line up the prominent North Corner and for the first time the seventh grade of difficulty appeared—several times—on an official topo of an Eiger route. The first ascentionists placed bolts for safety on most of the stances that were capable of withstanding loads in excess of one ton. They also placed intermediate bolts; these were not to serve as aid but as protection for the difficult free climbing sections. In 1982 Slovenian Franč3́ek Knez—climbing solo—and the Swiss rope of Kaspar Ochsner and Urs Brunner successfully prospected for new routes on the section of the Face west of the Geneva Pillar. When viewing the Eiger from Männlichen, this part of the North Face looks small and insignificant, yet at this point the Wall still has a height of 600 meters, and the cold, serious atmosphere of this steep and featureless zone of rock, broken by rubble-strewn ledges, conveyed to the climbers the requisite "North Wall ambience." The year 1983 brought no less

than three very different new routes. On 20 March, Slovakian Pavel Pochylý set sail on his epic thirteen-day odyssey, climbing the direct fall line from the summit. This so-called "Ideal Direttissima" had already been attempted in 1977 and 1978 by Czech teams. The second team's climb had ended below the Fly on the summit wall when the lead rope fell. The lower part of the Ideal Direttissima follows the route climbed back in 1935 by the Germans Karl Mehringer and Max Sedlmayr; they made it as far as the Second Ice Field, before a snowstorm forced them to remain—forever—on a ledge above the Flatiron, a place which later became known as Death Bivouac. Despite miserable weather conditions, Pochylý fought his way up the Face and, with indescribable good luck, survived the adventure.

From 9 to 12 July 1983, after a day spent preparing the route, Swiss climbers Pierre-Alain Steiner and Paul Maillefer put up the first real sport climb on the Eiger. These two outstanding climbers simply abseiled from the West Ridge down the north side and traversed across ledges to the foot of the compact steep wall of the Geneva Pillar. Their route "Spit verdonesque édénte" is protected almost entirely by bolts and calls for demanding climbing up to Grade VIII. For the first time, a route on the Eiger could be approached in training shoes or lightweight rock boots without having to cross patches of snow; to this day, the climbing can be done in one day with no problem and is limited to nine interesting pitches.

At the end of July of the same year, after several abortive attempts over the previous few years, Michel Piola and René Ghilini finally succeeded on a direct route up the highest and most prominent rock spur above the Rote Fluh. It gave Grade VII free climbing interspersed with sections of aid, and on some sections the etriers had to be hung from "cliffhangers" placed carefully in tiny holes, like steel fingers, since the compact nature of the rock refused to accept normal peg placements. Bolts were placed only on the stances, and in places where progress could not be made by any other means. A retreat from the almost continuously gently overhanging Pillar would require awkward rope maneuvers. In 1983 rescuers were unable to offer much assistance even from a helicopter.

In March 1985 Jiří Šmíd, with exiled Czechs Michal Pitelka and Čestmír Lukeš, claimed his third Eigerwand route, this time between his 1976 climb and the Japanese Route. The first ascent team christened their route the "Toni Hiebeler Memorial Route"; it involved difficult aid, steep sections of ice, and a lot of mixed ground. In the summer of the same year, Slovenian Franček Knez returned to the North Face. Together with Mayan Freser and Dani Tic, this new-route specialist opened up a new direct route on the left-hand section of the Face, giving mainly extremely difficult free climbing; climbing like an express train, he did it in only two days.

Climbing Boom on the Western Part of the Face

In the jubilee year of 1988 there was a renewed onslaught on the right, or western, side of the Wall, with several first ascent parties bustling about one after another. A group of Indonesians was attempting to find a new line based around the North Corner, climbing in expedition style and installing a chain of fixed ropes. After a month they had completed their route, which follows the Howald Route in parts, or a line very close to it.

On 5 August 1988, laden with heavy sacks, Michel Piola and I climbed up and over the initial rocks of the Face, heading for the Geneva Pillar. After the first steeper rock band we moved off leftward to the foot of a steep and compact cliff, more than 100 meters broad and leading a quiet and undisturbed existence between the North Corner and the Geneva Pillar. This roughly 400-meter-high wall never gets a single ray of direct sunlight the whole

year long. While we were preparing a narrow ledge for the bivouac, we gazed longingly across at the North Face, where the warming red light of the evening sun briefly alleviated and dissolved the stark contrast that reigns between the serious atmosphere of the rock and ice on the Face, the cowbells on the green alpine meadows, and the antlike movements of the tourists down at Kleine Scheidegg.

The next morning two other climbers turned up further across on the initial pedestal at the foot of the Wall. The Czech brothers Miroslav and Michal Coubal were making strenuous headway up the ill-defined pillar between the North Corner and the Piola-Ghilini Route. Pitch by pitch they climbed higher, first equipping the difficult sections, then abseiling back down

Kaspar Ochsner on the 1983 sport route "Spit verdonesque édenté." *Spit* means "bolt," *verdonesque* is a reminder of the French climbing paradise the Verdon Gorge, and *édenté* means "toothless." But there is certainly enough bite to this route, which finds a way up a vertical to overhanging zone of slabs, with sections of climbing up to Grade VIII, even if the approach can be made in training shoes.

again, with one of the climbers finally redpointing the whole pitch on the lead—that is to say, climbing it without hanging on any of the protection and without using artificial aids to make progress. So two new routes were being climbed almost simultaneously, with the Swiss team using tried and tested practices imported from the Alpine crag scene, and for the first time on the Eiger employing a portable drill to place the necessary bolts. Most of the belays were equipped using the drill,

(above) The constant search for new territory. In the summer of 1997, Italians Andrea Forlini and Gianni Faggiana finished the extremely difficult new route, "Yeti," on the West Ridge Pillar.

(facing page)"Mr. Eiger" is undoubtedly Michel Piola. With four new routes to his credit between 1979 and 1992 (Le Chant du Cygne pictured), the Geneva Alpinist epitomizes modern times on the Eiger.

but the climbing itself was protected where possible with nuts, Friends (special camming devices used in flared cracks), and normal rock pegs, with the second removing the gear again. Only on exposed and very hard sections would interim bolts be placed and these would then be left *in situ*. The route finished close to the rock mushroom on the West Ridge where in 1974, during the shooting of his Eiger action film, Clint Eastwood had had to cut his rope while dangling out over the abyss. The new route thus received the name "Eiger Sanction."

One week later I was back at work on the Eiger again. Together with Michael Gruber, I was prospecting for a climbable line up the compact collection of walls on the extreme right-hand side. Of course, the crux sections

should also be climbable without recourse to aid. Our luck was in, and the steep and solid mountain limestone turned out to be peppered with a lot of nice little pockets. Protection was almost exclusively from bolts and cams. With seven pitches of climbing, interspersed with rubble-strewn ledges, "Löcherspiel" is an ideal route to get used to the rock structure and the gloomy atmosphere of the north side of the Eiger.

The Development Is Not Yet Finished

In the 1990s the trend toward sport climbing began to be applied more and more to the Eiger. The most recent ascents have concentrated almost exclusively on the Heckmair Route and on the sport climbs that can be done in a day. A glaring exception to the trend was accomplished by the well-known American climber Jeff Lowe. Over thirteen days on the Wall, Lowe showed everyone what adventure can be. Alone and without bolts he worked from 19 February to 4 March 1991—with one day's break—on his own route, somewhere between the Japanese Direttissima and the Pochylý Route, straight up to the summit.

Also in 1991, Michel Piola and I climbed the slabby plinth at the base of the Wall directly below the Geneva Pillar. The line gave interesting climbing on compact rock up to the soaring vertical Pillar, and the approach no longer involved hundreds of meters' height gain over dangerous, loose ground and steep snowfields. For the continuation up the upper section of the Wall in July 1992, we decided, in view of the heavy rucksacks, on an approach from half height, coming in from the West Flank. Several abseils and traverses saw us passing beneath the start of "Spit verdonesque édénte" and arriving back at our project. The aim was no longer simply to get up it any old how; for us, it was important to free climb every meter of the route if at all possible. We were really happy when

we actually managed this, adding ten very steep sport climbing pitches right up to the top of the Geneva Pillar. Nor were we shy about using the drill to place the necessary protection; now, anyone wishing to repeat "Le Chant du Cygne" can do it with only Friends and nuts for additional protection—these can be stripped again by the second without any great loss of time.

In 1998, a new route was established by the Italian team of Andrea Forlini and Gianni Faggiana—the "Yeti." Forlini and Faggiana finally topped out on 29 August after several forays and a total of twenty-six days spent on the wall, including the time spent preparing the route in 1997. The Yeti Route starts at the so-called "dynamite hole" on the lower section of the North Face, and takes a line between the existing climbs "Eiger Sanction" and the North Corner to join the West Ridge. The route exits to the right of the Mushroom, a rock tower which overhangs the North Face. The Italians' route is 800 meters high and eighteen pitches long, and involves mandatory free climbing sections of Grade VII. Forlini warns that the aid climbing sections, on which they were obliged to use etriers, would be Grade IX or even X if climbed free.

In the summer of 1998, the Swiss pair Daniel Anker and Stephan Siegrist set off on the twenty-fifth route on the North Face of the Eiger—and from a free climbing point of view, technically the hardest. It traces a line from the Gallery Window and up the Rote Fluh (at its highest and most overhanging point) and the Czech Pillar direct to the West Ridge. It will be finished in 2000.

What might yet happen on the Eiger, then? For new routers, the extensive central section of the Wall certainly holds the promise of climbable, as yet untouched rock; the routes will, however, cross each other more and more frequently. A grade push seems possible on the western part of the Wall, with very hard free climbs still to be done. In addition, many existing routes still await a repeat, a first winter ascent or first solo. Sixty years after the first ascent of the North Face, there are still things to do on the Eiger.

Daniel H. Anker (born 1959), teacher and mountain guide, climbed ten different routes on the Eigerwand between 1982 and 1992, among them four first ascents ("Eiger Sanction," "Löcherspiel," "Le Chant du Cygne") and a first solo (North Corner). He has also climbed new routes in Colombia, Peru, and Patagonia, and done many new free climbs in the Alps. To avoid confusion with the journalist of the same name, he uses the name Daniel H. Anker in his articles.

(left) Doctor Michiko Imai is the first woman to have taken part in a first ascent on the North Face. With her five companions, she climbed for sixteen days without a break on the new Japanese Direttissima. (The bad weather continued on the descent but she still managed a smile for the camera.)

(facing page) Swiss mountain guide Evelyne Binsack solo on the Lauper Route. For the 1999 television program "Eiger Nordwand Live" she was one of four actors, and the only woman.

Women on the Eigerwand

In September 1964 the first woman successfully climbed the North Face of the Eiger. This was Daisy Voog, Estonian by birth and living in Munich, accompanied by German Werner Bittner. They took four days.

Voog was not, of course, the first woman on the Wall. As early as 21 July 1937, Swiss climber Loulou Boulaz, the sole woman to become involved in the race to climb the North Faces of the Matterhorn, the Grandes Jorasses, and the Eiger, got to a height of 2700 meters with Pierre Bonnant. In 1962, Boulaz made a renewed attempt on the route, this time with Michel Darbellay and Yvette and Michel Vaucher, but sudden bad weather forced them to retreat from the Ramp. The second ascent of the classic '38 Route went to Frenchwoman Christine de Colombelle; the first Swiss women were Yvette Vaucher and

Natascha Gall, in 1975, each accompanied by men. The first British woman was Alison Hargreaves, who did the climb in 1988, when six months' pregnant. In the summer of 1993 she returned to the North Face, this time quite alone. The first winter ascent by a woman fell in February 1980 to Claudia Heissenberger. The first solo—and thus the first winter solo—was made by Frenchwoman Catherine Destivelle on 9 March 1992, in just seventeen hours.

Women have also written their names into the history books of the North(east) Face on routes other than the Heckmair Route. In August 1937, Swiss mixed doubles team Lucie Durand and Hans Haidegger set out to make the second ascent of the Lauper Route. Due to the bad weather conditions they traversed left at the Lauper Schild, reaching the Mittellegi Ridge at the so-called "Hick" at the foot of the steep upsweep at about 3650 meters.

The first female ascent of the Lauper Route was only made in 1966, again by Daisy Voog. On the first ascent of the 1969 Japanese Direttissima, a woman, Michiko Imai, was on the team. Women were also part of the Czech Direttissima (Sylva Kysilková in 1976) and the North Corner (Christel Howald in 1981). The second ascent of the Messner-Hiebeler Route on the North Pillar was made by the all-woman Polish rope of Wanda Rutkiewicz, Danuta Wach, and Stefania Egierszdorff in September 1973. They were the first women to climb the North Face without male accompaniment. On 29 and 29 August 1999, Daniela Jasper-Klindt and her husband, Robert Jasper, made a new combination with the lower part of Le Chant du Cygne with the Spit verdonesque édenté. Though this is not really a new route, the couple named it "Symphony of Liberty."

First Ice Field

I was not the first man to tackle the Eigerwand alone. Two others had tried in recent years, but both had died in the attempt. The aura of fatality and blood that hangs over this killer mountain seemed painfully distinct to the eyes of a solo climber, restoring it to the atmosphere of the early years.

I appeared on the first snowfield simultaneously with the first thundering salvo of boulders, and I just had time to dodge smartly back into the Swallow's Nest before they came shooting by. The incident did not surprise me; it is natural on a face like this that as soon as the upper snow slopes are touched by the sun they should start to unload their wares, and it was by chance that with the whole wide face available they had fallen exactly where I happened to be. No harm had been done. So I started again up the first snowfield, which in fact consisted of bare ice.

Walter Bonatti, *I giorni grandi (The Great Days)*, 1971.
Eigerwand attempt in 1963.

(facing page) Ueli Bula belays his climbing partner at the edge of the First Ice Field. After the hot summer, there is not much left of the ice. But it is cold nevertheless when the wind sweeps the refrozen thaw snow down the Wall.

The Eiger on Skis

(right) Eiger (on the right), Mönch, and the Eiger-gletscher between them on a poster by Paul Lecomte from the year 1930. Said Walter Amstutz, son of a Mürren hotelier, ski pioneer, Director of Tourism, and advertising expert: "With Lunn, we tried to popularize alpine skiing and downhill racing and I did the ski tour on the Eiger to prove that downhill was an important discipline."

(facing page) Frenchman Bruno Gouvy visible as just a tiny dot on the West Flank on 21 April 1985. The same day, he snowboarded down the East Face of the Matterhorn and the South Flank of the Grandes Jorasses.

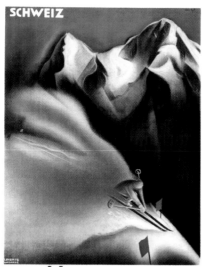

On 18 May 1924, Englishman Sir Arnold Lunn, known as the inventor of the downhill and the slalom, with porter Fritz Amacher, a lift boy at the Hotel Baer in Grindelwald; Mürren hotelier's son Walter Amstutz; and his Bern University colleague Willy Richardet, set out with their skis to climb the savagely crevassed Eiger-gletscher to the Northern Eigerjoch (3614 meters). From there they continued on foot along the South Ridge to the summit. This brave ski tour took place in the golden year of Alpine skiing and is described by Lunn in his publication _British Ski Year Book_. The following account, a shortened version of Lunn's text, originally appeared in _The Mountains of Youth_.

I spent my winters in full view of that great curtain of snow which falls from the Eigerjoch to the Scheidegg. The sight irritated me. I knew that I should have no peace of mind until I had imprinted on these snows the signature of my skis. . . . May seemed to be the most promising month for the climb. The Eigergletscher faces north, and even in April many of the snow bridges might still be formed of loose winter powder. Not until these bridges had been melted and refrozen into compact crust could there be any chance of success.

We roped up and left the Eiger-gletscher Station at 10:15 P.M., followed by tearful forebodings....We climbed rapidly, threading our way through countless crevasses. The false corridor which I had spotted from below did its best to lure us to a cul de sac, but we avoided the temptation and pressed steadily upward. We had been climbing for about four hours when we were pulled up by a formidable obstacle: a wall of ice separated from us by a crevasse that was not too securely bridged. Amstutz and I were leading, and I suggested a frontal attack up a convenient crack which seamed the face of the Wall. Amstutz preferred to try conclusions with a pinnacle, the summit of which was connected to the opposite wall by a rickety snow bridge. I followed him reluctantly. He murmured something about "giving him a shoulder," but giving a shoulder had lost its charm since the invention of crampons, and I received his suggestion very coldly. Meanwhile, Richardet had arrived and settled the matter by

promptly attacking the wall of ice by the route that had struck me as feasible. He crossed the crevasse and was soon busy chipping handholds in an ugly bulge of ice which led into the crack. I watched him with pleasure . . . .

The crack, once reached, was wide enough to admit his body. He worked himself upward, using the feeble friction between the ice and his back, chipping an occasional handhold, and helping himself with his crampons. We heard him breathing heavily, and then at last came the shout of triumph which told us that he had won through. The ski came up on a rope. Fritz and Amstutz followed, and then my turn came . . . .

We reached the North Eigerjoch at 6:30 A.M., eight hours after starting. The view was wonderful. We looked down on to the great glaciers which flow from the Mönchjoch toward Grindelwald and beyond them to the Schreckhorn and Wetterhorn. We could see almost the whole extent of one of the loveliest of all snowfields, the Ewigschneefeld. The Mönch and Jungfrau were looking their best . . . .

The last rock ridge leading to the summit was easy enough, excepting for two steep pitches which required care. We reached the summit at 9:30 A.M., eleven hours after leaving the Eiergletscher Station . . . .

We left the summit at 11 A.M., scrambled down the rock ridge, and found, as we had expected, the ice slope leading to the Eigerjoch in bad condition. The superficial snow was melting and called for the greatest care . . . .

We put on our skis at the Eigerjoch and ran down to the head of the icefall, a perfect run on ideal snow. Had we been on foot we would have had an arduous tramp under a burning sun. All went well until we reached the "Drop and Check" pitch, where a nasty surprise awaited us. The bridge we had crossed in the morning had succumbed to the heat and disappeared. One other

Arnold Lunn on 18 May 1924 at the Northern Eigerjoch.

bridge still survived, but its appearance was not encouraging. The snow that composed it was melting in the heat. It presented a quaintly dissipated appearance and sagged visibly under the strain of keeping itself up. Fritz, who was leading, started shuffling across. Suddenly his right leg broke through; he gave a cry of anguish and retreated. We passed him down two pairs of skis. He laid the first pair across the bridge and shuffled forward again, pushing the other pair ahead of him in order to prolong this bridge of skis. Not for the first time that day we were grateful to our skis.

Very gingerly Fritz proceeded on all fours, keeping his hands and knees firmly on the skis. The situation was complicated because he had to cope not only with a large single crevasse but also with a whole network of intersecting crevasses, most of which were partially or entirely concealed. And as soon as he left the skis and stood up, he broke through again. Finally, in an exhausting process, he picked his way to solid ground . . . .

We had spent an hour crossing the crevasse and it was getting late. I had hoped to reach the Eigergletscher Station shortly after midday, for I knew that the lower slopes are liable to be swept by tremendous snow avalanches. We were four hours late and I felt distinctly nervous. The snow was easy but the ground was difficult, and roped skiing reduces one's speed considerably. We were tired, and I was feeling the strain. The labyrinth of crevasses seemed unending. Stemming turns and Christianias followed in unending succession, while we strained every nerve to avoid falls and to waste no moment of time in the race for safety. Our anxiety was not unreasonable. An hour after we reached the Eigergletscher Station a tremendous avalanche peeled off the buttresses of the Mönch and thundered down the slopes that we had descended.

The remains of this avalanche were still visible in the late summer. Had the avalanche fallen an hour earlier nothing could have saved us . . . .

We reached the Eigergletscher Station just after 4 P.M., nearly eighteen hours after we left . . . .

The Eiger on skis by the Eigerjoch is a magnificent expedition. The interest is sustained from start to finish. There is not a dull moment on the climb. I have seen no view that impressed me more than the view from the summit as we saw it in May. The icefall by moonlight stands out among a host of Alpine memories, unique in its severe beauty. Nor was the skiing a disappointment. We enjoyed in all some 4500 feet of running, of which about 2000 feet was easy and pleasant, and the remainder difficult but intensely interesting.

The expedition was severely criticized in certain quarters. We were told that the climb was an anomaly, neither justifiable as a ski tour nor sound judged by normal canons. . . . If every expedition that involved a risk of ice or snow or rock avalanches had to be ruled out as unjustifiable, some of the greatest climbs in the Alps would never have been attempted . . . .

But I am very glad that we were not dissuaded from leaving our ski tracks on the slopes below the Eigerjoch, for no day among the mountains has left a more enduring impression on my memory, and there is no climb to which I look back with greater pleasure than those eventful hours among the snows and icefalls of the Eiger.

Sir Arnold Lunn (1888–1974) made the first ski-ascents of many summits, wrote the first two ski touring guidebooks to the Bernese Oberland, and was the inventor of the modern ski race. At age ten he was one of the first to ski in Chamonix. He organized the first international ski races—encompassing downhill, slalom, and combination events—held in Grindelwald and Mürren on 4 and 5 January 1924. At the end of the same month he founded the Kandahar Ski Club in Mürren. That same winter the first Winter Olympic Games were held in Chamonix (without the Alpine skiing events, however), the international ski organization FIS was founded, and the first Parsenn Derby took place in Davos. And finally, in November 1924, Lunn's ski companions Amstutz and Richardet, together with Hermann Gurtner, held the inaugural

Snowboard extreme. Bruno Gouvy snowboarding the Eiger West Flank in 1987.

Is the Eiger Really a Ski Mountain?

The Englishman Frank Smythe, one of the best Alpinists of the period between the wars (two new routes on the Brenva Face of Mont Blanc, first ascent of Kamet), described the route across the heavily crevassed Eigergletscher chosen by the Lunn party as "extremely dangerous, and anyone wishing to climb the Eiger by this route should be unmarried and have no children." In spite of this, Smythe made the first winter ascent of this route—on foot, even though he was a wild man on skis—in January 1929, with T. Y. Kagami, of Japan.

On 13 April 1951, the English woman Angela Stormonth-Darling and her guide Oskar Gertsch reached the Southern Eigerjoch from the easier Jungfraujoch side of the mountain. A descent to the north from the Southern Eigerjoch across the ice field was out of the question, however. Thus, they removed their skis, lashed them together, and for four hours climbed up the exposed

and corniced connecting ridge to the Northern Eigerjoch. The two skiers were back down in Wengen in time for afternoon tea.

"He'll never get down alive!" the spectators at Kleine Scheidegg are alleged to have said; they were watching through the telescope on 9 March 1970 as Sylvain Saudan started off from the summit of the Eiger on his ski descent of the West Flank, which in its upper reaches has an average angle of 45 degrees.

On 21 April 1987, Frenchman Bruno Gouvy surfed down it on a snowboard. On 16 and 17 May 1983 the Italian pair Toni Valeruz and Bruno Pederiva skiied down the 1700-meter, up to 60-degree-steep North East Face of the Eiger—the so-called Lauper Route. They did this not once but twice, since the descent was being filmed by various television crews. Where it was not possible to ski, they abseiled.

We now wait for the first descent of the North-East Face of the Eiger on a snowboard.

Ice Hose

After two pitches, the snowfield lies below us and we come to a damned awkward section. The First and Second Ice Fields are connected by a 100-meter-long gully that is completely iced up. It is massively steep and sometimes almost vertical.

The Wall shows itself as it really is. One step after another has to be cut; ice pegs must be placed. And all this on almost vertical ice. With my right hand, I cut a series of steps upward and rightward at full stretch, then again up and left, and so on. Reaching rock I belay on an old piton and bring Zdeno up.

While Zdeno hammers the pegs out so we can use them again, I enjoy the panoramic views. The first train crawls up to Kleine Scheidegg. Around the hotel, little black dots swarm—the tourists. A long snatch of an old shepherd's melody reaches our ears. We know the originator. Day after day he stands before the hotel and blows an ancient long alphorn. The idyllic tones accompany every climber on his passage up the Wall....

Suddenly, the sound of an engine! An airplane flies the breadth of the Wall. It disappears behind a rocky rib, turns, and comes back. It looks as if we have been noticed down at Kleine Scheidegg and the press have been informed. The theater begins.

Radovan Kuchař, *Deset Velkých Stěn (Ten Big Walls)*, 1967.
Eigerwand in 1961.

(facing page) Martin Grossen on the Ice Hose, at a time when it certainly lived up to its name. Nowadays at this point climbers often encounter awkwardly sloping rock which is often covered in a thin veneer of ice.

West Side Story on Ice

Back in the days when no one spoke of the greenhouse effect and the Eigergletscher had not yet melted back, tourists at Eigergletscher Station—opened in 1898—would take to the slippery slopes and the cool grotto for a little fun. There was no danger involved, except perhaps to the delicate shoes the ladies wore.

It has become one of the best-researched hanging glaciers in the Alps. The reason? If, as feared, our climate does become warmer, the Eiger ice could start sliding. Peter Krebs summarizes the situation.

Ignored by tourist brochures and mountaineers in equal measure, the west side, in direct comparison to the North Face, appears less precipitous. Yet it is still steep enough. Right in the middle stands the Kleine Eiger. Behind the back of this subsidiary peak the ice world of the Eigergletscher extends.

On the other side of the Kleine Eiger, the one facing us, one can make out a second short glacier, high up, 1000 meters above the station, breaking off abruptly halfway down the Wall. For years, it did not even have a name. Now it is known to glaciologists and climatologists everywhere as "the hanging glacier on the west flank of the Eiger."

Suddenly in the Spotlight

Like all glaciers, hanging glaciers are fed from above with new ice, which then flows downhill. The glacier grows. Due to the steepness of their situation, hanging glaciers—unlike valley glaciers—do not extend down to warmer zones, where the snout melts. The mass of ice achieves its balance by periodic "calving" at the front edge; in rare cases, huge and destructive icefalls occur.

In spring 1990 a larger icefall seemed imminent on the Eiger. Observations were sent to the VAW, the hydrology and glaciology institute of the ETH in Zürich. This marked the start of a comprehensive program of research. The objectives were twofold. The Jungfrau Railway wanted to clarify whether or not the glacier posed a threat to its Eigergletscher Station, while for the scientists it was a rare opportunity to take a closer look at a hanging glacier.

The 30-degree, steep hanging glacier on the Eiger is prone to avalanches, but favorable conditions in May 1993 allowed a research team of ETH glaciologists to land by helicopter. The expected icefall had indeed happened in August 1990, without causing any damage, and the ice had since restabilized. Working with specialized equipment, and under unusually difficult conditions, the glaciologists measured the ice masses, took temperature readings, and determined the flow rate at the surface.

A Hot Surprise

The whole glacier rapidly renews itself and consists of "young" ice. Even at the bed of the glacier, where it creeps forward more slowly, the ice is only several hundred years old. The glacier lies at an altitude of between 3200 and 3500 meters, where the mean yearly air temperature is -6 degrees. Astonishingly, most areas of the main body of the glacier are distinctly warmer, often reaching melting point. The glaciologists attribute this to the fact that when rain and meltwater penetrate and freeze, and through the movement of the ice, heat is given off.

The coldest part is located at the bed of the glacier, near the front edge, where the lowest outside temperatures penetrate. In this area the ice of the substratum is frozen; thus, the glacier is relatively firmly anchored. The mass of newer ice above cannot disturb the equilibrium; it does, however, cause considerable tension and loads the ice of the lower stratum to the limit of its breaking strength.

Cool Enough in the Future?

It appears uncertain whether the hanging glacier will be able to withstand this pressure in future. Glaciologists are attempting to determine what effect the expected worldwide temperature rise will have on its stability. The Intergovernmental Panel on Climate Change's preferred scenario estimates that by the year 2100 the greenhouse effect will cause global warming of between 2 and 4 degrees. This would cause the surface area of the glacier to shrink by some forty-five percent. A general rise in temperature would also result in more rain and meltwater penetration. This would place an addi-

tional load on the front edge. In all probability, critical stability would be reached. The front would no longer be able to hold back the ice masses. The glacier would start to slide . . . .

According to one survey, the railway itself lies outside the danger zone. However, ski lifts and footpaths might be in danger from a large collapse.

For this reason, both the Jungfrau Railway and the VAW have been keeping the hanging glacier under close scrutiny for several years now. At Eigergletscher Station, an automatic camera has been installed that takes a photograph every day. Annual aerial photographs and helicopter reconnaissance flights supplement the safety program.

Peter Krebs (born 1953) is a freelance journalist and editor of the Swiss Federal Railways magazine *Via*. In 1997, with Dominik Siegrist, he published a walker's handbook, *Klimaspuren: 20 Wanderungen zum Treibhaus Schweiz* (Rotpunktverlag Zürich).

(above, upper) The Eigergletscher comes down from the Eigerjoch and flows beneath Kleine Scheidegg in the direction of the Eigergletscher Station. (above, lower) The hanging glacier on the West Flank of the Eiger, showing the break-off zone.

(left) Fear of a larger icefall in spring 1990 led to a sign being erected warning people in four languages of the danger of straying onto the area behind Eigergletscher Station.

Second Ice Field

The First Ice Field, then the long Second Ice Field. Small stones whistle down at us from above. One of these many little ones gets my right index finger. Only nine fingers left for climbing. That's enough. The sun has reached the rack railway station; trains are coming up and down regularly. It looks like it's going to be a good day for the tourists: They can watch us through their binoculars. "Can they do it?" they will ask themselves over lunch, while the two little ants move incessantly upward. That's us. On the Second Ice Field we are moving in the center of the arena. We are not on a wall of death, but we have already begun to move into something like a death zone. While, down below, the drudgery of everyday life mechanically moves along, up here we are totally dependent on ourselves. Only we can help ourselves. Toward midday we reach the "Bivouac." Time for a break. We have no fear. Nevertheless, the tension remains. The Ramp and the crumbling Traverse of the Gods. My God, what kind of rubble heap is this mountain.

Reinhard Karl, *Erlebnis Berg: Zeit zum Atmen,* 1980.
Eigerwand in 1969.

(facing page) Oswald Oelz balances up the black ice of the Second Ice Field on the front points of his crampons. Stones are visible imbedded in the ice—mute witnesses to the stonefall which repeatedly peppers the Ice Field.

Rescue in the Third Dimension

The helicopter is already approaching, in order to fly the injured Japanese Kenji Kimura directly from the summit to hospital. But he still has to be rescued from the Wall using a cable winch and then carried on the back of Grindelwald mountain guide Rudolf Kaufmann.

Without the dozens of direct helicopter rescues from the Eiger North Wall—the first successful one was in 1971 off the Second Ice Field—countless alpinists would have remained on the Wall, as did Mehringer, Kurz, and Longhi before them. But even today every helicopter rescue carries a certain risk. Climbers who rely upon modern rescue technology rather than realistic estimations of their own personal ability and conditions on the Eiger endanger not only their own lives but also those of the rescuers. Marco Bomio follows the development of flight rescue technology.

August 1935. Swiss military pilots repeatedly fly their planes as close to the Eigerwand as they can. But it is neither military nor tourist reasons that force the pilots to carry out these delicate flight maneuvers. It is to try to spot Max Sedlmayr and Karl Mehringer, who climbed onto the Wall more than five days ago so that they might be the first people to solve this "last problem of classical Alpinism." After a change in the weather it is no longer possible for the many onlookers to see them from Kleine Scheidegg, and one can only assume the worst. In mid-September German A1 pilot Ernst Udet and his passenger, Grindelwald mountain guide Fritz Steuri, discover one of the two mountaineers standing in the snow, frozen to death at the upper end of a distinctive ledge; there is no trace of the other. Later this ledge becomes know as the "Flatiron" and the spot where the other mountaineer froze to death as "Death Bivouac."

When the North Face of the Eiger was climbed for the first time, in 1938, a plane was also included in the party. On 23 July, the third day of the successful undertaking, Bern photographer Hans Steiner took a picture of the four German-Austrian climbing partners on the traverse from the Ramp up to the Traverse of the Gods. During the first two decades of Eiger North Wall history these planes were used for research and photo flights. While in September 1957, on the occasion of the dramatic rescue of the Italian Claudio Corti, a plane was used merely for a reconnoiter flight, in July 1959 a plane was used for the transport of rescue equipment. This transportation of rescue equipment facilitated the recovery of the body of Corti's rope mate, Longhi, who was

(preceding page) Using a rope of up to 227 meters on the end of which the rescuer hangs with a radio and an anchor pole, the helicopter no longer needs to fly into and remain in the rockfall zone. Thanks to the longline technique it is also possible to access vertical and over-hanging wall sections directly. But when the weather conditions remain so treacherous for such a long time as in the case of Mehringer and Sedlmayr, even the most modern rescue methods are useless.

unable to be rescued alive during the drama two years earlier. A plane transported the equipment to the upper part of the Eigergletscher, about 500 meters beneath the Eiger's summit. From there the rescuers had to carry the equipment on foot to the summit. They recovered Longhi's body with the help of a cable winch.

The First Helicopters on the Scene

The use of planes to transport equipment or even people during mountain rescues has very narrow limits, even when glacier flight pioneers like Hermann Geiger (1914–1966) were able to land and take off again on incredibly small and steep snowfields. A limited maximum permitted load and a rapid loss of power at great altitude prevented helicopters from being successfully used until the 1960s. A helicopter was used for the first time to transport equipment onto the Eiger in 1965. A plane was used for the unsuccessful rescue of Japanese mountaineer Tsuneaki Watabe. In July 1967 the first recovery of bodies by helicopter took place. The bodies of four mountaineers from the former East Germany who all fell at the Hinterstoisser Traverse had to be recovered from the foot of the Wall.

Helicopters Make Their Mark as a Means of Rescue

On 25 January 1970 the Japanese climber Kenji Kimura, who broke his lower leg while attempting the Exit Cracks of the Eiger North Wall, was evacuated from the Eiger summit in an expensive rescue operation. It was the first-ever winter rescue on the Eiger summit; once again the tried and tested cable winch was used.

This operation demands the utmost skills of the pilot, as the rescuers must climb out of the swaying helicopter onto the narrow summit ridge at a height of 3970 meters. Only a few months later in a similar rescue operation (of Sergio De Infanti from the Exit Cracks) this method had already been refined and the rescuer was winched down from the swaying helicopter onto the summit ridge.

On 12 September 1971 the first serious helicopter rescue took place.

The Germans Martin Block and Peter Siegert were surprised by a sudden change in the weather, and at night they sent an emergency signal with their lamps toward Kleine Scheidegg. They were plucked directly from the Second Ice Field by helicopter.

When Eiger Rescues Become Routine

After the first direct rescue from the Eiger North Wall in autumn 1971, mountaineers, both male and female, have been rescued practically every year directly from the Wall.

"Rescued by helicopter without any problem" wrote Kurt Schwendener, head of mountain rescue, in the records for the rescue. But not all of the twenty-five direct rescues from the Wall between 1971 and 1987 have been without problems. This is shown by remarks such as "helicopter rescue impossible," "heavy rockfall, never again," or "operation abandoned for safety reasons!"

Date: 18 November 1977; Place: Ramp

In a nerve-wracking operation two Spanish mountaineers, Jesus Fernandez and Miguel Angel Perez, the latter with two broken lower legs, are rescued from the Ramp at the last possible moment. Once again the rescuers take an enormous risk—not least of all because of the danger that they may not be able to be flown off the Wall in time because of the threatening weather conditions. This whole tale has been made into an impressive story in the book *From the Diary of the Swiss Air Rescue Team:* "My friend could no longer walk. Both his legs were broken. It felt like this was the end. We had had nothing left to eat for ages. Snow, which fell in excess each day, served as a thirst quencher. The tenth day was the day of our reincarnation: We saw a helicopter. 'It looks like they've seen us,' I called to Miguel, 'they're signaling.' . . . One of the rescuers made signs from the helicopter which we read as 'We'll get you out tomorrow.' Then the 'red bird' disappeared. What joy we felt that night. At nine o'clock in the morning we finally heard the helicopter in the distance. The helicopter did a loop, presumably in order to find a place from which to attempt the rescue. Then the rescuer was lowered onto a tiny ledge . . . . 'Our rescue has begun, they will get us out.' . . . We had to endure thirty more minutes in this igloo, which had offered us protection for so many nights, until the men were finally able to grant us the certainty of our rescue. I stared at them. I could find no words. I reached out my hand to greet them, a greeting with almost no strength left in it. I was completely exhausted."

Fiftieth Anniversary of the First Ascent—the Film and the Reality

The fiftieth anniversary of the first ascent of the Eiger North Wall was in the summer of 1988. All around the Eiger a hive of filming activity had already started a year earlier. Various television channels wanted to be able to present their own Eiger film in time for this jubilee year. Swiss Television was no exception. The Grindelwald mountain guides were able to convince television executives that it was not just another Eiger history program that was required but, rather, a production focusing on the rescue services. Thus the greatest and most time-consuming Eiger summit "rescue operation" of all time came about. Although in past years the majority of Eiger rescues had been carried out using a helicopter, it was decided that this exercise should take the form of a cable winch rescue. This was realistic in so far as there are some places on the North Wall where a direct rescue would have been impossible with the technology available at the time. After extensive preparatory work the first part of the exercise was started on 22 June 1988 and recorded by Swiss Television as if it were a live broadcast. Two helicopters were used to fly over thirty mountain guides, with more than a ton of rescue equipment and several television and telecommunications technicians to the mountain summit. A third was used as a camera helicopter. Unexpected fog hampered the work, but nevertheless they managed to winch down four men into the Exit Cracks in order to finish off the preparations for the actual exercise the following day.

An "injured" solitary climber was winched from the Exit Cracks to the summit ice field. There he was "rescued" directly by helicopter. That is said to have been the last cable winch rescue off the Eiger summit to this day.

On 24 July 1988 all hell suddenly breaks loose on the Eiger: In spite of bad weather conditions, several ropes have started up the Eiger, presumably to celebrate the fiftieth jubilee in their own way. The alarm goes up on the North Wall. An English climber has fallen and has serious head injuries. His survival is dependent upon a speedy rescue. The constant rockfall suggests an immediate rescue would be unwise. The head of mountain rescue, Kurt Schwendener, has learned always to postpone direct rescues from the Eigerwand until the early

Research, reporting, and, above all, rescue flights all form part of the Eiger's dramatic history.

Spaniard Miguel Angel Perez, who had broken both legs during a fall into the Ramp on 12 November 1977, was airlifted by helicopter six days later. Before that, mountain guide Hannes Stähli had put his legs in splints and dragged him to a ledge from where he could be attached to the winch cable. Bad weather had prevented an earlier rescue.

morning hours when the lower temperatures limit the risk of rockfall to a minimum. The doctor and mountain guide Bruno Durrer goes on foot to the injured man on the lowest part of the North Wall. From the Gallery Window of the Jungfrau Railway he reaches the scene of the accident at the Shattered Pillar. It is the same Gallery Window that was used fifty-two years earlier for the dramatic attempted rescue of Toni Kurz. The doctor's words on the radio sound urgent. "For God's sake try to get the injured man out of here. He won't last the night. The rockfall has let up." The pilot of the Swiss Air Rescue team REGA approaches the scene of the accident. Acting rapidly the doctor is able to attach the injured man to the winch cable. After a short flight to the Eigergletscher Station he is prepared for the longer journey to hospital. His condition appears to be stable. The injured man is in a coma for six weeks, then the redeeming news: He has survived the accident and it has not caused any permanent damage. An uncomfortable feeling remains. Had the boundary of risk been exceeded in this rescue and recovery operation on the North Wall, or was it justifiable to risk a direct rescue in this situation? One thing is certain: Rockfall represents the greatest risk in

direct rescues by helicopter. A rock in the rotor blades can cause the machine to crash. In addition the pilot must fly incredibly close to the Wall in order to lower down the rescuers with the winch.

Thanks to Emergency Radio and the Longline, (Almost) Anything Is Possible

In the years after the Eiger North Wall fiftieth jubilee celebrations, alpinists have again and again needed to be rescued from the Wall. And again and again, questions about risk must be asked. However, the mountaineers who have got into difficulties hardly seem to think about this risk anymore. More and more frequently they also pack radio equipment, with which they can almost always "send for" help in the form of a helicopter, often by giving false information. What frequently happens is that the person who has got into difficulty is lacking nothing other than better judgment of their own capabilities or better knowledge of the weather. Thus the development of a new method of rescue comes to the aid of the rescuers at the start of the 1990s: the "longline" rescue.

The first to try out this new rescue technology were the mountain guides from the Hasli Valley. The rescuer is attached to the helicopter by a rope (the so-called "longline") of up to 227 meters, depending on the situation. The man hanging below on the rope is almost a second pilot, as he must let himself be maneuvered into the correct position with precise instructions from the helicopter pilot, an incredibly demanding task and one which is also difficult for the rescuer. This means the helicopter is able to stay out of the rockfall area and usually to maintain a sensible distance from the Wall. This longline method is the one that the Hasli Valley mountain guides use for accidents on the vertical or even overhanging faces in their rescue area. That the use of the longline method could be of great significance on the Eiger North Wall as well was recognized immediately by head of mountain rescue Kurt Amacher, who succeeded Kurt Schwendener in 1993. He made sure that various mountain guides from the Grindelwald rescue station became familiar with this method. Its first trial on the Eiger was not long in coming.

A few months after the first Grindelwald mountain guides had been trained to use the longline technique—26 July 1994—employees of the Wengen mountain railway hear calls for help coming from the right side of the Eiger North Wall. During the reconnoiter flight two climbers are discovered on the uppermost part of the Geneva Pillar: One of them is clearly injured. Time is pressing on, it is already 5 P.M. and a storm is brewing. For these reasons the head of mountain rescue, Kurt Amacher, decides upon a rescue using the longline, the first such operation on the Eiger. Mountain guide Edi Bohren is taken up to the height of the injured mountaineer on a 180-meter-long rope. The rescue specialist is only able get on to the Wall, which is overhanging above them, by swinging in. He can no longer see the helicopter! The mountaineer who had injured his foot was flown to hospital and immediately operated upon.

Rescue Technology at the End of Its Development

Kurt Amacher believes that the air rescues on the Eiger North Wall will not change considerably in the foreseeable future, but that there will be improvements, above all in the equipment sector. Thus, for example, the rope's properties of expansion and torsion are currently being worked upon. Only with regular training in this demanding rescue technology and constant exchange of experiences among the different rescue stations can the risk brought on by man be kept to a minimum. Better than the best organized rescue would be that no rescue is necessary. And to this end Kurt Amacher has made very clear recommendations to all mountaineers and above all to prospective Eiger climbers. They should

make sure that family or friends have good information about proposed tours and routes in order to avoid unnecessary search flights. Climbers should show more understanding if they get into difficulties and cannot be rescued immediately—the weather is always the deciding factor as to whether it is safe to fly or not. And in general they should show more respect for the mountain, for the conditions, and the weather—an age-old precept that is valid even in the age of the longline.

A cable winch rescue had already been prepared for the two Spaniards Perez and Fernandez when Günther Amann, the pilot, did then manage to lower down four mountain guides, including (left) Ueli Frei and (right) Edi Bohren.

Flatiron

While Hannes dug away and flattened the fresh snow, I unpacked my tripod, cameras, and lenses. Five minutes after that I was ready, and there was Eric climbing toward us. If I had been anxious for him before at a distance, it was nothing to what I became now, watching him up close. His only rope was coiled over his shoulder and he was moving without any form of protection. I concentrated on the filming. So far, so good. Everything had gone according to plan, and I had filmed him coming across the last 500 feet of the Second Ice Field. Then he disappeared from sight below the Flatiron . . . .

It was an hour before Eric emerged again, coming up the side of the Flatiron. He had had a problem leaving the Second Ice Field in one of the chimneys flanking the buttress, and had almost fallen off in his haste . . . .

Although the two had spoken on the phone, Eric and Hannes had not actually met.

"Hello, Hannes, I'm Eric."

"Yes . . . I know . . . pleased to meet you."

Leo Dickinson, *Filming the Impossible,* 1982.
Eigerwand in 1980.

(facing page) Martin Grossen climbing the heavily iced Flatiron using two ice hammers. Latter-day alpinists, with superior ice tools to Grossen's, prefer the ice to the smooth, awkwardly sloping limestone of the Eigerwand.

Filming the Impossible

(above) Lights, camera . . . action. The Eiger has been a subject of documentaries, feature films, and television broadcasts since 1911. The filmography runs to a record 95 titles.

(facing page) Hannes Stähli looks back over a long career as a cameraman and actor for Eiger films (left, upper and middle). In 1987 he was there at the Jubilee film *Alptraum Eigernordwand* (North Face Nightmare); the crew was dropped by helicopter on the Flatiron (right, lower); Wolfgang Brög celebrates at Death Bivouac (right, middle). Later, he filmed the climbers in the Exit Cracks (right, upper, and left, lower).

From early days, the mountain film became an important element in film history. On the Eiger, and particularly on the North Face, which presents itself as a spectacular theater and is steeped in mystery and danger, the film as a medium has taken a prominent position center stage. Markus Schwyn presents us with a close-up.

The muffled chattering of the rotors of a helicopter can be heard just above the Flatiron, hovering perilously close to the snow- and ice-plastered Wall. At this time of the day, surely, the fusillade of stones has begun to strafe the Wall, so what are they doing up there when there has been no rescue scheduled? Who would dare venture onto the Wall, that world of snow and ice, just for pleasure?

It turns out to be the Swiss pair, Hannes Stähli from Wilderswill in the Bernese Oberland and the German Toni

Freudig from Pfronten in the Allgäu who have had themselves flown in with a film team. To mark the fiftieth anniversary of the first ascent, they are to climb, and film, all of the crucial sections of the route. Filming starts at the Flatiron, since at this point the team can be landed on the Face without any great problems. For the potentially dangerous abseil maneuver, the pilot has to fly close in to the Face, right into the stonefall zone. Immediately, the rotor is hit by a falling rock; the helicopter starts to list slightly, and then it happens—the rotors make contact with the cliff. The pilot just manages to tear his machine, shaking and spinning, away from the Wall and, in spite of the damaged rotor, carry out an emergency landing on a flat piece of the meadow at the foot of the Wall.

Filming under such conditions is certainly a risky business, but spectacular images can be captured which hold the promise of nerve-tingling excitement and high drama. The Eiger is a filmmaker's mountain and its North Face a vertical hemisphere containing everything a good set designer might require. Behind the precipitous Wall, the Jungfrau Railway skirts the edge of the stage almost like a kind of "runner" or "key grip." Entry and exit to the Face is possible via any of several holes. A perfectly equipped stage with an incomparable set—take one . . . action!

North Face Nightmare

The year 1895 saw the birth of film, as the Lumière brothers committed to celluloid the first images, and the new medium spread like wildfire around the world. Shortly afterward, hand-cranked

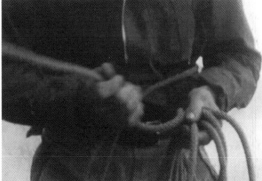

In 1936—two years before the successful ascent—a Swiss-German crew made the first Eiger North Face film. Of the original 60 minutes, only 35 remain, yet this is nonetheless a unique document in alpine filmmaking.

cine cameras appeared sporadically in the mountains. Then, the ill-fated Eiger-wand attempts of 1935 and 1936, on which six young climbers lost their lives, aroused interest in the mountain and the one-hour film *Die Eiger Nord-wand* was made. It showed the Munich Rescue Team recovering the body of Toni Kurz, a young climber who had died within sight of his rescuers. The cameraman, Max Herrmann from Bern, accompanied the Munich Mountain Rescue Team on their call-outs over several weeks in summer 1936.

"Back and forth, up and down, the line of rescuers moved across the Face, often frozen in inactivity against the cold stone. Icy water, howling stonefall, treacherous icy ledges, sudden blankets of mist followed by blinding sunshine, and always the biting cold—these were the enemies waiting to catch us out at every step. Each phase of Sedlmayr's uncanny journey of 1935 and of this year's Expedition of Death could be relived." This passage appeared in the newspaper after the film's premiere at the Hotel Freienhof in Thun on 29 October 1936. The film crew, led by Thun mountaineer E. O. Stauffer, had pushed the route to within 60 meters of Mehringer and Sedlmayr's first bivouac, with Herrmann using a miniature camera. The film also shows footage of the Normal Route on the Eiger, described as "a comfortable ascent."

In 1948, Swiss Otto Ritter made a documentary film of a special kind. In *Grat am Himmel* he accompanies a team climbing the Eiger's Mittellegi Ridge. He experiences all the hardships of the ascent but remains a detached observer, documenting the mountaineering feat and adding his own commentary through his images. For a long time, filmmakers had toyed with the idea of making a film about an ascent of the North Face by the classic Heckmair Route. The technical and mountaineering difficulties turned out to be so great, however, that several times the attempt had had to be aborted. Lothar Brandler had failed in 1958. Adolf Derungs and Lukas Albrecht had indeed been filmed on the Spider from the safety of the

Ridge, but the remaining shots in the film *Eiger-Nordwand* with Toni Hiebeler and Lothar Brandler had attracted fierce criticism due to the posed nature of the scenes shot later. In 1969, the BBC had filmed Chris Bonington and Dougal Haston at several points on the Harlin Direttissima, which they climbed for a television broadcast, but here, too, the crew had been unwilling to venture onto the Face itself; the camera was directed at the climbers from the safety of the West Flank. Although by summer 1969 over 250 climbers had done the North Face, a comprehensive film portrait of this great mountaineering challenge had yet to be made.

The Monster Is Tamed

Finally, in 1970, there was to be a new attempt made. Up above Grindelwald a young cavalier, in the shape of Leo Dickinson, took the stage, utterly convinced that—with his three partners, Cliff Phillips, Pete Minks, and Eric Jones— he would film an ascent of the '38 Route. An undertaking of this caliber required a professional behind the camera, someone not only possessed of above-average skill as a filmmaker, but who was also an exceptional mountaineer, with a feel for dramatization and direction. In addition to the climbing gear, the team had to strap the film equipment on their backs: two film cameras with several lenses, batteries, 3000 meters of film, a tape recorder, and five cameras for documentary stills.

Right from the start, the project seemed cursed by bad luck. Cliff Phillips slipped off one of the lower snow slopes near the First Pillar. Unbelayed, and with nothing to grab hold of, he was unable to brake with his ice axe and slid off down toward the valley. And as his friend slithered toward certain death, Dickinson kept filming, without once taking his finger off the shutter mechanism, until Phillips disappeared from view. Phillips eventually managed to arrest his death slide before plunging over a cliff edge. As soon as he reappeared, he shouted up to Dickinson, "Did you get it all?" Dickinson replied, "Of course, idiot! Stunts like that will go down a bomb with the viewers." In the following weeks the team climbed the Wall in several stages, braving every adversity—stonefall, sudden bad weather, cold, lightning strikes, and thunder. Finally, it was in the can.

Immediately after its screening on British television, journalist William Keenan wrote in the *Daily Mirror* of 9 December 1970, "This film was for me—and I am sure the same goes for all the other viewers—the most dramatic mountaineering film ever made."

Leo Dickinson was to return to the Eiger in 1980. Eric Jones wanted to make the first British solo of the Wall. And Leo Dickinson was not about to pass up the chance of filming a solo ascent. But how best to do it? If he

(above) Feet firmly on the ground, Clint Eastwood (left, front) recovers at Kleine Scheidegg from his vertigo-inducing cutting of the rope with the Swiss Army knife (below left) on the vertical precipice of the Rote Fluh. Reinhold Messner, Heidi Brühl, and Peter Habeler provide the company.

(following pages) For the Bond film *Goldeneye*, a few hot scenes were filmed with the Eiger as a backdrop. In the actual film, the action was transposed to Siberia.

were to go along on the climb it would no longer count as a solo. There was only one thing for it—the helicopter. Since the first successful helicopter rescue from the North Face, in 1971, filmmakers, too, had been able to profit from this new possibility. The Flatiron was the key to the problem—it was not only well situated between the Second and Third Ice Fields but could also be reached relatively "comfortably" from the air. Hannes Stähli, with fellow guide Edi Bohren, had already been dropped

by helicopter on the Flatiron back in 1978 during the filming of Friedrich Bach's *Der Tod klettert mit*.

The Route Is the Destination

The documentary and the feature film are very close relatives, particularly in their portrayal of historical events. In several Eiger films, the directors have inserted historical scenes or built their film on the basis of a reconstruction of the events of 1935 and 1936. Here, clothing, equipment, and climbing techniques from a bygone age are the props of imagination. In his documentary series *Der Weg ist das Ziel (The Journey Is the Destination)*, Gerhard Baur reconstructed the historical events on the Grandes Jorasses and the Eiger. In February 1982, Leo Dickinson replayed events from 1935 and 1936 at their original locations and built the scenes into the film he had made in 1980 of Eric Jones's solo climb. The resulting film, *Eiger*, included as its

(above) British climber and filmmaker Leo Dickinson kept his viewfinder firmly trained on the Eiger. In 1970, he climbed the Face with three friends, filming as he climbed—a world premiere. Ten years later, for a new Eiger film, he used a life-sized (and lifelike) model to reconstruct John Harlin's fall (below right).

dramatic high point a reconstruction of John Harlin's fatal fall from the Direttissima. With free-fall parachutist Paul Applegate, who was dressed as a climber for this scene, Leo Dickinson made several jumps from the helicopter, filming Applegate in free fall with the camera strapped to one hand. When level with the Hinterstoisser Traverse, both men opened their parachutes and landed in Alpiglen. In order to get a wrap on the lower part of Harlin's fall—and the final impact—a dummy was thrown out of the window of the Eigerwand Station.

Drama on the Eiger—Not His Best Film

There are only two feature films in which the Eiger is more than just a pure backdrop, but is the location for the storyline itself. Lean pickings. In summer 1962 a film crew caused uproar at Kleine Scheidegg when Luis Trenker, the grand old man of the "homeland film," chose the Eiger for his last feature and spent several weeks at Scheidegg with his crew. *Sein bester Freund (His Best Friend)* or *Drama am Eiger (Drama on the Eiger)* dealt with the ascent of the North Face of the Eiger and was, of course, framed by a spicy little subplot of love and jealousy. However, the film brought Trenker only derision and mockery. He was unable to appeal to an audience—for some it was too melodramatic, for others simply too banal. In addition, he received a stern reprimand from the mountaineering camp, who took up arms against the commercialization of climbing as

portrayed in the film. Climbing for money—nowadays the norm under the title of "sponsoring"—was not a matter for public discussion in 1962. The film hardly registered and is nowadays little known.

In 1974 there was great excitement again at Kleine Scheidegg, with the arrival of Clint Eastwood from Hollywood. Undaunted by the long journey with his team to the Bernese Oberland to shoot his spy thriller *The Eiger Sanction,* Eastwood remained unable to get on friendly terms with the Wall itself. Hannes Stähli relates how, as he stepped out of the Gallery Window into the middle of the Wall with Eastwood, he heard him curse, "Oh shit! Let's get out of here."

(left) Luis Trenker (background) worked both behind and in front of the camera and was well known for doing the dangerous scenes himself. In the film *Sein bester Freund,* his leading actor, Toni Sailer, follows his example. Yet even the artificial blood did nothing for Trenker's Eiger film; it remains rather anemic.

Markus Schwyn (born 1963) is the curator of the Swiss Alpine Museum in Bern where twice a year a series of events on the theme "The Alpine Film" takes place.

Eiger North Wall Live—Reality TV at its Best

In 1997 the Swiss Television, SF DRS, together with the third German Channel, Südwestrundfunk SWR, put forward the following concept for a program: To show in a live report how two pairs of climbers climb the North Face of the Eiger—in about thirty hours from the start to the summit, by the route first climbed by Heckmair and his companions in 1938.

In 1975, the BBC attempted to transmit the first live climb of the Eigerwand. The Swiss authorities, however, put a stop to it at the last minute, saying the date coincided with a national public holiday. The Scotsman Hamish MacInnes, who hatched the plan during an Everest expedition with Dougal Haston and acted as a safety advisor, suspected, "that the Swiss had got cold feet in view of the reputation of the Eiger." When the authorities finally agreed to the project, the attempt by the American television organization Transworld International failed due to financial reasons.

It was different in 1998. At the end of

August the team was ready for the transmission of "Eiger—Live." The alpinists chosen for the project—two male and two female, all mountaineers—were accustomed to using cameras and helmet-mounted microphones. The camera positions on the Wall, on the summit and on the Western Flank were installed, and the camera crew and two mountain guides from Grindelwald were used to working together. The operations center was up and running, the deployment of the helipilots was planned down to the last detail, and the Grindelwald mountain-safety guide team was prepared. Only one incalculable factor—the weather—hindered the plan. In a three-week time span, a period chosen because of past experience, there was not one stable period of good weather. The team proved that trying to maintain "greatest possible safety" were not merely empty words; and no, they did not cancel the project, but postponed it for another year, an option that the producers had left open from the start.

The patience of the team was rewarded: On 9 September 1999, at 9 A.M., Evelyne Binsack (born 1967) and Stephan Siegrist

(born 1967) from Interlaken; Hansruedi Gertsch (born 1966) from Grindelwald and the German Ralf Dujmovits (born 1962) set off onto the Face. All four are mountaineers. That the afternoon they reached the bivouac site at Death Bivouac; at 3:30 P.M. On 10 September 1999, the four stood on the summit.

When he reached the summit, Ralf Dujmovits, expressed his great respect for the achievement of the first ascentionists sixty-one years earlier. And down below on the sun patio of the mountain inn in Männlichen, only a few meters away from the large screen television, in front of which the Presenter Röbi Koller congratulated the climbers, there sat one man who particularly enjoyed Dujmovits' praise: Anderl Heckmair, almost 93-years-young, a glass in one hand and in the other his beloved Toscanelli cigarillo.

Freddy Widmer (born in 1947) is the editor of the Basler Zeitung. He frequently writes about mountaineering topics. He is an avid mountain walker, particularly in the Bernese Oberland and in South America.

Death Bivouac

So we waited. Precious time was slipping by, wasted. On this sinister, murderous face, the rusty pitons and rotten ropes dating from the early attempts, the stone wall which surrounded us as we ate, and which sheltered Sedlmayr and Mehringer before they died—all these combined to remind us that the moment you cease climbing toward the summit, success and safety itself are compromised. That is more than a painful and depressing impression—it is literally true. You are lost in the hollow basin of this curving wall; it is vast, and the line of advance is tortuous. Already we had passed a third of our time in horizontal traverses which did not gain us a foot of height.

Gaston Rébuffat, *Etoiles et tempêtes (Starlight and Storm)*, 1954.
Eigerwand in 1952.

(facing page) Stephan Siegrist belays his companion up to the roomy ledge of Death Bivouac while, far below, the village of Grindelwald enjoys the sunshine.

Karl and Max: On Blank Ice, in Blank Verse . . .

(above) Karl Mehringer (left) and Max Sedlmayr traveled to the Eiger in style and in high spirits.
(facing page) But the mountain is an unpredictable monster, showering down infernal streams, stones, and little avalanches that spew forth from its innards.

The first tragedy on the North Face of the Eiger had always moved writers, and none more so than Zürich author Roland Heer. His piece "Karl and Max," written in 1997, is, in his words, "a polyphonic discourse, a musical score of fragmented words, a poetic, brachial singsong, a spoken opera." During the performance, the playwright requires that both stage management and actors refrain from well-intentioned realism, stipulating that the greatest possible distance be maintained from the conventional tone of Alpine epic storytelling à la Luis Trenker or Reinhold Messner. According to Heer, the piece fluctuates between various opposite poles: the hopelessness of the situation versus the excesses of megalomania; borderline versus continuum; nothing versus everything; the lyrical versus verbal machismo; the fragility of the figures versus the robustness of their pretense; life versus death. Stark changes in tempo are apparent as the play proceeds, from *presto furioso,* through *andante* to *lento gelato* as toward the end the dialogue freezes almost solid.

It is 25 August 1935. The two Munich climbers Max Sedlmayr and Karl Mehringer, both between twenty-five and thirty years old, have been ensconced on the still-unclimbed North Face of the Eiger for five whole days. The two climbers had set out during the night of 20/21 August in perfect weather and, watched through the big telescopes at Scheidegg by many spectators, at first made rapid progress. After two bivouacs, however, everything started to go more slowly, presumably because of stonefall or because one of the pair had been injured. Then, on the third day, a dreadful storm hit the Face. On Sunday, 25 August, the two men are seen alive for the last time, moving slowly up toward the so-called Flatiron. At this point the play begins.

Karl and Max: A Spoken Opera in One Act
Characters:
KARL: the younger of the two climbers
MAX: the elder of the two climbers

(A long, deafening crash, then daylight)

MAX: God! Where are you, hey! Say something! Can you hear me? You still there? Karl, you all right?

KARL: Yeah. I'm OK. Ow! My head, damn it . . . it got me . . . *(he climbs across, half crawling, kicking steps)* . . . on the head, it got me. The rucksack . . . you . . . it's . . . bastard stonefall . . . ow, my hand, my head. *(They cower together on a very exposed, sloping ledge.)*

MAX: Let me just tie you on here first, shift to the side a bit. My God, the sack! Gone. Ripped off your back. And there, you're bleeding there, under the hat.

KARL: Shit, man, that hurts . . . I told you I didn't like that gully, damn it. Bloody idiot, should've stayed put instead of hanging my ass out to dry up there. And my head, obvious with those avalanches. Carry on climbing, making progress? Oh, sure. You, it's all spinning round, I'm getting the shakes now.

MAX: Easy, Karly, just stay calm lad. Nice and calm. You're right, there's no way up here, but further right . . . come on . . . when you're feeling a bit better . . . you're a lucky bugger it's only the rucksack you lost.

KARL: What? Lucky? Don't make me laugh. My arm's bust, my head's killing me, the rucksack's gone, it's storming . . . and there's half a mile of rock below us . . . damn. Fuckingwall, fuckingweather, fuckingstonefall, fuckingworld!

MAX: Come on, let's have a look at you . . . you're covered in blood here.

KARL: Ow!

MAX: Show it to me, I'll strap it up with this cloth here. *(He ties a grotesque ribbon around Karl's head as if he had toothache.)*

KARL: I told you there was no way, we should stay where we are, I said, where we were safer from the stonefall, I said. I told you . . . when it's been snowing nearly two days . . . *(shocked)* . . . damn . . . in the ruck-sack . . . damn it . . . the stove . . . and the food . . . .

MAX: The stove? No, surely not . . . and the food . . . it can't have . . . OK, forget it, it's done . . . we'll just have to eat snow! . . . We have to keep going, whatever. There's nothing else for it. Keep going, hang in there, without the stuff. No one's coming to help us, Karly. No point waiting. Believe me, it's not going to get any better.

KARL: Maybe it'll buck up, who knows? It can't stay like this for ever. Hey, it's summer, my God, August . . . if it gets better, who knows, from the Gallery, they should be able to do it . . . the more dangerous it gets, those guys on the rescue just get better . . . .

MAX: In this snow, no one could manage it—out of the question. There's no one coming up here, even if it does get better—and there is no way we are getting down from here, either. Five days we've been messing about already . . . so, hell, let's just get out of here now, whatever the cost! This

"We are deeply indebted to Frau Jossi for her hospitality. She was always there with a helping hand. From two poor climbers, with our warmest thanks." Entry by Karl (right) and Max in the visitors' book of the Hotel des Alpes, Alpiglen.

filthy wall is just taking the piss . . . up and out, now! We've got to climb out, Karl, waiting around is just wasting time.

KARL: No, I'm staying here!

MAX: You're coming with me!

KARL: Don't take another step. Wait there.

MAX: Come on, Karl. I'll lead it, I'll belay you, we have to . . . .

KARL: What do you mean, "have to"? I don't "have to" do anything. Stay where you are. I'm not risking my neck again . . . it's useless.

MAX: Useless? It's getting later and later.

KARL: Then let it get later! Shit, my head is hurting. Shit, I feel sick.

MAX: Pull yourself together. Grit your teeth. Come on, Karl lad, don't be a stupid prick. *(He stands up)* We've got to try it. Now.

KARL: Go on your own then, try your luck.

MAX: Ha! With no rope? We've still got almost half of it to do, and nobody knows what's up there. Solo it now . . . and leave you here? Crazy!

KARL: I'm not budging. I can't now. Need a rest. Can't keep my eyes open . . . can't . . . won't . . . I'd sooner freeze to death here than fall off.

MAX: Freeze to death? Nonsense! We're going up! Karl, please!

KARL: Can't climb any more . . . .

MAX: Please!

KARL: Can't do any more . . . I haven't got the strength . . . don't want to move. I've . . . had it. Kaputt.

MAX: So what, then? *(Starts climbing)* If you don't come up there with me now, right now . . . .
(the noise of avalanches and stonefall again; it grows dark)

KARL: Hey, where are you? Say something! Are you still . . . hey, Max!

MAX: Yeah, yeah, I'm still . . . ow! My leg! Damn it, Karl, it got me, that one . . . got me on the leg . . . .

KARL: Come here, sit down, I'll make room next to me.

MAX: I think it's broken . . . swelling up like a balloon . . . can't

Base camp Alpiglen. Karl (left) and Max slept in a shepherd's hut from 16 August 1935, waiting for good weather. After they set off on the route, a reporter paid a visit to the hut. "Lying there in open view on a block of wood were the passports, made out in the names of one Max Sedlmayr and one Karl Mehringer, the travel documents for the car, parked at Grindelwald-Grund Station, and next to them 60 Swiss Francs in cash."

bend it any more . . . bad luck, damn it.

KARL: I'm telling you, man, it's useless in this weather. Here is where we stay. We've got no choice.

MAX: Come on, help me with the sack, tie it on, right? I just need to take a breather before we try . . . aagh! . . . careful . . . damned leg . . . wait a bit, till the pain goes . . . man, Karl, the stonefall here . . . whatever, what's down there is down there and can't get us any more. Damn this storm . . . bloody steep everything here as well. If only the visibility got better . . . damn it . . . my leg, still . . . .

KARL: I never touched you.

MAX: Damn it, it's got to be possible . . . and even if it isn't . . . it could've . . . not packing it in now . . . shit . . . my leg.

KARL: It'll be OK . . . we'll just have to wait.

MAX: Man, Karl, it's, like, I can't see any way . . . .

KARL: Right now, I can't see bugger all. Don't know shit. Sitting here. Can't do anything else. Just want some peace and quiet.

MAX: My leg's fucked, constant avalanches, shit stonefall, ropes as stiff as a horse's dick . . . what an idiotic way to end up . . . don't believe it . . . so bloody mean . . . from behind . . . we make it? . . . Karl!

KARL: Karl, Karl, what's this Karl? I'm not Karl any more. Karl is freezing to death from the fingers in. Karl feels like a snowman, just missing the carrot nose.

MAX: Are we to just perish here in silence, no songs, no words? Make friends with the enemy like cowards? Without a fight, just let the Wall have us, or what?

KARL: Your fight, dear is fought. I don't want this any more.

(The End)

(above) At the telescope in Alpiglen. Together with rescue man Ludwig Gram-minger (left), Heini Sedlmayr, the brother of Max, scans the North Face to no avail.

(right) The journey is the aim, but they aimed too far and too high. The fate which befell Karl and Max was reconstructed in an Eiger film of 1982. Bernese Ober-land mountain guides Hannes Stähli and Jürg von Känel (with the hat) played the two Munich high-altitude tourists.

"We are just dreaming and then we will wake up . . . you're right . . . just wait . . . it'll be all right . . . yes. And tomorrow, maybe, we will be sleeping in the warm, with a full belly, on straw. It's worth waiting, isn't it?" The (fictitious) last words spoken by Max to Karl at Death Bivouac.

After a long period of bad weather, in the second half of September 1935, the German pilot Ernst Uder flew a foolhardy mission close in to the Wall. He and his passenger, Grindelwald mountain guide Fritz Steuri, both spotted one of the two climbers—frozen and up to his waist in snow up on the Flatiron. Since then the place has been known as Death Bivouac. The following year, during operations to recover the body of Toni Kurz, the remains of Max Sedlmayr were found at the foot of the Wall by his own brother. Those of Karl Mehringer were only discovered twenty-seven years later, at the edge of the Second Ice Field.

Roland Heer (born 1959), from Zürich, is an author, German teacher, and alpinist. His "Kadash am Berg," a concert of words with a seven-piece jazz band and vocalist first performed in 1995, is the musical and verbal representation of a fatal fall in the mountains.

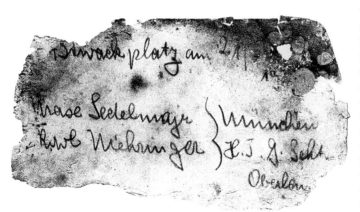

The last message of the dead heroes. "Bivouac on 21/8/35. Max Sedelmajr, Karl Mehringer. Munich H.T.G. Section Oberland." H.T.G. stands for "High Tour Group." It was probably Mehringer that penned the note, since he misspelled the name of his climbing companion. A Czech rope team found the cigarette packet with the yellowed note on 21 June 1976.

Third Ice Field

At exactly twelve o' clock midday I start up the Third Ice Field. We now have more than half of the Face behind us. Belayed by Lois, I climb out onto the 60-degree ice slope. Here, we find signs of the Tyrolean climber Adi Mayr, who fell to his death on this climb. The over-large steps cut into the ice must be his, for only a man seized by mortal fear would make such steps, to fool himself into believing that he was a little safer. It must have been here that his nerves finally gave up on him. Up near the Ramp he finally fell to his death. We do not have the time to reconstruct the accident, but in our thoughts we say farewell to Adi Mayr. The man had had the same intentions as we, yet Fate had not been as merciful toward him. About 300 meters above the Ice Field is the Spider. Missiles of every caliber are funneled down from the summit wall and shoot off down to the valley. Seconds before their impact, you can hear the rocks and lumps of ice howling past. You get used to it.

Leo Schlömmer, *Meine Welt die Berge,* 1973.
Eigerwand in 1961.

(facing page) Hans Kessler traverses across the Third Ice Field in the afternoon sun. The sea of clouds illustrates his loneliness on the huge precipice of the North Wall.

Alpine Trilogy

In 1949, the German Anderl Heckmair (second from right) published the classic *Die letzten Probleme der Alpen (The Last Great Problems of the Alps)*. Frenchman Gaston Rébuffat (second from left) was the first to climb all three big North Faces: Grandes Jorasses in 1945, Matterhorn in 1949, Eigerwand in 1952; Hermann Buhl (far right) was on the Eigerwand at the same time as Rébuffat. Also pictured are Georges Tairraz (left) and Léon Claret-Tournier (middle).

The dictionary is clear on the issue: A trilogy is a group of three tragedies with a single theme and, by extension, three works that follow each other and form a whole. Of course, the three North Faces that constitute "the" Trilogy—those of the Eiger, the Matterhorn, and the Grandes Jorasses—are not short on tragedy. Yet the story of the Trilogy is more or less exempt from drama, as Sylvain Jouty discovered.

At the beginning of Alpinism, people were content quite simply to climb a summit by one route, to come back down by another, and to start all over again a few days later. But soon was born the taste for collecting: One summit did not suffice; several of them

were needed, linked by a certain geographic, temporal, or even thematic proximity. Perhaps the big North Face Trilogy has known such a success because it unites these three criteria: It is a matter of three famous mountains, three walls that are among the most imposing in the Alps, three mythical itineraries, conquered at intervals of a few years. These three North Faces, austere and frozen, represent a sort of quintessence of Alpinism, such as it had developed up to the 1960s.

It is true to say this is not the first trilogy that mountaineering has known. For example, there was the one involving the great routes to the same summit climbed by Graham Brown on the Brenva Face (the Sentinelle Rouge, the Route Major, and the Pear); or the lesser-known one, done by the Spanish climbers Alberto Rabadà and Roberto Navarro (the West Face of the Naranjo de Bulnes, the eastern spur of the Gallinero, and the Las Brujas Route on the Tozal del Mallo)—the three "last problems" of the Pyrenees, solved over three years by a formidable roped party that from that moment onward judged itself equal to attacking the North Face of the Eiger—an error that was to be fatal for them, because they lacked experience on ice. After a six-day ascent, they died of exhaustion in the Spider on 15 August 1963.

Kasparek and Heckmair Speak of the Three Great Faces

It is in 1938, in a book sponsored by the Nazi Party, that the question of the three "Grosse Wandprobleme" represented by our three big Alpine faces appears for the first time. And the most difficult problem posed is that of the Eigerwand. Heckmair takes up the theme in order to give a title to his celebrated 1949 work, *The Last Great Problems of the Alps*. It has been a fixed idea since that time that the conquests of these three Walls represent the major events in Alpine mountaineering before the Second World War.

Rébuffat Climbs Six North Faces

After the war, the Alpinists could find no better task than to repeat these great routes. In 1954, Gaston Rébuffat published *Etoiles et Tempêtes (Starlight and Storm),* an account of the ascent of six famous North Faces: those of our Trilogy, but also those of the Piz Badile, the Cima Grande di Lavaredo, and the Petit Dru—six faces conquered between 1931 and 1938, all of which Rébuffat was the first to climb. In so doing, he becomes the first trilogist.

Schlömmer Does Them All in a Year

There was however no "hexalogy": The distances were too great, the disparities of ambience, style, and commitment too evident. It also quickly became apparent that of the six North Faces climbed by Rébuffat, those of the Trilogy were by far the most formidable. To have climbed all three established you as an Alpinist. It was logical that they should come to be climbed within the space of a year. The Austrian Leo Schlömmer achieved this exploit from summer 1961 (Eiger) to summer 1962 (Grandes Jorasses), including the first winter ascent of the North Face of the Matterhorn in February 1962.

Hasegawa and Ghirardini Fight It Out

The era of the great winter climbs was ushered in. The Trilogy in winter?

Bonatti or Hiebeler might have thought about it, but things moved so quickly in the 1960s and 1970s that it was the solo winter ascents that really established the reputation of the Trilogy. There was certainly something new in the air in 1977, with a strange Franco-Japanese duel. Tsuneo Hasegawa was first on the scene with the first solo winter ascent of the Matterhorn North Face in March. He was imitated, in December, by Yvano Ghirardini, who followed on in January 1978 with the first solo winter climb of the Croz Spur on the Grandes Jorasses, to which Hasegawa replied with the first winter solo of the Eigerwand at the beginning of March. Ghirardini followed him several days later, thus becoming the first Alpinist to have climbed the three North Faces, solo, in winter and in the course of the same season. It is he, therefore, that one can consider the real inventor of the Trilogy. Hasegawa took his revenge by achieving the first winter solo of the Walker spur on the Jorasses. A draw: the Trilogy of solo winter climbs in one season for one, the first three winter solos for the other.

Profit Does Them All in a Day

It is during these years that the first modern enchainements take place. The first links concern neighboring routes, but soon, with the aid of a parapente, itineraries increasingly more removed from each other geographically form the links in the chain. It is however a real "conceptual leap" that is proposed by Christophe Profit in 1985: Having been the first to climb the North Face of the Eiger, solo, in winter and within a day (March 17), he now believes it possible to climb the three Faces one after the other! A challenge that Profit rises to masterfully; on July 25, he descends from the summits on foot and the intermassif links are made by helicopter. However, caught out by the weather at the foot of the Jorasses, the French Alpinist chooses to climb the Lincuel

(above, upper) In 1977/78, Frenchman Yvano Ghirardini became the first climber to solo climb all three big faces in one year, in winter.

(above, lower) Slovenian climber Tomo Cesen repeated the feat in 1986, in only six days. He was unable to go any faster, since he was obliged to use his old Zastava to transport him from one mountain to the next.

goes awry—he gets lost in the night on the North Face of the Matterhorn. Failure. Bad weather prevents Escoffier from taking up the challenge.

During this time, a young Slovenian Alpinist, the then unknown Tomo Cesen, unobtrusively achieves the first winter sequence . . . not in twenty-four hours, but in six days, because it is his old Zastava that provides the transport from one massif to another.

Escoffier Loses the Winter Duel with Profit

The Escoffier-Profit duel recommences the following winter. To make things more exciting, the two competitors set out on the same day, 11 March 1987. Profit starts off with the Croz Spur of the Grandes Jorasses, descends by parapente, takes time out to have a shower and heads off to the Eiger, which he starts at 4 P.M. He knows the Face well but this time he has to climb it at night. At 9:30 A.M. he is on the summit but the parapente take-off is impossible due the wind; Christophe flies to Zermatt by helicopter. At 8:23 P.M. he is on the summit of the Matterhorn, forty-two hours after starting out. It is a long way off twenty-four hours, but the performance is impressive all the same. Escoffier launches his attack on the Eiger at midnight on 11 March. Having never climbed the Face he gets lost while searching for the Hinterstoisser Traverse and decides to go back down again. A new start the following day; he reaches the summit after seventeen hours. He travels to Zermatt by car. Profit, meanwhile, has succeeded. It has snowed during the night and the Matterhorn is plastered. On the evening of Friday, March 13th—an unlucky day, as we know—Eric is 400 meters from the summit of the Matterhorn, with no bivouac equipment, and he loses an ice axe. The fresh snow will prevent him from climbing the North Face of the Jorasses at a reasonable speed. The only solution is to abandon the attempt. The duel is terminated.

(above) Christophe Profit solo climbed the Eigerwand three times: in 1985 in both summer and winter, and again in the winter of 1987. He set off at 4:00 P.M. and topped out at 9:30 A.M. Then it was off to the North Face of the Matterhorn.

(facing page, below) Profit raced up the three North Faces in twenty-two and a half hours on 25 July 1985. When attempting to do the same in winter, a competitor appeared in the shape of fellow countryman Eric Escoffier. Profit won the race on his second try in 1987, in under forty-two hours.

(Shroud), a much quicker and easier route than the Walker Spur. After twenty-two hours and thirty minutes it is done.

Cesen Strolls up the Face

Christophe then announces his intention to reclimb the Trilogy in winter and again in under twenty-four hours. It is then that an outsider appears, in the shape of his rival, Eric Escoffier. On 8 March 1986 Christophe attacks the Croz Spur, a route which he does not know, and descends by parapente. Transferred by helicopter—and here the scheme

Gouvy Does the Trilogy on His Snowboard

Bruno Gouvy, a fanatical pioneer of snowboarding, takes up the idea of the Trilogy again in 1987. The idea is rather far-fetched, since the nature of the Trilogy is defined more by the three North Faces than by the summits themselves. That makes no difference to him and 22 April 1987 sees the successful completion of his sequence—snowboard descents of the West Flank of the Eiger, the South Flank of the Jorasses, and the East Face of the Matterhorn (from the Shoulder).

Up to that time the history of Alpinism has been a history of men, as well as one of winter climbs and solo ascents. It is Catherine Destivelle who establishes a new category in the record of Alpine achievements: the first solo winter climb by a woman. Between 1992 and 1994 she climbs the three North Faces, at the rate of one per winter, ending with a flourish with the

repetition of the Bonatti Route on the Matterhorn. This first Trilogy by a woman has somewhat eclipsed the exploits of Great Britain's Alison Hargreaves, who, during the summer of 1993, soloed the six North Faces so dear to Gaston Rébuffat in a kind of return to the origins of the enchainement.

(above, upper) Without the aerial assistance, fast enchainements of the Grandes Jorasses (pictured here), Matterhorn, and Eiger are hardly possible. Nor are they marketable—modern trilogists must be photographed and filmed.

The Ramp

It is appropriate that we climbed the Eiger North Wall in the time between 30 July and 2 August 1964. Only our parents and one of our best friends knew of our intentions, in order to avoid the usual intrusion by the press. My father, a post office official in Engelberg, was kept up to date about proceedings on the Wall—as far as possible, given the weather conditions that were bad at times—by Mr. Mich, the post office official in Grindelwald. . . .

We climbed over a small overhang, then through a gully onto the edge of the Flatiron and from there to "Death Bivouac." Then came the traverse of the Third (60-degree-steep) Ice Field up to the Ramp. The rain had stopped and we started climbing, rope length after rope length—it was difficult but enjoyable—until a large black chimney pulled us up short due to a waterfall shooting down through it. It was now 8 P.M. and the sun had begun to set, glowing red on the horizon. We looked for a place to bivouac, but there was not much choice, as there was nowhere very flat. The most favorable place was a sloping slab of rock. We hammered in two pitons on which we were able to hang up our rucksacks and secure ourselves.

Letter from Kurt Güngerich to the Resort Management at Grindelwald, 1968.
Eigerwand in 1964.

On the official list of all the North Face climbs to mark the fortieth anniversary of the first ascent, there was no mention of Kurt and Rolf Güngerich.

(facing page) Ruth Baldinger climbs a wintry Ramp. Down below one can just make out the snow-covered tracks of the rack railway to Kleine Scheidegg.

Telescope Directed Toward the Icy Hell of the Eiger

Paul Etter writes about his fellow climber Ueli Gantenbein, with whom he and Sepp Henkel undertook the first descent of the Eigerwand at the end of December 1963: "Now it had finally gone dark he had first of all to relieve himself. It had been bothering him all afternoon. But in the daylight he did not have the courage to perform this act publicly. His just suspicion, that many people were watching through the telescope, made it impossible."

"An important task falls to the press in the fight against this North Wall fever. It should strive not to satisfy the public's unquenchable desire for sensation," declared Samuel Brawand—Grindelwald mountain guide and first to climb the Mittellegi Ridge of the Eiger—in the summer of 1937, when the Wall was once more besieged by climbers, journalists, and tourists after the total exploitation of the tragedies of 1935 and 1936. Brawand's appeal in the *Neue Zürcher Zeitung* was to no avail; the Eigerwand and its climbers remained uncontrollably in the limelight. Daniel Anker, himself a mountain sports journalist, has looked at dozens of articles.

The Wall has to be the reason. Three years before the commotion began, Hans Lauper wrote this about the 1932 first ascent of the Eiger North East Face,

by the route that now bears his name: "When I looked down toward Grindelwald, for a moment I had the unpleasant sensation that I was being watched. But the only person who knew of our intentions was Mr. Seiler from the Hotel des Alpes on the Kleine Scheidegg. A mountaineer himself, he had kept silent until our return as promised."

When the press was not informed about a first ascent they were critical: "It is a pity that nobody knew about the route, as it would have been a rare pleasure for many people to follow this climb with cameras."

"Hopeless Situation on the Eiger North Wall"

From 1935 onward, the situation for spectators and readers improved dramatically. Under the heading "Hopeless situation on the Eiger North Wall," the *Oberländisches Volksblatt* of Interlaken printed an appropriate announcement from the resort management in Grindelwald on 27 August, according to which the climb was the talk of the day and would be followed precisely. It was said that the rescue station in Grindelwald had organized a rescue plan in advance, yet the decision to set off could only be made after an improvement in weather conditions. We can also read in this short announcement that after the heavy, persistent high mountain storms it was hoped in mountaineering circles that these two brave climbers would escape with their lives. The alphorn player with whom the two Alpinists had arranged a "call sign" was indeed said to have heard shouts, complaining about insufficient provisions, after playing his horn.

"The Dead of the Eigerwand"

We know that Sedlmayr and Mehringer did not come back alive. What we do not know is whether or not they heard the horn player. He wanted to create a contact between the observers and the observed, between below and above. A few days after the sounds of the alphorn had faded away a Swiss military plane tried in vain to maintain this contact. A few weeks later the German war and film hero Ernst Udet and his passenger, Grindelwald mountain guide Fritz Steuri, were luckier. From the air, the two of them discovered a body at a spot on the Wall which since then has been called "Death Bivouac."

And according to Steuri, in his interview published by reporter Hans Jegerlehner in the *Volksblatt* of 28 September under the title "The dead of the Eigerwand," "To my great horror Udet even let go of the controls and took pictures from 20 meters away. He will let me know by telegram tonight whether or not they have turned out all right."

But we do not know that either. It is a pity. The photos would have been unique documents. The first dead man on the Wall, photographed from a plane. And down below the local rescue team, hesitating.

The following year the Eiger spectacle really took off.

"The Tragedy on the North Wall of the Eiger"

"Lull in the fighting on the Eiger" the *Oberländisches Volksblatt* announced in its edition of 18 July 1936. This had to be corrected the next day to "New attacks." And on 20 July 1936 under the heading "Oberländische News/About the Eigerwand" the following is written: "The attack on the Eigerwand has failed." And then on 23 July 1936, the shock: "Tragedy on the North Wall of the Eiger. All four mountaineers dead."

Since that time the Eigerwand has claimed many more victims. In 1967, for example, four mountaineers from the the former East Germany fell to their deaths at the same time. This hardly made the headlines, not merely because

the public had by now got used to the triumph and tragedy in the Wall. The deciding factor was that in contrast to 1936 the sense of drama was missing . . . .

The merciless end met by Toni Kurz is, after the deaths of four mountaineers on the first ascent of the Matterhorn in 1865, the most famous accident in Alpine history. The *National-Zeitung* of Basel for example dedicated more than the whole front page to the story in its morning edition of Thursday, 23 July 1936, showing pictures of the four dead men while they were still alive. The magazine *sie und er* showed on its title page of 25 July a large picture of the Eigerwand and a smaller one of Toni Kurz smiling into the lens of Hans Jegerlehner's camera. A week later the readers see more. What they see is Toni Kurz hanging lifeless on a rope.

The photographer of this picture, which to this day has lost none of its horror, was Walter Gabi of Wengen. He had accompanied the rescuers from the Gallery Window to the site of the accident. His photos formed the basis of a special edition of the *Schweizer Illustrierte Zeitung* of 29 July to mark the mountain tragedy on the Eiger and the beginning of the Spanish Civil War—a happy coincidence of chance incidents that provided a great boost to sales.

"On Monday Longhi's heavy, lifeless body hanging from the rope was observed clearly, not only by the glacier pilot Geiger but also by the spectators watching through the telescope at Kleine Scheidegg. Without a doubt he had passed away in the night." Press report of 1957 about the Corti-Longhi tragedy, during which the photo was taken. For two years both journalists and spectators were able to fight their way to the telescope to see the body hanging there. When the recovery operation took place there was even more pushing and shoving.

Das Bergsteiger-drama an der Eiger-Nordwand

Der Der der Tragödie: die Eiger-Nordwand, die wieder vier Todesopfer forderte; mit den eingetragenen Routen ihrer Opfer. Die ausgezogene Linie zeigt die Route der vier Kletterer Rainer und Angerer, die als österreichische Emigranten in München wohnten und der Berchtesgadener Andreas Hinterstoisser und Anton Kurz, die alle vier nach bewundernswürdigen Kletterleistungen den Bergsteiger-Tod in diesen Tagen fanden. Die gestrichelte Linie markiert die Route der beiden im August 1935 tödlich verunglückten Münchener Alpinisten Max Sedlmayr und Karl Mehringer. Die kleinen Kreise geben die Biwakplätze an. Rechts der Berchtesgadener Bergsteiger Toni Kurz, der nach heldenhaftem Ausharren beim Abseilen vor den Augen der schweizerischen Rettungsmannschaft, den Bergführern Christian und Adolf Rubi, Hans Schlunegger und Glatthard die für dessen Rettung ihr Menschenmöglichstes einsetzten, am Seil hängend verschied.

(above) According to the *National-Zeitung* of Basel on 25 July 1936, "When it was announced on national radio on the Wednesday afternoon that there would be a direct transmission about the attempted rescue whole neighborhoods got together wherever there was a radio available."

(right) "The environment in which they grew up is to blame. Their heroism had taken a wrong turn." Author Otto Zwahlen's final edict in the first North Wall publication of 1936. It ran to many reprints and cost 90 centimes. The comment in a reader's letter: "The fact that money should be made out of such a tragic and widely disputed case is disturbing."

"Exploiting the Eigerwand"

The reactions to the publication of pictures of the hero hanging on a rope and to other photos of rescue and recovery (the pole with the knife attached, which was used to cut down Kurz's body; the transportation of the bodies in sacks to the foot of the mountain and then on the train) were inevitable. "Why should such pictures be published for the sake of the masses?" one *Volksblatt* reader asked. The "exploitation of the Wall" (as was the title given to one reader's letter in the daily paper *Der Bund,* of Bern) continued without wavering. One month after the tragedy, a forty-eight-page magazine appeared on the market: "The fight for the Eigerwand. An illustrated report about the tragedies of 1935 and 1936 on the Eiger North Wall."

Yet this was not enough. In 1936 the first Eigerwand film was released. It was made with the help of the Munich Moun-

tain Rescue team and mountain guides from Grindelwald. After its premiere in Interlaken the *Volksblatt* gave the following commentary: "The film closes with pictures of the recovery of the remains of Toni Kurz. However impressive this ending may be, one cannot help thinking that when death has come so tragically the camera should keep away."

"Record the Besieger's Every Arm Movement and Ice-axe Blow"

One of the next team to attempt the route took a camera: Ludwig Vörg. Of all the newspapers, it was the *Sport*—in which Othmar Gurtner from Lauterbrunnen had described attempts to climb the Wall as "insanity" and "eastern Alpine technocracy"—that was the one to carry "an authentic picture report about Rebitsch and Vörg's German rope team," after they had laid siege to the Eiger's North Face in 1937. Gurtner remarked proudly that the *Sport* was the first Swiss newspaper to publish "Ludwig Vörg's Contax Photos." Matthias Rebitsch could be seen on the hand-traverse ("the crux") and on the lower ice field; the names Hinterstoisser Traverse and First Ice Field had not yet gained currency. A few weeks earlier in an article in the *Sport* Gurtner had written: "In order to lessen the desire for sensationalism the press will continue

Illustrierter Bericht über die Tragödie 1935 und 1936 in der Eiger-Nordwand

Preis 90 Rp.

to record each and every arm movement and ice-axe blow made by the besiegers." In order to solve the problem of "delicate reporting" a "Committee for Official Eiger Reports" was founded in Grindelwald in the summer of 1937. On 22 July 1938 at 10 A.M. this committee announced that there were "two parties on the North Face of the Eiger."

"North Face of the Eiger Conquered!"

In order to steer clear of the North Face commotion Anderl Heckmair and his then companion Toni Lesch had stayed at Interlaken's swimming baths in 1937. Nevertheless, they were caught by photo journalists, who published a photo with the caption: "Two anonymous Eigerwand candidates who do not want to give their names." Perhaps his desire for anonymity was also the reason that Heckmair protested against Vörg taking his Contax with him when they were collecting their equipment together prior to the first successful attempt to climb the North Face in July 1938. "Wiggerl, however, insisted, saying that any photos that might be brought out would be important documents." They were.

Vörg took photos during the snowstorm on the upper part of the Wall and was able to supply pictures as proof of the "Icy Hell of the Eiger" for a newspaper article published on 24 July 1938. When it became known that Heckmair, Vörg, Kasparek, and Harrer were going to attempt to climb the Face, the *Münchner Neuesten Nachrichten* immediately sent a journalist to Switzerland. "At six o'clock we were at the large telescope near the Grindelwald Station, hurrying to focus on the four up there." The ascent was not only watched from below but also from an airplane. The Bern photographer Hans Steiner chartered a plane while the weather was still good and photographed the four Alpinists on the Brittle Ledge and in the Brittle Crack. This picture was published by the *Schweizer Illustrierte Zeitung* in the supplement to the thirtieth edition under the title "The North Face of the Eiger Conquered!"

"Chronicle of the Eigerwand"

After 1947, Rudolf Rubi continued the "Chronicle of the Eigerwand" with his own self-published pamphlets. To date there are seven in total, crammed full of articles.

"Drama on the North Face of the Eiger" was the title that the *Schweizer Illustrierte* magazine gave to its "exclusive report about the rescue operation" of two fallen climbers, Franz Moos-

müller and Manfred Söhnel, in the summer of 1956. Even before the arrival of the rescue team the reporter had already climbed to the foot of the Wall. It goes without saying that the hard-nosed press stayed with the Eiger story until well into the following year when the Corti tragedy took place. The photographer Hans Steiner

"Barry Brewster was unconscious most of the time. Once he was able to say, 'Brian I am so sorry, so sorry,' I knew that my time had come too." It had not, otherwise the *Blick* would not then have been able to interview Brian Nally.

(above) Anderl Heckmair fought in vain in 1938 against Ludwig Vörg taking his Contax onto the Wall and even carrying it ready to shoot on the bivouac on the Ramp. The Munich magazine *Der Illustrierte Beobachter* published a report after the first ascent "with photographs taken by the four brave mountaineers themselves; pictures as never seen before by human eye."

(right) The photo from Heckmair's personal album shows him together with Theo Lesch (behind) at the swimming bath in Interlaken where they were hiding from curious reporters in 1937.

climbed to the Eiger summit with the rescuers. "The Eigerwand is to keep its victims," the *Volksblatt* had to inform its readers. Two years after Claudio Corti's rescue, mountain guides from Lauterbrunnen recovered the body of his partner, Stefano Longhi. This event was financed by a Dutch press concern, which made the rescue team give it exclusive coverage—even the air space was out of bounds for other reporters. Such "repulsive" accompanying conditions, as they were criticized by *Der Bund,* heated up the atmosphere beneath the North Face, on the viewing terraces and at the kiosk.

"Reporters' Aircraft with Three Occupants Crashes"

In 1958, Kurt Diemberger and Wolfgang Stefan were accused of profiteering with information and photos of the Wall. The North Wall hopefuls had no respite, not even on the Wall itself. There they were spied upon by airplanes. Anyone who wanted to embark upon the climb and anyone who was able to make the descent from the summit, had to—or was allowed to—give a full explanation of their actions to radio and newspaper journalists.

In 1962, Chris Bonington sold the story rights of the planned first British ascent with Don Whillans to the *Daily Mail* right from the start. They did not succeed because they had to rescue Brian Nally, who had got into difficul-

ties, from the Second Ice Field. That was of course a much better story. "Brewster is dead," *Blick,* the Swiss gutter-press newspaper, printed in big fat letters on its front page. In 1961 the events had already come thick and fast. The *Emmentaler Blatt* announced: "A dramatic weekend on the Eiger. 8 men conquer the Wall. Reporters' aircraft with three occupants crashes."

"An End to Climbing on the North Face of the Eiger!"

It is no wonder that the local newspaper *Oberhasler* of Meiringen demanded "an end to climbing on the North Face of the Wall" to deal with the "constant new outbreaks of Eigerwand psychosis." On 12 September 1961 the *Echo of Grindelwald* printed a request that "this dance with death on this icy, rocky wasteland" should stop once and for all. The *Oberhasler* henceforth consistently refused to print any more reports on the Eiger. For his part the editor of the *Echo,* however, believed that "if the Swiss press were to come to an agreement no longer to print any more reports about the Eigerwand, it should come as no surprise how quickly the strength of this magic mountain would ebb away!" For these reports are for Eigerwand climbers "one of the main reasons why they attempt their climbs—to make their names known!"

The *Wiener Arbeiter-Zeitung* demanded the "complete 'civilization'

and licensing of this Wall, which it is, however, impossible to keep free from those who have had enough of this life." The *Volksblatt* reprinted this sarcastic suggestion from Austria for the solution of the Eigerwand Problem: "It would be good if all those looking for fame on the Eiger were to pay a hefty entrance fee which could be used to put up concrete shelters for the mountain rescuers which were easy to reach by cable cars and where the mountain rescue team could warm themselves, drink tea, and stamp passes; this would save any arguments in court as to who had climbed the "Wall and who had not. Steep couloirs could be made safe with nylon nets which would render the expensive task of looking for bodies unnecessary."

"They Wilfully Risked Death"

On 3 August 1962 the *Basler Nachrichten* soberly recognized that "as regularly as the turning of the summer sun the sensationalist reports about the latest escapades of Eiger North Wall hopefuls appear in the news. And at the same time, statements of displeasure from truly expert mountaineers to whom this whole activity is abhorrent and who rebel against the fact that Alpine special achievements should attract such media attention."

For example, 1963 was one of those summers.

"'A great mountain' said the victor" was the title *Blick* gave to the article about the first solo ascent of the Eigerwand by the mountain guide Michel Darbellay. No sooner was this triumph out of the headlines than came the tragedy of the two Spaniards, Alberto Rabadà and Roberto Navarro, who, with no experience in ice climbing, lost their lives in the Spider. The commentary from the daily news in Bern was as follows: "They wilfully risked death." The Swiss Paul Etter, Ueli Gantenbein, and Sepp Henkel recovered the bodies of the two Spaniards on the first descent of the Wall.

"The Desire for Sensationalism Is Paid for With Death"

And the next sensation followed immediately, the attempt at a direct

route in the bitterly cold January of 1964. Four Alpinists allowed themselves to be sponsored by the German gutter-press *Bild*. However, they did not make it to the contractually determined minimum height. An extract from the well-respected German weekly newspaper *Die Zeit*, reprinted by the *Volksblatt*, said, "The four young Munich craftsmen had 'died': For the magazine *Quick*, which had offered them 4,000 Deutsch-marks for the right to be second publisher, and for a Swiss agency, which sought to acquire the worldwide rights for the Direttissima climb."

Exclusive report in *Quick* on 20 September 1964: "More courage than a thousand men." They were talking about the "twenty-six-year-old girl" Daisy Voog, who was the first woman to climb the North Face, "cold-blooded and confident." The title in *Blick* was even more impertinent: "Blonde secretary Daisy from Munich Broke the Taboo on the Murderous North Wall."

The American John Harlin, on the other hand, would not have been pleased with the title printed by the *Thuner Tagblatt* on the occasion of his fall due to a snapped rope on 21 March 1966. "The desire for sensationalism is paid for with death: Fall on the Eiger." *Blick* gave a preferable title in its description of the death of the North Face victim, age twenty-eight: "Blond, happy, masculine, strong as a bear. A complete man. A man who gave his life to the mountains." After his death the

(left) Chris Bonington and Don Whillans set off from Hampstead on a motorbike to attempt the first British ascent of the Eigerwand; they had sold their story to the *Daily Mail*.

(below) Toni Hiebeler, lead climber of the first winter ascent team, ran an exclusive report in the magazine *sie und er* with the title "The Wall and Us." The report also appeared in other magazines, even in the United States. The only silly thing was that Hiebeler tried (in vain) to keep quiet the fact that he and his companions had—thanks to the Gallery Window—climbed the Wall in two stages with a one-week break in between. The scandal was great and Ulrich Link asked the question in the *Münchener Merkur*: "Will Munich ask the four climbers to give back the awards they have been granted?"

two teams who were competing for a direct route joined forces and completed the Harlin Direttissima, the first new route next to the classic Heckmair Route.

"An Accident on the Eiger North Wall"

"The Eiger North Wall continues to tempt," said the Bernese newspaper *Bund*, according to which Swiss and Japanese ropeteams were planning winter ascents of both the direct routes, the Harlin Direttissima and the 1969 Japanese Direttissima. Oddly, the more new routes were done the quieter the press became about the Wall: Thanks to the constantly improving helicopter rescue service the number of dramas had decreased. They did, however, still exist. In the *Berner Tagblatt* of 21 July 1970 I read the following Eiger story: "The Italian mountaineer Sergio Insanti [correct: De Infanti], rescued from the Eigerwand on Sunday, owes his life to chance. The owner of the Hotel Kleine Scheidegg, Fritz von Allmen [Almen], was observing the Wall on Saturday afternoon through his telescope when he knocked the telescope by accident. When he looked through it again he could not believe his eyes. On a rocky ledge just beneath the so-called Exit Crack somebody was waving desperately with a handkerchief in order to attract attention to himself. It later transpired that this was the twenty-six-year-old alpinist Sergio Insanti [De Infanti] from Udine, Italy, who had secretly started up the Face eight days previously with his partner Angelo Urdella [Ursella]. Von Allmen [Almen] immediately alerted the rescue services, who were able to rescue a frostbitten Insanti [De Infanti]. All help came too late for his partner Urcella [Ursella]. He would surely have been alive also if the two mountaineers had informed the appropriate authorities of their planned climb." That is where the journalist was wrong: According to the rescue report Ursella had broken his neck during the fall. De Infanti remained at the side of the dead man just as Kurz had once done next to Willy Angerer.

"In the Face of Death"

The *Schweizer Illustrierte* entitled its report about the Czech Route of 1978 "32 days staring death in the face." This is true even for those who do not climb. Hans Jegerlehner saw this as clear as day in his report "The Attack on the North Face" (*Neue Zürcher Zeitung,* 14 July 1937): "As the crow flies, only a few kilometers separate the mountaineers, whose battle ground is as lonely and deserted as the North Pole, from places and towns where people of many different nationalities bustle about, spoilt by all the latest acquisitions of the tourist trade. I still remember today with a certain dread this contrast, when on the day after Kurz's death ladies in their Sunday best and gentlemen sporting fancy national costumes, fresh from the tailors in London or Paris, were led by the magic of the telescope to the horrors of the Wall, where the curtains of the dust avalanches fluttered down unceasingly. And how they then turned round again, pleasantly filled with horror, and with an increased perception of the warm shelter which the hotel had to offer."

The fascination of the Eigerwand: Mountain guide Edi Bohren, who was the first man from Grindelwald to climb the Face, in 1978, summed up this special situation precisely at the fiftieth anniversary celebrations of the first ascent: "If the Wall had been turned around 180 degrees, there would not have been such a commotion."

Waterfall Chimney

From the Ramp I could see the hotel they were in at the Kleine Scheidegg very clearly, and I had never felt so keenly the contrast between life down there and the precarious situation I was in up here. I was speaking to them over the radio; just one tiny mistake and only half a second later I might slip off and cartwheel 1000 meters down the Wall....I had no possibility of belaying myself, everything was covered in snow, and I was forced to carry on climbing and trust luck. It was a bit like Russian Roulette. I was standing on the front points of my crampons, and anything could happen. The radio was my packet of cigarettes and instinctively, without hesitation, I called in. Then I came to the crux section of the Ramp—the chimney: Here things got really nasty. Three big icicles of well-hardened snow, one above the other, blocked the chimney.

Christophe Profit, *La trilogie en hiver,* 1987 report.
Third Eigerwand ascent in 1987.

(facing page) Kobi Reichen bridges (stems) up the Waterfall Chimney, one of the crux sections of the Heckmair Route. It was while attempting the first bridging maneuver at the start of the Chimney that aspirant soloist Adi Mayr fell to his death on 28 August 1961.

Alone in the Vertical Corridor

Catherine Destivelle: "Toward the top it started getting harder, meaner. Horribly unstable heaps of snow, loose rock, deceptive ledges. I really had to watch out. On terrain like this it is impossible to self-belay, and you cannot allow yourself to make even the tiniest mistake."

"The Eigerwand solo? You'd have to be nuts to do that!" The comment is understandable if we take a look at the balance sheet, the fatal falls taken on the early attempts to solo the North Face. In more recent times, however, candidates for the big solo seem to have realized that, quite apart from outstanding technical ability, a special type of "Eiger psyche" is required. Daniel H. Anker, author of the chapter on soloing, has also climbed the Face alone.

During the postwar years, the North Face of the Eiger lost some of its prestige among the very best Alpinists as the greatest challenge, as more and more successful ascents were made. A generation of young climbers was looking for new and higher challenges.

There was, of course, the seductive lure of the eight-thousanders of the Himalaya, but it was only a select few mountaineers who were given the chance to participate on an expedition. In the 1960s, the young climbers proved their courage and skill on winter ascents, new routes, and first solo ascents in the Alps.

But, just as it had done during the first ascent attempts of the 1930s, the Eiger proved to be a tough and unpredictable adversary. Yet again, it was not the pure technical difficulty of the climbing that cost various soloists their lives, but the psychological demands and the requirement to spend at least one bivouac in the oppressive atmosphere of the North Face.

Dangerous Games: The Scramble for the First Solo Ascent

German climber Günther Nothdurft recognized the dangers on his solo attempt in July 1957. As the weather was deteriorating he retreated from the start of the Second Ice Field, climbing down through the night. A few weeks later he climbed the Wall with Franz Mayer, in dramatic circumstances. While their Italian companions Stefano Longhi and Claudio Corti stayed put, hoping for rescue after first Longhi and then Corti had fallen, the German team reached the summit in a storm and died of exhaustion descending the West Flank in mist.

In August 1961, watchers at the Kleine Scheidegg telescopes thought they could see Austrian Adi Mayr up on the Ramp; after a difficult traverse, he seemed to be trying repeatedly to bridge across onto a foothold that was presumably coated in water ice. Why did he not climb back down while he still had the strength and try the section again with a self-belay? Was it that he did not want to lose any more time, having already spent a long, nerve-corroding night at Death Bivouac? No one will ever know the full story. Only one thing is clear: Adi Mayr, twenty-three years old, slipped off and fell to his death.

On 31 July 1962, Adolf Derungs, who had already made the sixteenth ascent of the North Face in August 1959 with Lukas Albrecht, started up the climb. On 27 August, that same summer, Austrian Diether Marchart followed suit. Both men fell from the lower part of the route, before the real difficulties had even started. Were they, in their mind's eye, much further up on the big ice fields or in the Waterfall Chimney, not allowing themselves the time to compose themselves and concentrate on tackling just the next few tricky moves?

On 28 July 1963, the very well-known and experienced climber Walter Bonatti made his own solo attempt. The media men who had tagged along specifically for the occasion had already trumpeted his first steps onto the infamous Face to the whole waiting world. Despite this, he decided to retreat from below the Second Ice Field. He did not at the time feel up to the route and withdrew with a supreme demonstration of skill. The great Walter Bonatti admits defeat—a psychologically mature performance. Or did the decision come easier for him because he was so well known?

On 2 and 3 August 1963, Valais mountain guide Michel Darbellay pulled off the coup that was to make him famous overnight. In one and a half days, with no apparent effort, he soloed the great North Face. He approached every difficulty with calm and concentration; after all, he knew the Wall well

enough from an attempt the previous year with Loulou Boulaz and Yvette and Michel Vaucher, which ended with them having to retreat in mist and snow from the Ramp. For him, every meter of the climb is important, not only the summit. Of prime importance is the mountain experience; only later comes the unavoidable spotlight of media attention.

From the First Winter Solo to the Trilogy

After the first solo ascent, the top climbers of the day had to find themselves a new challenge on the Eiger. They found it in the 1966 Direttissima. As early as March 1967, Frenchman Roland Travellini had set out to solo the Harlin Direttissima—a daring undertaking, even though Walter Bonatti had shown what was possible with his 1965 first winter solo of the North Face of the Matterhorn. But the Eiger is not the Matterhorn, and Travellini was no Bonatti. Nothing more has been heard or seen of the Frenchman since he set foot on the initial rock pitches of the Wall.

The time was not yet ripe for such a difficult undertaking, for even the first winter solo of the classic Heckmair Route was another ten years coming. Then, in March 1978, came two successful solos, in quick succession. Japanese Tsuneo Hasegawa spent a total of seven days on the Wall, from 3 to 9 March, followed by Frenchman Yvano Ghirardini, who climbed it from 7 to 12 March.

Other Alpinists, male and female, contributed new aspects to the history of solo climbing on the Eiger. In 1980, Eric Jones was filmed by Leo Dickinson making the first British solo of the Face. In summer 1981, Swiss climber Ueli Bühler inadvertently started the race for the fastest ascent, while 1985 saw a new game with Christophe Profit's enchainment of the North Faces of the Grandes Jorasses, Eiger, and Matterhorn in the space of twenty-four hours. It must be said that in this case a large

(above) Michel Darbellay: "I was at the Exit Cracks and dripping wet from the water that was running down them. I did not want to arrive at the summit, with the wind blowing from every direction, in this state. I had also found a really good place to bivouac. I just wanted to smoke a cigarette, to calm myself down. But it was not to be. Although I did have a full packet of cigarettes, it was soaked through."

(following pages) On the Ramp: Catherine Destivelle makes the first female solo ascent, and in winter. The crux of the climb is the Waterfall Chimney, where in 1961 Adi Mayr had taken his final step, while down below the watchers crowded round the telescopes.

support team, with helicopter involvement and interviews conducted during the connecting flights, was unavoidable. Profit went one step further in March 1987; his linking of the Big Three in winter and in under forty-two hours represented both the high point and a fitting conclusion to this form of mountaineering. Swiss climber Michel Wirth took six hours to solo the Lauper Route in winter conditions on 10 February 1989, and on 9 March 1992 French climber Catherine Destivelle made the first female solo of the North Face, in a single day!

The Quest for the Ideal Direttissima

On 15 July 1982, Slovenian Franček Knez opened up a new route—solo—to the right of the West Pillar. Meanwhile, as the solo-sprinters were busy establishing new record times for the Heckmair Route, Pavel Pochylý was searching for a new challenge of a quite different kind. In March 1983 he was to become the first soloist to attempt a big new route alone. Admittedly, he was able to profit from two Czech attempts on his route made in 1977 and 1978. On 29 April 1978 the leading rope of Jiří Pechous and Jiří Slégl had fallen to their deaths from the Fly, the ice field above and to the right of the Spider. The two surviving climbers, Heinz Skopec and Viktor Jarolim, had abseiled back down the line of the route, leaving equipment and fixed ropes behind.

After weathering a weeklong snowstorm, Pochylý reached the steep step between the First and Second Ice Fields. To save time, he used one of the old Czech fixed ropes. While dangling below an overhang, working his way slowly up the old rope with his jumars, he suddenly discovered that further up the rope was more of a thread than a strand; the wind had caused it to chafe over the rock and it was worn almost through. Pochylý held his breath,

offered up a short and fervent prayer, and reached the next belay in one piece. In spite of the incident, the Slovakian worked his way indefatigably higher and higher up the route. On the lower part of the summit headwall he was helped by fixed ropes left by the Czechs and still fit for use. The loss of his two ascenders was made good by finding three of the Czech team's jumar clamps below the Fly.

Thereafter, the climb increasingly took on the proportions of a walk on—or even beyond—the edge. Pochylý was tough, honed by many long and very difficult solo climbs in the Tatra. Although he had hardly trained at all for two years he was obviously right up there psychologically and refused to allow anything to interfere with his calm, neither the loss of his last remaining glove, nor his crampons breaking twice. He endured two nights of storm in only a down sleeping bag but without a bivi bag; this he had jettisoned, together with other items of gear, in the belief that he would reach the summit that same day. On 2 April, after thirteen days on the Wall, he reached the summit, totally exhausted, in darkness and mist, and with no knowledge of the descent down the West Flank. Despite sliding off, executing several somersaults on the way down, and a loud crack from his neck on impact, he reached the Eigergletscher Station at midnight. On Pavel Pochylý's solo adventure, not only courage and endurance had played a part. He had also had a whole squadron of guardian angels with him on the climb.

My Adventure on the North Corner

It is the beginning of September 1985. After an unsettled night in my sleeping bag between the buildings of the Eigergletscher Station, I set off across the lower rocks, heading up toward the North Corner. At a short, steep band I unintentionally stray onto a patch of water ice, the heavy ruck-

Pavel Pochylý: "Above me I see the strand of a fixed rope being blown about in the storm. It had been left there five years ago by the Czechs. Should I? To climb the second steep section in this awful weather would cost me a whole day. I wonder, is the rope still all right? In 1966, poor John Harlin fell to his death when a fixed rope broke and that had only been hanging up there on the Wall for a few weeks."

sack restricts my freedom of movement, and the next thing I know I am several meters further down on a steep, rubble-covered ledge. That could have been a costly slip, like many other fatal mistakes on solo attempts. Why am I here, why do I still carry on climbing? Only the day before I had had an impressive adventure, climbing the route "Spit verdonesque édenté" with friends. After the climb all three had commitments elsewhere—or maybe they had just had enough of the Eiger for one year. And me?

Actually, I suspected it well in advance and had already toyed with the idea of doing a solo climb. I intend to self-belay on all the difficult sections and to take my time. I am well aware of the fact that, deep down, I am really quite frightened of it all and for a true solo—without a rope—would need a wide safety margin. A sprint up the Heckmair Route would be too dangerous. And so I have selected a route on which the technical difficulties and the unknown factors are great enough to have thus far failed to capture the interest of the solo climber. The magic appeal for me is to stand the test alone, without the physical and psychological support of a partner. To meet the challenge and face my fears completely alone.

As soon as the terrain gets steeper and more difficult, it is I who will decide when to belay and when not. Do I feel sure enough of my abilities to go for it, with the rucksack on my back or left standing at the last stance, connected to me by the rope so that I can haul it up after me? Or should I climb it roped up, belaying myself as I go, and then abseil back down and jumar the pitch with the heavy sack on my back?

The weather is splendid. I do not need to waste time worrying whether a Christophe Profit would free-solo the same pitch in half the time. If such considerations were to take up too much space in your thoughts, solo mountaineering would become a dangerous game. Pitch by pitch I climb up toward the West Ridge. My arms and shoulders are getting tired from sack hauling; my hands are swollen from contact with the rough rock. In the evening of the second day I climb out of the darkness of the corner into the setting sun.

Record Time on the Harlin Direttissima

In January 1990, Slovenian Slavko Sveticic climbed the Harlin Direttissima in an "impossible" twenty-seven hours. This exploit became reality through the consistent application of the motto "as light as possible, as fast as possible." But what does this really mean on a technically very difficult route like the Harlin Direttissima, for which a roped team of climbers would normally require several days? Sveticic admits that the Harlin Direttissima is the most often repeated route on the central section of the Face, after the classic Heckmair Route. Since after every repeat ascent a few additional new pitons are left behind, the number of *in situ* points of protection has increased. On 31 July 1983, French climber Jean-Marc Boivin had climbed the section of the Harlin Direttissima from Death Bivouac to the

Daniel H. Anker: "At a short, steep band I unintentionally stray onto a patch of water ice, the heavy rucksack restricts my freedom of movement, and the next thing I know I am several meters further down on a steep, rubble-covered ledge. That could have been a costly slip, like many other fatal mistakes on solo attempts."

Jeff Lowe: "Never in my life have I been so in the line of fire. Every five minutes, a huge avalanche shot down. I could not move, even if I had wanted to. Nevertheless, I somehow had to wriggle out of there and find a better place to bivi. Circumstances simply dictated it."

summit in a very short time to complete his solo ascent of the Face. For Sveticic, himself a top-flight mountaineer, this meant that he, too, would be able to dispense with that stretch of the route in a reasonable time. Sveticic also had one further advantage: In the winter of 1990, the North Face had been enjoying dream conditions since December. A period of thaw after the early snowfalls and a prolonged period of fine weather had consolidated the snow into firm neve.

Searching for His Own Identity

It was an Eiger adventure of a very different kind that Jeff Lowe had in mind in the winter of 1991. For the past year, everything had been going wrong for him: His own company went bankrupt, an affair with Catherine Destivelle (they climbed a new route together on the Nameless Tower in the Karakorum) finally caused the breakdown of his marriage, and as a result he had to part company with his three-year-old daughter. In addition, his fortieth birthday was looming. While he sank into depression, plans for a special type of "mountain therapy" were crystallizing in

his mind: "A route on the North Face of the Eiger—a clean, direct line between the Czech Route and the Japanese Direttissima. Solo. In winter. With no bolts." But the very experienced Lowe was no suicide candidate; he was looking for a personal confirmation, a way back to himself, back to his identity as an extreme mountaineer. In this mood, he managed to achieve the utterly impossible. On his first foray he reached the steep band below the First Ice Field in just four days. He then descended, in order to rest and stock up on equipment. Two days later on 24 February, in fine and mild weather, he went up onto the Wall again. At first he made swift progress. Then, at the foot of the summit headwall, a snowstorm overtook him. Thanks both to information received by radio and to his own wise predictions he was able to dig himself a snow cave and sit out the torrents of powder snow, emerging unscathed apart from the wet clothes and the frozen equipment. Despite every untoward incident that befell him, he worked his way slowly but surely up the headwall, somewhere between the Pochylý Route and the Japanese

Direttissima. With great patience, endurance, and consummate technical skill he managed to climb the most difficult passages, and even sections with appallingly bad protection. The last few pitches became a race against time and bad weather. Just a few meters short of the West Ridge and the summit, Lowe ran out of rope. A tedious search failed to uncover a single possible placement for a nut, piton, or ice screw—the rock was all completely loose. After contacting his team down at Scheidegg, he untied from the rope, leaving all his gear on the mountain. With no rope, he climbed the last few meters up to the West Ridge, where a short while later he was lifted off by helicopter. The concluding part of the ascent did not fit in well with Jeff Lowe's climbing ethics, but it does show that here was a man not only in love with adventure but with life itself, in equal measure.

Whether or not Lowe's route was really new or identical in parts with other existing routes is immaterial; the performance was—in the same way as Pochylý's—absolutely brilliant and hard to comprehend. Clearly, these elder gentlemen (Pochylý was thirty-eight when he made his climb, Lowe forty) find more satisfaction in such murderous undertakings than younger, technically outstanding climbers. Or is it that experienced alpinists of more mature years are simply better suited to the special demands of the Eiger?

One thing is clear. The following two options remain for the soloist— male or female—wishing to contribute something new: Either attempt a lightning-fast ascent of a well-known route, or get brave and go for a multiday adventure on one of the many, as yet unrepeated, routes.

Thomas Bubendorfer: "I no longer had to think about which hold to grab with which hand, or where the best pick placements were; well before I was capable of rational thought, body and instinct had taken over and without question done the correct, the only, thing."

Who Is the Fastest?

As early as 1969, the famous South Tyrol climber Reinhold Messner attempted to solo the classic '38 Route on the North Face in one day. Stones cascading down from the party ahead of him caused him to abandon the attempt. On 15 August 1974 he set the balance straight, climbing the route in ten hours—a new record—this time with a rope and in the company of Peter Habeler.

On 25 August 1981, the young Swiss climber Ueli Bühler did the Heckmair Route in just eight and a half hours.

Over the next few years, the following solo climbers raced up the North Face:

1982: Slovenian Frančck Knez, in six hours

1983: Austrian Thomas Bubendorfer in four hours and fifty minutes (the record still stands today); a few days earlier he had "learned" the route with Peter Rohrmoser

1983: South Tyrolean Reinhard Patscheider in five hours

1983: Frenchman Jean-Marc Boivin in seven and a half hours (climbing the upper half of the Harlin Direttissima from the Flatiron to the summit, the first time this section had been soloed)

1984: Slovenian Slavko Sveticic in eight hours and in bad weather

1985: March, Christophe Profit accomplished the third winter solo ascent of the Heckmair Route in ten hours

1988: The seventeen year-old Frenchman Jean-Christophe Etienne in nine hours and twenty minutes

1992: Without any attendant media hullabaloo or helicopter accompaniment, and after careful and hard training, exiled Czech Michal Pitelka climbed the Heckmair Route in eight and a half hours.

Thereafter, things went quiet on the classic North Face route as the record attempt dwindled.

Postscript: Swiss climber Kobi Reichen ran up the shorter Lauper Route in three hours in 1986!

Ramp Ice Field

At midnight we discover a halfway acceptable bivouac site on the ridge at the right-hand edge of the couloir. We are 2 meters apart. This second bivouac is exceedingly uncomfortable. Our clothes and the contents of our rucksacks are wet through....

A sleet shower draws across the Wall. We are close to thinking that our names are about to be added to the macabre list of our predecessors. Lionel reckons that we might be able to descend before the bad weather really sets in. Personally, I am counting on a moderation of the elements and think we should try to climb out....

At five in the morning the weather is still dismal. Not very happily, we search for the line Terray suggested yesterday across the system of ledges. Our bodies are stiff from the tiredness of the previous day and the cold of the night and it is unutterably difficult to master the immediately serious difficulties. After a traverse of two rope lengths across very slippery slate we experience huge pleasure. We happen upon a rock piton and a barely rusted lantern. They had been left here by the Krähenbühl-Schlunegger rope and mark the high point of their attempt.

Louis Lachenal, *Carnets du vertige*, 1956.
Eigerwand in 1947.

(facing page) Ueli Bula arrives at the upper rim of the Ramp Ice Field. The two Swiss mountain guides who attempted the second ascent of the North Face in 1946 had to retreat from here in bad weather—a long and dangerous descent.

Should Mountain Guides Be Allowed to Guide the North Face of the Eiger?

(from left to right) Brothers and mountain guides Karl and Hans Schlunegger from Wengen and their client Gottfried Jermann from Dittingen climbed the Eigerwand on 4/5 August 1947. This third ascent was also the first Swiss ascent and the first time the route had been guided.

Mountain guides who go about their business on the fearsome North Face of the Eiger: Are they heroes, breakneck lunatics, pushy and negligent fame merchants, or the most able practitioners in their chosen field? Could they not simply wait until the time is right for such a tricky job of work, until adequate preparations have been made, the conditions on the Face are good and the form of both guide and client are absolutely right? Ueli Kämpf, himself a guide, gives us a feel for their work.

Three headlamps appear at the Gallery Window, at the uppermost edge of the initial rock wall on the North Face. It is 2:30 A.M. on 5 October 1997 and a party has just started up the classic Heckmair Route.

The Oldest Client

The Italian client Benedetto Salaroli, a longtime Swiss resident, is at seventy-two a good five years older than Jean Juge, who set the age record for the Wall back in 1975. His two guides are old Eiger hands, with impeccable credentials. Kobi Reichen, thirty-seven, from Lauenen has done, among other routes on the Eiger, the third ascent of the Piola-Ghilini Direttissima and an early repeat of the North Corner. In addition, he has proved his abilities by making the first ascent of the Direct North Face of the Jungfrau and the first ski descent of the North Face of the Mönch. Ueli Bühler from Gsteigwiler is thirty-one years old and has recently become a father. He has many extreme Alpine routes to his name, including several first ascents on the Wendenstöcken in the Bernese Oberland and, in February 1989, he and his brother Heinz ascended the Japanese Direttissima in only fifteen hours.

The stable weather patterns and warm autumnal temperatures—even at altitude—allow the three climbers to make their ascent without worrying about any meteorological surprises. Kobi leads; he does not need to search out the line, he knows the route well from three earlier ascents with friends and clients. Ueli climbs alongside Benedetto, removing the ice screws, cams, and rock pegs, pointing the way to allow a smooth and even climbing tempo. As day breaks they begin the long traverse across the Second Ice Field. The ice demands a great deal of concentration; while up on the Ramp, they have to use every climbing technique in the book. Their sprightly and vigorous client is in the best possible physical shape and takes this difficult terrain in his stride; technically, he climbs supremely well, mastering even the hardest cracks and bulges under his own steam, without recourse to jumars or etriers. At midday the rope of three moves along the iced-covered rock of the Traverse of the Gods and onto the Spider, and just three and a half hours later climbs the Summit Ice Field in the gentle evening light, emerging onto the 3970-meter summit at 7:00 P.M.

The First Client

In the mid-1940s no one knew the Face better than the Wengen man Hans Schlunegger. He had been there in 1936 during the attempts to rescue Toni Kurz. During the first ascent of 1938 he had followed Heckmair's party up the West Ridge to the summit. On 16 August 1946, Schlunegger had intended to make the second ascent with the Bern mountain guide Edwin Krähenbühl but they were foiled by bad weather and had to retreat from high on the Face, climbing down and abseiling to reach the safety of the Gallery Window. Two years later, Schlunegger was back, this time with his brother Karl and a client, the excellent Jura climber Gottfried Jermann. On 4 August 1947, at 2:00 in the morning, they set off to attempt the third ascent of the Eigerwand. Two weeks earlier, the French guides Louis Lachenal and Lionel Terray had made the second. The Eiger gave away nothing to the Schlunegger brothers and their client. Sudden bad weather, with rain, snow, and high winds and the resultant snowslides and stonefall, plagued their ascent from the Ramp Ice Field onward. Their wet clothes froze stiff with ice, but they kept moving anyway, reaching the summit after thirty-eight hours of torment—the shortest time thus far.

Almost His Very Last Climb

On 9 August 1975 a group of eight climbers made their way onto the North Face: Michel Darbellay (who eight years earlier had made the first solo ascent) with his client Louis Frote, Tomas Gross with Natacha Gall, Yvette Vaucher with Stéphane Schafter, and finally Michel Vaucher with his sixty-seven-year-old client Jean Juge. At the first bivouac on the Ramp Ice Field, Jean Juge dropped the rucksack with the clothing, the crucial bivouac equipment, and crampons. Continuing the climb, he suffered badly with the damp and the cold brought on by the increasingly poor weather, slowing the whole group down on the way up to the summit. While the others began their descent via the West Ridge, Tomas Gross and Michel Vaucher stayed with the by now totally exhausted Jean Juge, hoping against hope for either a break in the weather or an airlift off the mountain. Only after a further two days could the helicopter rescue Juge and his mentors. These trials and tribulations, however, could not satisfy the North Face hunger of the former professor of chemistry and president of the UIAA. Three years later he died from a heart attack on the descent after climbing the North Face of the Matterhorn.

Ueli Kämpf (born 1955) is employed as a mountain guide. During the winter he organizes ice climbing courses and guided ski-mountaineering tours. He knows the Heckmair Route well from a winter ascent he made, without a client.

The Price for the North Face of the Eiger

The costs of a climb of this magnitude are arranged between guide and client, and vary considerably. In 1947, the wages paid to Hans and Karl Schlunegger were 1000 Swiss Francs. In his book *Eigerwand*, Toni Hiebeler writes that present-day guides can command three times this fee. If all goes well, the time-scale for the guide—including reconnaissance, preparations, route, and recovery time—is roughly one week.

(above, upper) Mountain guide Edwin Krähenbühl photographed his colleague Karl Schlunegger on one of the crux sections of the Face. They set off on 16 August 1946, intending to make the second ascent. A sudden worsening in the weather forced them to retreat only 300 meters below the summit.

(above, lower) Guide Kobi Reichen and Italian client Benedetto Salaroli, photographed by guide Ueli Bühler on Sunday, 5 October 1997, at 7:00 P.M. At seventy-two, Salaroli is the oldest to have climbed the North Face.

Brittle Ledges and Brittle Crack

Then it was the Ramp Ice Field, the Brittle Ledges, and the Brittle Crack. Mark had described the Brittle Crack as "pretty scary," so I belay myself again. For the first time, I take the crampons off. The climbing is appallingly exposed, for just here you have a particularly steep part of the Face right below your feet that intensifies the impression of height enormously. Despite the brittle rock, the first few meters up from a little snow-covered ledge into the crack are really overhanging. But the pitch, leading up to the Traverse of the Gods, is not actually as difficult as feared and, more important, I have now worked out how to set up the self-belay so I can pull the rope through from above. It really is such a great pleasure to climb so many famous features in a single day. All the sections highlighted here can be reeled off by heart by just about every mountaineer, since they crop up in all the stories, books, and tragedies written about this most famous route and its sixty or seventy victims.

Malte Roeper, *Auf Abwegen,* 1995.
Eigerwand in 1988.

(facing page) Stephan Siegrist moves along the Brittle Ledges, where an old fixed rope still hangs. This section of the climb is immediately followed by the Brittle Crack.

The Far Side of the North Face

(above) After the opening of the Eismeer Station in 1905 (note holes in rock directly above lead climber), tourists would often clamber down to the glacier with the aid of a rope ladder.

(facing page) Werner Burgener on the most recent South East Face route.

Where else in the Bernese Oberland —or the rest of the Alps for that matter—can one find an 800-meter-high, almost 200-meter-wide cliff with only two routes on it? And with rock that, while it is not always perfectly sound, is nowhere near as loose as first impressions and prejudices would have us believe? And do not forget: The start of the climbing lies only thirty minutes from the Eismeer Station of the Jungfrau Railway. North Face specialist Hannes Stähli comes to grips with the little-known backwater of the South East Face of the Eiger.

September 1987. As Werner Burgener and I leave the dark tunnel at Eismeer Station it is not only the view that undergoes a radical change. We feel as if our facial expressions have altered, too, from "North Face preoccupied" to "South Face cheerfulness." Maybe that is the reason why we underestimated the climbing and overestimated our own abilities. Whatever, we reckoned we could have the 800 meters more or less in the bag by evening! The approach to the foot of the face is no problem, but the step across from the glacier to the start of the route is less simple, and it is only at the second attempt that we touch rock and take off on our voyage of discovery. After all the time that has elapsed since the idea of a new route on the eastern sector of the South East Face was first mooted, the thought that we might not be the first still persists. But we find only unclimbed, rough rock.

After the first two pitches we arrive at the lowest and easier-angled part of the Face and from here we can see most of the continuation line. The next 150 meters are dispensed with quickly and this inspires confidence. But all too soon the "easy stroll" is over as, unlike the central section of the South East Face, our bit of the cliff gets steeper and steeper the higher up we climb. In profile, it may best be compared to a huge ski jump, steep at the start followed by an easier-angled section and a final "take-off zone" ending on the Mittellegi Ridge.

The limestone is good and at times reminds us of the rock on the Engelhörner. Water-worn slabs alternate with corners and cracks. A cave at the start of the steeper middle section looks inviting as a bivouac site, with the view across to the Schreckhorn, Finsteraarhorn, and Fiescherwand included in the price of the overnight stay. But now

Shady Goings-on on the Sunny Side of the Mountain?

Was Ludwig Vörg, one of the rope of four that first climbed the North Face of the Eiger in 1938, also part of the team comprising Otto Eidenschink, Ernst Moeller, and Hias Rebitsch that had the previous year done the first ascent of the South East Face of the Eiger? The records show as much, yet the route was done on 11/12 August 1937 and at the same time—namely between 11 and 14 August 1937—Rebitsch and Vörg were on their third, and highest, attempt at the North Face, reaching a point a few rope lengths beyond Death Bivouac. After the weather broke they retreated, becoming the first men to return alive from the central section of the Face.

One thing is clear: Mid-August 1937 all four of the aforementioned climbers were indeed on the Eiger, but not on the same face! The confusion perhaps stems from the fact that a few days earlier, on 6 August, the four men had climbed a north face together; namely, that of the Grosser Fischerhorn. This lies but a stone's throw away from the South East Face of the Eiger. What is not certain is whether or not Moeller and Eidenschink really were the first to climb the South East Face.

On 24 August 1934 the local press

Adrift on a sea of rock. "Eidenschink at work. Leica photograph by Moeller" reads the original caption from the Zürich magazine *Sport* on 1 September 1937.

ran a story about the "Conquering of the South Face of the Eiger." A Dresden team was said to have climbed it prior to their unsuccessful attempt on the North Face but the reports were inexact and the claim was greeted with suspicion in Grindelwald.

Back, then, to the ascent made by Eidenschink and Moeller. There is no doubting the abilities of these two men. In 1934, Eidenschink— with Rudolf Peters, one of the party that did the first ascent of the North Face of the Grandes Jorasses—had established an exceptionally difficult new climb on the West Face of the Totenkirchl in the Kaisergebirge. Before the Eiger, Eidenschink and Moeller set about repeating the climbs of Willo Welzenbach on the North Faces of the Gspaltenhorn, Lauterbrunner Breithorn, Grosshorn, Gletscherhorn, and Grosser Fischerhorn, often as second ascents. They were, therefore, best prepared for the Eigerwand and only the bad summer of 1937 prevented them carrying out their plans. Instead, almost as an afterthought, they turned their attention to the sunny side of the mountain, climbing the South East Face in just twenty-four hours, with a twelve-hour bivouac just above half height.

The second ascent of the original route was made in 1964 by the Swiss Albin Schelbert and Geni Steiger. From 21 to 23 December 1972, Kurt Haas, Walter Müller, Ernst Ott, and Markus Wacker bagged the first winter ascent and on 24 August 1974 Müller, with Karl Moser, established a new direct start up the central crack system. The third (and at VI/A0, the most difficult) route, "Panorama Route," was the work of Werner Burgener and Hannes and Ueli Stähli.

the "take-off zone" gets steeper and we realize that we are unlikely to finish the route in the day. After climbing about half of the route we abseil off to catch the last train down. We only have the one day . . . .

September 1988. Werner and I return and push the route again as far as the last steep section, where we have to give up for a second time. First, it snows and second, we do not have the right gear. Over the next couple of years I get used to the idea that I will not go back on the route and even tentatively christen it "The Unfinished." A bad idea.

September 1991. Film work on the Eiger again, this time with Americans on the summit. It occurs to me that I could abseil from the Mittellegi Ridge to the high point of our route on the south side and finish off the remaining few pitches. Festooned with enough gear, my brother Ueli and I abseil to the big ledge. Gliding past, I can see what is waiting for us. Five pitches of exposed and strenuous climbing see us back on the Ridge. Some things are worth the wait.

September 1997. I still want to do the route in one push, from the bottom, as recompense for all the hours spent on the mountain, the shredded hands and the uncertainty that goes with making hard first ascents. Ueli and I decide to go for the comfortable "bivi" in the warmth of the waiting room at Eismeer Station and start climbing in the first grey light of morning. The first rays of sun reach us shortly afterward. The settled autumn weather, the light rucksacks, and the certain knowledge that we are up to the route make the ascent an unforgettable experience. After eight hours we are standing on the Mittellegi Ridge, that impressive blade of rock poised between shadow and sunlight. To one side is the North Face, the adventure playground for mountaineers the world over; to the other is the south side, free of the media hype and mass

ascents. We called the route "Panorama Route," the third climb on the South East Face of the Eiger.

Hannes Stähli was born in 1947 in Grindelwald and has lived since 1952 in Wilderswil, gateway to the Lütschinen Valleys. He is a sculptor, mountain guide, and ski instructor and for many years worked as a mountain guide instructor and ski trainer. He has also worked as a cameraman and extra on several Eiger films and has been involved in numerous rescues. He has done over fifty first ascents of rock and mixed routes, particularly in the Bernese Oberland. On the Eiger, he was not only responsible for a new route on the South East Face but also did the first ascent of the South East Buttress of the Ostegg on the Eigerhörnli with Edi Bohren in August 1977.

Four attempts and countless abseil maneuvers were necessary in order to establish a third route on the 800-meter-high South Face. In September 1997, Hannes and Ueli Stähli climbed the new route, the "Panorama Route," in one push and then abseiled back down to the Eismeer Station.

Traverse of the Gods

"Would you like to join us—we can all go up together. I think we should push on tonight as far as possible."

"No. It is quite all right. We shall stay here and go on tomorrow."

We left them with a feeling of relief mixed with guilt, and started across the Traverse of the Gods, a line of rubble-strewn ledges, clinging to the sheer wall. We could hear the cow horn at the Kleine Scheidegg blow a lugubrious tune and, nearer, the rattle of the rack railway; the sounds emphasized the isolation of our position more than the wildest mountain could have done. We seemed so close to safety, and yet, if anything went wrong, nothing could help us.

Chris Bonington, *I Chose to Climb*, 1966.
Eigerwand in 1962.

(facing page) Michel Wirth gets cold fingers on the Traverse of the Gods during a winter ascent. In order to climb a tricky section he has to remove his gloves briefly.

Drama on the Wall of Books

164

"Behold the struggles and cares heralded by a new dawn: Avalanches strike, rockfalls resound, tatters of fog abound—Comrades, the time is come!"—Margrit Volmar, *On the Eiger North Wall* (circa 1936)

There are only a few summits which are the object of literary fiction: Mont Blanc, the Matterhorn, Mount Everest. . . . And of course the Eiger. Thirty-four literary works have been devoted to it, only four not concerned with the North Face, as they were published before the first tragedies in the 1930s. But even the first novella of 1892 has the prophetic title *The Hero of the Eiger*. Daniel Anker has climbed his way through the mountain of books.

At the end of the 1970s Jörg Binder, a twenty-three-year-old mountain guide from Wengen, made a discovery which almost made him fall a second time. A few moments earlier an avalanche had almost swept him and his climbing partner down the Eiger North Wall. There, cowering on a narrow ledge just below the Traverse of the Gods, was a dead man. Binder approached him with care.

On his head the dead man had a cap as worn by the mountain soldiers of the German Alpine Corps. As Binder approached the well-preserved body he saw the eagle symbol from Nazi times on his anorak. Around his neck there was a locket on a chain. Binder was able to make out a name and a date on the back of it: Erich Spengler, October 1942. Then he opened the locket: Inside there was a photo of a very pretty woman, whose name the mountain guide was able to read on the reverse: Helene Rössner.

The thriller *Traverse of the Gods* by the Englishman Bob Langley thus begins dramatically. Why a German soldier of the Second World War had to die high up on the Traverse of the Gods on the Eigerwand, the readers discover during the remaining 250 pages. It is an outrageous story and yet so well told that at the end we almost believe that Spengler and Rössner were successful in the second ascent of the Wall. But Spengler is dead—or is he?

"The Hero of the Eiger"

One really cannot imagine a better or more exciting setting for a mountain espionage crime thriller than the North Face of the Eiger. The author Trevanian also uses this in his book *The Eiger Sanction,* which was filmed with Clint Eastwood in the leading part. The fictitious hero of both women and the mountains, Jonathan Hemlock, is the only one of his team who survives the fight against the Wall and against his companions. "The Hero of the Eiger" was the brilliant title given to a story from the work *Tourist Novellas* by the author Joseph Victor Widmann from Bern. The hero is a twenty-four-year-old

Englishman, Sir Robert Doll, who with his guide has conquered the Eiger without troubles or difficulty; he reminds us of the first Eiger climber, Charles Barrington. The latter's name is given to a North Wall climber in the novel *The Ice Mirror* by Charles Machardy. Only this Barrington does not make it to the summit; he dies. But back to our first Eiger hero. Feeling happy about his deed, which was so easily accomplished, Doll returns to a hotel in the Lauterbrunnen valley, where there is an assortment of different people around the guest table. This is when the trouble starts. Doll defends Miss Angélique, a pretty Frenchwoman, against the verbal abuse of a German professor, and as he does this so vehemently and at the same time charmingly, the reactions from person to person are greatly varied: One responds with a gun, another with kisses. Widmann's novella is very amusing and still worth reading nowadays.

The tourists, the "birds of the Eiger" as Trevanian calls them, play an important role in the Eiger: "All heads peer silently up at the Eiger ridge, to the razor-sharp edge, scarred and hacked to pieces by the weather and dashed by lightning strikes." The Swiss author Johannes Jegerlehner powerfully depicts the Mittellegi Ridge of the Eiger and its first ascent in his 1929 book *Melchior the Mountain Guide: A Jungfrau Novel*. By 1935 the book had sold 10,000 copies. But it was precisely then that the Mittellegi Ridge disappeared from the view of the readers and the spectators and the North Face came into the focus. And how!

"The Drama on the Eiger"

The publishers had by no means finished working on the Death Bivouac misfortune of Mehringer and Sedlmayr in 1935 when, the following year, there was the tragedy of Toni Kurz and his companions. Only a few months after the last survivor of the attempt to climb back down due to bad weather had uttered his last words, "I can't go on," and collapsed on his rope before the very eyes of his rescuers, two books tried to portray the tragic event in words. Theo Lütolf called his epic poem *The Drama*

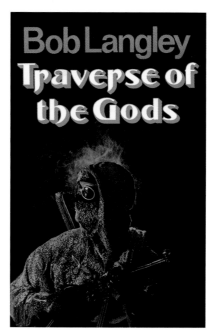

Langley: "There is no doubt. Your arm is completely broken. If you want to get off this ledge, you will have to crawl on your belly. Fine, then I will crawl, he said to himself. For Helene, for Henke, and for Dr. Lasser. I will crawl up through this wretched 'Spider' and if necessary through this wretched Exit Crack."

on the Eiger. Erika Jemelin took another approach. She wrote the fictitious diary of Toni Kurz, which was found "when the mountain released you and your young body was found cold and stiff at the foot of the snowy rocks. Your lips are silent, closed forever, but this small book tells of your heroic fight and your wait for the horrors of death." It goes without saying that Gustav Renker, who has written so much about the mountains, could not miss out on such heroic material. In his novel *Misfortune on the North Wall* he writes about "this one unattained target in the Alps, which have otherwise been conquered; the last symbol of the fight between great nature and little man" (jacket blurb). The author Edgar Winkler and his comrade Peter Lohmayer take up the fight; the former dies in the bivouac, guides rescue the other. When the book came onto the market in 1938 the North Face, "this horrendous marvel" (Renker), had not yet been climbed. It is well known that Fritz Kasparek and his three companions did not stick to the guidelines of pulp fiction. But Renker was not angry with him and wrote a foreword to Kasparek's work *A Mountaineer,* published in 1939, which spoke to loyal mountain soldiers from the heart.

ROMAN VON
OTTO ZINNIKER

Zinniker: "'Forward!' insisted Fred. He is a devil of a chap, a fiercely resolute fighter. What he would like best of all is to devour the mountain and grind it to sand in a grinding machine."

"Alpine Dance with Death"

I managed to dig up thirty literary works in which the Eiger North Face is either a central part or a background theme. Thirteen of those are novels (including four crime thrillers), six short stories, two plays, seven poems, one epic, and one linguistic work. Categorized by language, we have fifteen works in German, twelve in English, three in French. Eight publications appeared between 1956 and 1963, when Eiger Fever, after its first climax in the 1930s, made a new and stronger comeback. In short, they concern: the Corti Tragedy, which we are reminded of by Longhi's body hanging above the Traverse of the Gods for two whole years; first winter ascent; women on the Wall; fatal solo attempt; and the Spaniards, Rabadà and Navarro, frozen to death in the Spider. Thirteen deaths in eight years. Definitely something to write about.

The *Alpine Dance with Death* (as, by the way, Konrad Falke calls his short story that takes places at the foot of the South East Face of the Eiger) was begun in 1956 by Ernst Nobs, town president of Zürich, the first Social Democrat federal councillor and a freeman of Grindelwald, with his novella *The Wall*. At the center of it is the rich American, Peggy, who is determined to do the Wall. The prudent mountain guide Menk Rubi (who can be compared with Hermann Steuri) tries to put her off this idea, but the "Woman of Satan" snaps up his more relaxed brother Petsch and the Wall opens its jaws too.

In his book *In the Shadow of the Great Wall* Oswald Frey makes mountaineer Adolf Derungs a literary monument. In 1959 together with Lukas Albrecht he successfully climbed the Heckmair Route. Five years later he tried it again, this time alone. We know about the bad results, but less about the good book. On the other hand Otto Zinniker's novel *The North Face* is hardly worth reading. In a much too "schoolmasterly" manner, he searches painstakingly for the reasons for extreme mountaineering.

The Wall of the Man-eater

Yes, why do Alpinists risk their lives on this damned wall? Again and again

authors have tried to find the answer. Georges Sonnier's answer is very literary and florid: He probes Vincent and Renaud's ascent psychologically right into the last little crevices and cracks. The pair just manage to get away with it. The readers too. In Simone Desmaison's *La face de l'ogre* their ascent is made considerably easier but nevertheless there are enlightening insights into the mountaineers' psyche. And in this case the novel, written by the wife of the extreme climber René Desmaison, is clearly above the others, an insight into the difficult life of a wife who has to wait below, while her beloved, who is easily seen through the telescope and can be reached on the radio, fights up above—and loses.

The Eiger as an "ogre," a man-eater, is a common description in French. Hélène, the heroine of Desmaison's novel, even calls the mountain "ogress." The summit is also feminine in Christopher Burns' novel *The Condition of Ice.* Here, Ernst Tinnion and Hansi Kircher want to climb the North Wall of the "Temptress." In her novel *The Climb,* in which the main theme is the catastrophic attempt by three men to climb the mountain for very different reasons, Diana Raymond calls the Eiger "Heide" and Grindelwald "Lundervald."

In *Man on a Nylon String* by Whit Masterson, the village at the foot of the Eiger is called "Zauberwald" and the mountain "Weis Drache." In order to take the alienation effect a little bit further, yet another Eiger crops up elsewhere. The name Zauberwald does not really tell the whole story at all: Local mountain guides beat up the hero, Seth Crow, who in return for payment wants to bring down Douglas Holden (alias Longhi) who is hanging on a nylon rope on the Drachewand. A few people want to prevent this, as then a crime would possibly be discovered and because the mountain village would have less income as the tourists, greedy for sensation, would stay away.

The Man on the End of the Rope

Even better than Masterson's work because it is closer to reality, and thus

PAUL TOWNEND

The man on the end of the rope

A COLLINS THRILLER

BARBARA WALTON

ruthless in its criticism of the whole Eiger North Face commotion, is Paul Townend's novel published in 1960 with the title *The Man on the End of the Rope*. Here, too, the author is using the Corti-Longhi disaster as a starting point, with the climbers and rescuers (and the journalists) in a race for life and death. And that is precisely the key point of the thriller: In it the part of the press, which plays a main role on the North Face stage, is questioned critically. The English chief reporter Paddy Chipperfield causes an accident on the Eigerwand during his hunt for an exclusive picture story with an observation plane, which he then proceeds to exploit totally. Right at the start of the book the unpleasant Eiger hero is sitting in a restaurant in Interlaken and thinking: "As far as making the news is concerned mountaineering is out. Today it is the private lives of royal families and film stars that make the headlines."

Nightfall

The only Eiger story, apart from Trevanian's thriller and Renker's novel, which has been translated into another language is Tom Patey's satire *A Short Walk with Whillans*. The Scotsman Patey, who met his death while abseiling on the Scottish coast, was one of the great ice climbing pioneers: He wrote two

Eiger poems as well as the satirical short story. In it he describes a (fictitious?) attempt at climbing the North Face with this legendary English climber who, in 1962, was attempting the first British ascent, when he had to rescue an injured man. Patey uses many ingredients which make for an average Eiger report, but then spices them up with cutting blows and amusing encounters.

Take cover! The Irish climber "R" sees rocks above the Rote Fluh falling down. And at the same time he hears on the earphones of his pocket radio the alarm being given to take shelter immediately. In his short story *Nightfall*, first published in 1983, the Irish mountaineer and author Dermot Somers combines the last ascent of the North Face with the outbreak of a nuclear world war. During their ascent of the Heckmair Route, the older "R" tells the younger "L" the story of the Wall. For example: "Toni Kurz survived for a night and a day hanging on a rope, injured and frost-bitten, slowly dying of exposure. He lived ten times as long as Christ on the cross, and the only thing he was missing was the crown of thorns. All the time he thought he could be saved." The two climbers hoped to reach the summit before the threatened meteorological and nuclear storms. The story finishes for them—and for us—when they meet with death on the Traverse of the Gods.

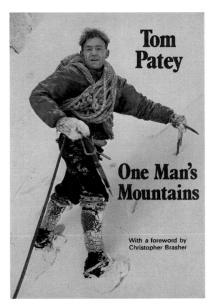

Tom Patey

One Man's Mountains

With a foreword by Christopher Brasher

Townend: "As far as making news is concerned, mountaineering is out. Today it is the private lives of royal families and film stars that make the headlines. Of course, if a well-known young man were able to persuade Brigitte Bardot or Marilyn Monroe to go climbing, then that would be news."

Patey: "Then a most unexpected thing happened. From an alcove in the wall emerged a very ordinary Swiss tourist, followed by his very ordinary wife, five small children, and a poodle. I stopped humming immediately. I had read of tearful farewells with wives and sweethearts calling plaintively, but this was ridiculous. What an undignified send-off!"

The Spider

The name "Spider" has been given to this steep patch of neve or ice high up in the almost vertical Face because of the white streaks spreading out from it in every direction like legs and clutching arms. These run more especially upward—in cracks and gullies up toward the summit snowcap—and down toward the "Death Bivouac." But nobody had discovered how apt the appellation was before we got there; nor had we, as yet, while we went up the first rope's length. We hadn't yet discovered that this Spider of snow, ice, and rock can become a fearful trap; that when hail or snow falls, ice particles and snow coming sliding down from the steep summit-neve get canalized in the cracks and gullies, shoot out on to the Spider under pressure, there to join up in a flood of annihilating fury, and then sweep across the Spider's body, finally to fling themselves outward and downward, obliterating and taking with them everything which isn't part of the living rock. Nor is there any escape from the Spider for anyone caught on it by bad weather and avalanches.

Heinrich Harrer, *Die Weisse Spinne (The White Spider),* 1958.
Eigerwand in 1938.

(facing page) Ueli Bühler climbs the black ice of the Spider. Tatters of mist still hang in the Exit Cracks, while a solitary ice screw provides some measure of confidence.

Climbing with Hitler

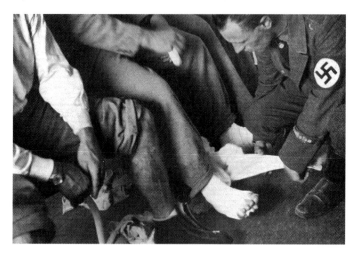

"The scars of battle" reads the original legend from the Eiger book published by the Nazi press. *Um die Eiger-Nordwand* was a total success and was reprinted several times.

The Spider: an ice field in the middle of the summit headwall of the Eiger. It is 1938. Sitting in the direct path of an avalanche of new snow, the Germans Heckmair and Vörg and Austrians Kasparek and Harrer try with all their might to prevent themselves being torn from their belays and swept away with it. The injured Kasparek is rescued and the four men team up as a single rope for the summit bid. Hitler makes political capital out of the success, using it as a propaganda tool to demonstrate the superiority of the German master race. Fifty-nine years later, this National Socialist past finally catches up with Eiger and Tibet hero Harrer. This time the former SS officer, who carried a Swastika flag in his rucksack on his ascent of the North Face, is no longer able to prevent his fall. Rainer Amstädter reports.

At the Berlin Olympics of 1936, Hitler promised to bestow the gold medal on the conquerors of the North Face of the Eiger. That summer it was already too late to mount a renewed assault, the more so since the tragedy which had befallen Toni Kurz and his three companions in July 1936 was still making the headlines. July 1937 again saw several German, Austrian, Italian, and Swiss teams ready to make their attempts on the route, among them one Anderl Heckmair, who had been observing the Face for many weeks and was waiting for better conditions. In his memoirs, *Mein Leben als Bergsteiger,* Heckmair relates how up to the summer of 1938 he had spent more than a decade with no fixed abode and no steady job.

In his alpine autobiography *Ein Bergsteiger,* which first appeared in 1939, Fritz Kasparek also reports on this unfettered mountaineering life. Kasparek is the Viennese example of a mountaineering youth shaped by the constantly growing numbers of unemployed. At the beginning of the 1930s Kasparek got to know the Carinthian climber Heinrich Harrer in the South Tyrol. Born in 1912 in Carinthia, Harrer joined both the Alpine Club and a gymnastics club. After high school he began studying for a teaching qualification in geography and physical education.

Harrer the Former Nazi

The world economic recession of 1930 saw the flourishing in Germany of the National Socialists and their party, the NSDAP. The wave of poverty in

Hitler, flanked by SS members Harrer (left) and Kasparek (right). Next to the Austrians are Germans Heckmair (far left) and Vörg (with bandaged arm). On the far right of the group are the Nazi officials von Tschammer-Osten (Sport Minister) and Frick (Minister of the Interior).

the wake of the world economic recession, and the hopelessness of the situation for countless young people who were unable to find jobs, were partially responsible for the influx of new NSDAP members. This recruitment was organized through numerous nationalistic bodies, in particular the German gymnastics clubs and the Alpine Club. Within these common interest groups, the youth of the day were schooled both mentally and physically as an elite force for great tasks to come. For example, during this time the greater part of the German nationalist–dominated student body of Graz joined the Austrian SA in a collective show of allegiance. Between 1933 and 1938 the SA (Schutzabteilung) and the SS (Schutzstaffel) mounted a systematic terrorist bombing campaign designed to destabilize the regime.

Well before the National Socialists seized power in Germany, on 1 January 1933, Harrer joined the NS teachers' federation. In October 1933 he also joined the SA, thus declaring his active involvement at the forefront of the illegal NS movement. Two days before the annexation of Austria, on 13 March 1938, Harrer applied for membership in the NSDAP, which he received on 1 May. On 1 April 1938 his proposal for membership in the SS was accepted.

Heckmair as Mountain Guide for the Ordensburg of the Nazis

Summer 1938 on the Eiger began with the death of the Italians Mario Menti and Bartolo Sandri, who fell while retreating near the Difficult Crack. After a series of training climbs in the Kaisergebirge, Heckmair and Ludwig Vörg arrived in Grindelwald on 12 July 1938. They had the best and most up-to-date equipment with them. In his 1938 Eiger book, published by the Central Publications Office of the NSDAP, Heckmair talks about this: "Help came at the last moment from the Ordensburg at Sonthofen! Just this year they were looking for mountaineers as sport instructors. We had both applied but at the same time had also requested deferment on the grounds that we had a big project in mind. The reply came swiftly: application accepted, good luck with your plans! If you are lacking any equipment, purchase it and have the account of the Ordensburg invoiced!" In the mountaineering classic of 1949, *Die drei letzten Probleme der Alpen (The Three Last Great Problems of the Alps)*, the lead climber of the first ascent team says that they acquired their equipment from Sporthaus Schuster. In October 1997 Heckmair wrote a letter to the publisher Michel Guérin, who was bringing out a lavishly illustrated French translation of his autobiography with

HECKMAIR · VÖRG · KASPAREK · HARRER

**Um die
Eiger-Nordwand**

2. Auflage
6.—10. Tausend

Schweiz. Alpines Museum
T 723
BERN

ZENTRALVERLAG DER NSDAP. FRANZ EHER NACHF., MÜNCHEN

"Thus it is that I salute the two members of the lead team, Vörg and Heckmair who, in association with the two comrades from the Ostmark, Harrer and Kasparek, conquered the North Face, as an expression of our will and as a symbol for the hard regime of education of our next generation of leaders of the NSDAP."
—Dr. Robert Ley, Federal Leader of the organizing body of the Nazi Party, in the preface to the 1938 Eiger book

the title *Alpiniste*. Extract: "Of course Wiggerl Vörg and I found a sympathetic ear among our superiors at the Ordensburg when we told them of our plans to attempt the first ascent of the Eigerwand. We were also offered money to finance the project, but this I strictly refused. I wanted to remain independent in my decision making and not feel obliged to be successful at all costs by accepting money. We merely accepted the offer of the materials we needed to complete our stock of climbing equipment (ropes, pitons, and carabiners)."

Details of Heckmair's work as a mountain guide for the Ordensburg at Sonthofen in the Allgäu are rather unclear. In his work of 1949 Sonthofen is not mentioned. In the 1972 *Mein Leben als Bergsteiger (My Life as a Mountaineer)* and 1991 *So war's (How it was)* versions, he admits that it was only after his North Face climb that he was admitted to the ranks at Sonthofen.

Yet in the letter mentioned above he writes, "My companion on the first ascent of the Eigerwand in July 1938, Wiggerl Vörg, was engaged as a sport trainer (particularly for mountaineering) at the Ordensburg at Sonthofen and arranged employment for me there as a mountain guide; a post I took up in spring 1938. That was the first time that I was employed as a guide, on a regular monthly income of 300 Reichsmarks."

What was this "Ordensburg"? In his letter to Michel Guérin, Heckmair writes, "The original purpose of the Ordensburg (the education of the Junkers) was unknown to me at the time. I was employed there until the outbreak of war in September 1939. Thereafter I was placed at the disposal of the army, due to political unreliability." In the Castles of the Order of the NSDAP, the Nazis imagined a birthplace for a new elite. In this way, Hitler wished to breed that barbaric strain of National Socialist footsoldier with whom he intended to flood Europe: "In my Castles of the Order a youthful generation will arise to cause the World to recoil in terror. A

mighty, imperious youth, unafraid and cruel. . . . In the most difficult tests they should learn for my sake to overcome their fear of death. That is the step to an heroic youth."

Like the mountaineering, the physical training as whole represented a significant factor in the expansion of power of the National Socialist regime. In the Allgäu Ordensburg, the aspirant future leaders were tested to the absolute limits of their courage, stamina, and powers of resistance through ski and mountaineering trips. This youth elite was selected from the whole of Germany. One of the young men was Hannes Schwarz, who is now in his seventies. He recalls the toughening-up processes and the requirement that to meet with death for the common good was to be regarded as the highest honor achievable. Schwarz had experienced Heckmair and Vörg as ski instructors and had been greatly challenged by them on their night marches. He also remembers that Heckmair had related to his charges the story of the first ascent of the North Face of the Eiger, classing it as a great deed—understandable, since he and his comrades were indeed Alpine heroes.

Kasparek the SS Member

"Through the roaring of unbridled avalanches they had fought their way to the end. With exemplary rigor, and in spite of all their detractors, they had achieved a splendid victory." This is how Viennese Rudolf Fraissl saw it, a man who, with Leo Brankovsky, had intended to be a part of the successful ascent but who had had to give up due to stonefall. As soon as he saw Heckmair, Vörg, Kasparek, and Harrer descending the West Flank, Fraissl rushed to the telephone at Eigergletscher Station "and a few moments later news of the victory was winging its way through the ether . . . Sieg heil, you brave lads!" Fraissl's praise for the Eiger lads can be found in his contribution to the little-known Nazi mountain book *Weg ins Licht (Into the Light)*. In retrospect rather more self-critical, he goes on to say a few lines later, "there was no time for reasoned thought." High time to redress the balance, then.

The National Socialist mountaineering world celebrated the solving of the so-called last great problem of the Alps as proof of the "unbendable will to win of our youth." And the Austrian Karl Prusik, inventor of the brilliant jamming knot that has saved so many climbers from certain death, declared proudly, "A people that has such sons can never perish!"

Hitler himself, who during the climb had had himself informed at hourly intervals about the team's progress, made political capital out of the success as his propaganda merchants used it as proof of the superiority of the German master race. In Bern, the German emissary Köcher arranged a gala evening and cars stood ready to make the drive to Sonthofen. Before the assembled dignitaries of the Castles of the Order, Heckmair delivered a personal report of the experience of the first ascent. Federal Sport Minister von Tschammer-Osten issued the invitation to the German Festival of Gymnastics and Sport, to be held from 29 to 31 July in Breslau, where the four men were paraded in front of a fervent and vociferous crowd. This first great festival of the National League of Sport, organized by Hitler, turned out to be a striking production of National Socialist mass manipulation. It ended with a speech delivered by von Tschammer-Osten, who called for the total mobilization of "the body populace" that would pass its first test of allegiance in the theater of war.

Hitler received the four men for a photo-shoot, presenting them with a picture of himself, complete with dedication, as a mark of his recognition and praising the joining together of the two ropes as a symbolic example of the annexation of Austria. Subsequently, SS man Felix Rinner accompanied them on a rest and relaxation holiday to Norway. In Breslau, he had been charged by von Tschammer-Osten with the duty of

presenting the four mountaineers to Hitler. Rinner was a middle-distance runner and was among those Austrian Olympic sportsmen who had publicly proclaimed their support of National Socialism at Berlin in 1936.

In 1938 the Central Publications Office of the NSDAP brought out the story of the German attempts on the Eigerwand, up to the first ascent in 1938, in book form. Harrer, in his piece, admits to having been moved to tears by Hitler's words in Breslau. Hitler had

(below) "The Gemeinschafts-führer Heckmair and Vörg are brought home to the Ordensburg at Sonthofen." The adoption of the climbers by the body politic—was it merely tolerated, wished for, conscious, or unconscious? Heckmair here looks proud and skeptical; Vörg is laughing. And what were the thoughts of the man in uniform?

remarked, "My children, what have you achieved!" Harrer's last sentence was, "We have climbed the North Face to the summit and beyond that to our Führer!"

When asked about his contribution to this book by the journalist Gerald Lehner in 1997, Harrer maintained that he had not drafted the article himself. At the photo-shoot in Breslau, Harrer and Kasparek, as SS members, were allowed to stand next to Hitler, while Heckmair and Vörg were positioned on the fringe of the group.

Kasparek, too, commended the North Face of the Eiger as a "symbol of German destiny." In Breslau, he received an offer to join the SS from SS Reichsführer Himmler in person. With the help of the National Socialists,

(following pages) At the upper edge of the gloomy Spider, Kobi Reichen belays himself and his client Oswald Oelz on new—and old—gear. For the Bernese Oberland guide the Eiger-wand is no longer a "last great problem"; he has done the Heckmair Route four times—three times with clients, twice in winter—and has intimate knowledge of seven additional neighboring routes.

Kasparek was now able to break free of his former existence as an unemployed mountaineering vagabond. Kasparek had earlier been a member of the mountaineering guild of the Social-Democratic Vienna Naturfreunde but after the organization was banned, and under the pressure of economic necessity, he switched allegiance.

Vörg the Victim, Harrer the Hero

At Christmas 1938, Heckmair was sent to Hitler by Reichsorganizationsleiter Robert Ley. During their conversation, Heckmair attempted to win over the dictator to grant permission for an expedition to Nanga Parbat. But Hitler "furrowed his brow and said, 'I need you for quite a different task'" (Heckmair, in *So war's*). In the war with Russia, all the SS Stammführer were scheduled to take part in a special operation. On 22 June 1941, a huge army swept across the Russian frontiers. The Eiger hero Vörg had already fallen, on the evening before the Eastern Campaign began. Heckmair spent the first months of the war as an infantry soldier on the Eastern Front. But the blitzkrieg in the East failed. Despairing of his situation, Heckmair approached Munich Alpinist and Grandes Jorasses victor Rudolf Peters for help. Peters was now

engaged as a trainer of mountain guides at the army's school of mountaineering at Fulpmes in the Stubai Valley and requested the Armed Forces High Command to allow Heckmair to join him there as a specialist trainer. And it was there that Heckmair remained until the end of the war. At the outbreak of hostilities in 1939, Harrer was taken prisoner far away from Germany. At the Breslau Festival of Sport, he had been invited by Himmler to join the 1939 Nanga Parbat Expedition. When war broke out, the German expedition was interned by the English. In 1944, Harrer managed to escape to Tibet; he returned to Graz in 1952.

Harrer's book *Seven Years in Tibet* became an international bestseller and was translated into forty-eight languages; his further expeditions, travelogs, and television films made him a national hero in Austria. The historical and political facts, on the other hand, demonstrate the inconsistencies between the image of Harrer the committed human rights activist and his contributions to Nazism. In 1997, Harrer was finally tripped up by the Nazi past he had always disavowed.

Yet it could all have turned out so differently. The Hollywood film of his experiences in Tibet, made at a cost of 90 million Swiss Francs, was to have been the final canonization of the icon that was Harrer. When, in 1997, the Austrian journalist Gerald Lehner exposed Harrer's Nazi past in the German magazine *Stern,* causing a huge stir in the United States, the film's director, Jean-Jacques Annaud, attempted to limit the damage by altering sections of the dialogue at the post-production stage. Confronted by Lehner with the evidence of his Nazi membership in May 1997, in an interview for Austrian radio, Harrer, after decades of silence and denial, disputed his association with the NS terrorist organizations right up to the last possible moment. After the *Stern* article appeared, in a damage-limitation exercise, Harrer condescendingly made

And All Because of a Swastika Pennant

In a special report for the inflammatory NS organ Völkischer Beobachter, penned on 31 July 1938, one "Andreas Heckmaier" writes about the arrival at the summit of the Eiger on 24 July, "Harrer, the SS man from Graz, takes from his rucksack a Swastika pennant and plants it in the snow. Victory is ours!" Today, Heckmair maintains he was not the author of this article (see page 185, "Problems with the Texts"). In an interview with the Austrian journalist Gerald Lehner, given in 1997, he says, "Heini did indeed have a Swastika flag in his rucksack, and he wanted to plant it on the summit. But he did not. Due to the high winds, all we could do on the summit was shake hands." And in a letter written on 13 July 1997 to Michel Guérin, the publisher of his autobiographies Mein Leben als Bergsteiger and So war's, he says, "I would in any case have torn down the flag immediately, because I considered it tactless to raise this flag in Switzerland and Wiggerl Vörg and I had not climbed the Eiger for nationalistic reasons. As far as I know, Kasparek did not have a Swastika flag in his rucksack."

Perhaps it was the one that had been left hanging on Kasparek and Harrer's tent, the one which Eiger contestant Rudolf Fraissl talks about in his report "Rund um den Kampf an der Eiger-Nordwand," written for the National Socialist mountain book Weg ins Licht: "Certain unprincipled rogues had paid a visit to the tent, which Heini and Fritz had pitched at the foot of the Face, and had stolen the food they found within. And all because of a Swastika pennant that hung from the gable end of the tent."

Ein Bergsteiger

Fritz Kasparek

Einer der Bezwinger der Eiger-Nordwand

erzählt von seinen Bergfahrten

Mit 71 Kunstdruck-Vollbildern

"I will never forget the North Face of the Eiger; it was at the same time the symbol of German destiny. Six German mountaineers had lost their lives on the climb. And it was our lot to grant those victims their last wish," reads an extract from Kasparek's 1939 book. In the later edition of 1951, which appeared under the title Vom Peilstein zur Eiger-Nordwand, "German destiny" was replaced with "mankind's neverending quest for great things, for the unknown," and "six German mountaineers" became "eight mountaineers."

magazine Der Spiegel in November 1997. However, he does admit to having been a member of the SS. And on the subject of the Eiger, he says, "I wanted people to notice me. And when Heckmair, Vörg, Kasparek, and I set out on the first ascent of the North Face of the Eiger in 1938, I surmised that if we were successful they would not be able to ignore me for the Nanga Parbat Expedition. But it is absolute nonsense that we climbed the North Face of the Eiger for the Nazis. We did it because it was a challenge."

Reinhold Messner, who has repeatedly clashed with Harrer over the latter's NS involvement, commented in 1997 in the Austrian periodical News on the superimposition of Nazi ideology on Alpine mountaineering, the magnitude of which is still to this day trivialized and even denied by both the German and the Austrian Alpine Clubs. Says Messner: "I do not understand why Harrer failed to question the extent to which National Socialism had taken root in mountaineering. Virtues such as the common bond of the rope, comradeship in the mountains, being as tough as leather, were synonyms for 'the German way.' With their 'Berg Heil ideals' they provided the food with which to feed the rise of Nazism and the war."

a partial confession while at the same time continuing to stress the harmlessness of his membership in various Nazi organizations.

He remains obdurate, just as he did all those years ago beneath the avalanches on the Spider. "I have never been in the SA," he maintained in an interview for the German current affairs

Exit Cracks

Since we could no longer risk a fourth night out in the open, we climbed on up the steep cracks despite the worst weather imaginable, being careful to climb only during breaks between avalanches. We had already made the observation the previous day that an avalanche broke loose every thirty to thirty-five minutes. During these short pauses we could press on unhindered. In spite of this we found ourselves in several awkward situations due to the masses of snow coming down the Face. Inevitably, they covered all the hand- and footholds, making our ascent substantially more difficult. Then it happened—Heckmair, in his crampons, accidentally jumped on his comrade Vörg's hand, causing him a desperately serious injury. Vörg just had to grit his teeth, since in our situation if any one of us had weakened, this would have affected the others and that would have been the end.

Fritz Kasparek, *Vom Peilstein zur Eiger-Nordwand,* 1951.
Eigerwand in 1938.

(facing page) Catherine Destivelle climbing the quarz crack on 10 March 1992. This is the hardest part of the Exit Cracks. The Frenchwoman became the first woman to solo the classic North Face route; it was also the first female winter ascent and the first female-only ascent of the Heckmair Route.

The '38 Ascent

The correct selection of equipment such as rock and ice pegs is crucial. Heckmair and Vörg had the best and latest gear, even down to their twelve-point crampons, while Kasparek had only ten-point crampons and Harrer none at all. And that on a wall that appears to be just a straightforward rock face.

"This Sunday at 7:45 P.M., the two German ropes—Vörg and Heckmeier from Munich and Harrar and Kaspareck—arrived safely back at Eigergletscher Station after conquering the Eiger North Face." This inaccurate, misspelled message was telephoned in by the rather overexcited special correspondent of the newspaper *Sport* to his Zürich editor on 24 July 1938. "For the last bit on Sunday they again met with terrible weather." How it really was is described by lead climber Anderl Heckmair in his classic report. This first appeared in 1938 in the controversial book *Um die Eiger-Nordwand* and is here translated into English for the first time.

It became necessary to leave our sheltered place and go out into the storm; a hard thing to do, but after a moment's reflection the decision was not a difficult one to make. Of course, we could have waited for an improvement in the weather, but how were we

to be certain that the weather really would get better? Often, you can wait for days, even weeks, on end and even then the Face is not in a good enough condition to allow climbing. We were thus all agreed that if Fate dictated that we were to fall, we would rather do so in battle than standing idly by.

So it was that, after packing everything again and roping up as a foursome, we stepped out calmly and confidently to tackle the last and most difficult hours on the Wall. Immediately we were confronted by an overhang plastered in ice, which we somehow had to cross. There followed a sideways traverse over to a rocky knob. On reaching this—I must have taken about half an hour on the traverse—I glanced down at my companions, who were below me and to one side, leaning motionless against the wall like icicles. Just as we were ready to set off it had in fact begun to snow more heavily. The wretched rock was coated in a smooth film of ice to which the new snow adhered. Two possible alternative routes remained: a gully line which, according to our observations, caught the main lateral force of the avalanches pouring down the Face, or a much safer shallow chimney. Since Wiggerl had now joined me I opted for the latter, but—alas!—in the first few meters alone I needed three rock pitons and thereafter could find no placements for any more.

"I'm going to climb the gully instead. Let's just wait for the next shower bath; there must be one due soon!"

To get to the gully it was necessary

to descend a little way, so I left one piton in and abseiled down.

Just up onto the top of a little pinnacle, and I would have a splendid and safe belay below the gully. But I was not on top of the pinnacle yet. I had a serviceable hold for my right hand but could find nothing at all for my left on the damned ice. As I tried to thrust my way up I slipped off and found myself standing 2 meters below on a little slab of ice; my crampons bit and I stopped dead in my tracks, like a tree rooted to the spot. Wiggerl, who had held me quite securely on the rope, grinned down impertinently. Straightaway I grappled with it again and slipped down again, exactly as before, only this time I did not come to rest on the slab, but swung across into the gully. This time, Wiggerl did not grin; he just held me. I had thumped my backside, but it had been used to worse pain. Nevertheless, I was now feeling small and humble and detoured around the pinnacle to the opposite side. Hardly had I chopped the icy crown off with my axe to make a level stance than the avalanche came sweeping down the Face. All of us stood belayed and under cover; it whistled around our ears a bit, but could do us no harm. After a time the last vestiges of the avalanche had also swept

past and I started up the gully down which the avalanche had roared only five minutes previously.

"It'll be an hour before we get another one. By then, however, I need to be above the steep, almost vertical, lower part of the gully." The ice was much harder than the previous evening and it took a lot of strength to climb it, without cutting steps and balancing only on the two front points of my crampons. After about 10 meters the gully fell back slightly and I could chop out a stance again. From here, I could already see that the gully did lead somewhere, so I dispatched a joyous yodel to my friends below. Wiggerl was soon standing next to me. Then it started again: This time, the white plume appeared first at the right-hand edge of the Wall. In about three or four minutes the avalanche would be upon us. And now we were standing right in the gully, where it would undoubtedly hit us, albeit with only one of its lateral arms. To be on the safe side, a second piton went into the ice.

Then it was upon us! The pressure wave did not tear us from the belay, however, but merely pressed the points of our crampons more deeply into the ice. We now had to make sure that there was no snow buildup between us and the ice of the gully, since this might

Up on the Brittle Ledges. Bernese photographer Hans Steiner took this shot of the two parties, climbing here as a rope of four, from an airplane on 23 July 1938. The photo shows (from left to right) Harrer, Kasparek, and Vörg; Heckmair has already started climbing the Brittle Crack leading to the Traverse of the Gods. From there, he and Vörg were to continue on their own, hoping to climb fast to beat the arrival of the bad weather. Up on the Spider, after an avalanche had almost swept both pairs away, the four first ascentionists finally joined together as one rope.

At the bivouac. On a narrow ledge, safe from stonefall and avalanches, the first ascent team spends their last night on the Wall. For Kasparek and Harrer, this was the third bivouac; for Vörg and Heckmair, the second. The stove still worked, but Kasparek's cigarettes were wet.

have forced us off the stance. There were no stones—we were already too high up for that—and the snow was quite fine grained and thus did not have much force behind it. We were soon in high spirits, happy at the way things had turned out. "Another one survived!"

We shook ourselves dry like wet poodles and while Wiggerl brought up Fritz and Heini I climbed another rope length. The gully now reared up steeply again. "Wiggerl, watch me here, it's getting hard again!"

The actual snow, which fell continuously, did not disturb us. It was only when the larger flakes came that we knew it was getting warmer. The avalanche would come a little later, but with renewed force.

It had been a long time since the avalanche. So, quickly up to the over-

hang. Swine—the ice was no longer as thick! The pitons would not hold any more! After the second hammer blow they fell through the hollow ice or bent uselessly on the rock beneath. At the overhang, I could only place my crampons one above the other, since the old ice had shrunk to a narrow strip and the new ice covering the rock was much too hard, smooth, and thin. The tip of the ice peg, which I held in one hand, only penetrated a little way; it was the same with the pick of ice axe. Suddenly, I let both the ice peg and the ice axe slip from my grasp. I could hold on no longer. "Watch out, Wiggerl!"— and I was off.

Wiggerl was there. He took in as much rope as he could, but I was heading straight for him, so he let go of the rope and caught me in his hands, taking one of my crampon points in the heel of his hand as he did so. The force of the fall was so great that it threw him off the belay. In this split second, he grabbed my rope again. There was a sharp tug, and I was standing upright— admittedly, without a proper foothold, but with all twelve points buried securely in the ice. With one step, we were back on the stance. The pitons had naturally been ripped out.

I immediately placed some more. Meanwhile, Wiggerl had removed his mitten. The blood sprayed out, but it was quite dark so it could not have been an artery. A glance up at the Wall: "No, thank God, no avalanche coming!" Off with the rucksack, out with the bandages and we got him all strapped up.

"You feel sick?" He was quite green.

"I don't know," he said.

I stood so that there was no chance he could fall off.

"Pull yourself together, it's all or nothing now!"

Rummaging around in the medicine bag, my fingers curled around a little vial of heart drops which a concerned lady doctor in Grindelwald had given me for just such an eventuality. There was something on the label about ten drops. I poured about half the bottle into Wiggerl's mouth. The other half I drank myself. A couple of glucose tablets to chase it down and we were back in business! There was still no sign of the avalanche.

"Right—I'm going for the overhang again!"

"Just don't fall on me again, OK?" said Wiggerl with a quiet laugh, his voice now very weak.

I summoned all my nerve and climbed in total safety through the difficult section. Not able to place any pitons, I ran out almost the full 30 meters of rope before I could at least get one of the small rock pegs to sit properly. Then it came—the avalanche. Good fortune had held it up for so long. But now it broke loose with real power. It could not really hit me, since the gully went off to one side, but Fritz and Heini caught the full force of it. Nor could Wiggerl complain that he got too little of it. The others protected themselves by pulling their rucksacks up over their heads, trusting to the wobbly ice pegs. I watched the strength of the waves of the avalanche and when it got really close, I shouted, "Now, now . . . hang on . . . it's coming down thick now!" I caught a bit of it again, knocking my head against the rock in the process. A few moments and I was free of it again. It still pattered down on my comrades. Then there was just wet snow, and the long pause.

"It's getting lighter . . . no . . . watch out! Watch out!" Then the main mass came down. Again, I got a bit of it.

"It won't last much longer, hang on—hang on!" After what seemed like an age to us, it finally stopped.

Wiggerl came up, the others fol-

lowed and I could continue climbing. Ow! My ankle. Must have twisted it during the fall. It couldn't be broken, or I would have felt it more. Not important anyway, even if it did hurt!

The gully became easier-angled, but the possibilities for running belays also grew fewer. It had to be the end up there. Suddenly, we clearly heard shouts from the West Ridge. "Don't answer," we whispered to each other in turn. We realized immediately that there was someone up there who wanted to help us and any sound we might have made could have led to a misunderstanding.

We were all too familiar with such things. First you get one individual alone who comes along, has a look and if he hears something the whole rescue apparatus is set in motion. With the sheer scale of this huge mountain it would

(above) In the upper Exit Cracks. Heckmair is just about to tackle the lower overhanging part of the crack. It was roughly at this point that he fell and tore Vörg from his stance. By a hair's breadth, the two escaped falling into the void. Could Kasparek have held them?

(left) At the belay. Harrer and Kasparek wait and Vörg finds time—despite snowfall, avalanches, and belay duties— to capture the miserable conditions for posterity with his Contax. Lucky for us that he did, otherwise we would have no photograph of the last day of the climb.

have taken hours before he was back down and the rescue team was up on the top. By then we would have made our own way out. To be sure, we had all been hit by the avalanche but we were not yet unfit for battle, not by a long chalk. We were nevertheless pleased with the sign, which showed that someone was concerned about us (we did not know, of course, that half the world was glued to the radio and that everything

that could be seen was being broadcast). As mountaineers, we respected the skill and the commitment of the lone Swiss guide in managing to get up there in that storm and in wanting to bring us help.

Shortly afterward we had reached the top of the gully. It was noon. By the time the last of us was up and out of the gully it was one o'clock. We were still a long way from the top. A steep ice field, where we used up the last of our pegs, led on upward. It continued to snow heavily, and it was getting thicker and thicker. The avalanches were now roaring down the Face uninterrupted. But they could no longer do us any harm. The higher we climbed, the harder the wind blew. I could no longer make

myself understood a rope's length away. The entire summit was so cloaked in ice that the moves could only be made sporadically. The straps on my crampons began to cut into my feet and the feet themselves lost all feeling.

But we were now off the Wall and now we would make it, come what may. It was just up to us now. We had survived the dangers of the mountain and the high wind was certainly not going to kill us! Nevertheless—pleasant it was not and we nearly toppled right over the summit cornice, too!

In its upper part, the ridge is nearly horizontal. But in the dim mist I thought it swept up steeply again. We had taken the last snow slope, now swept bare by the wind, in zigzag fashion. I was just about to put in another turn, when the very next step saw me standing on top of the cornice. A few meters behind me, Wiggerl did the same thing. Suddenly he roared "Stop! Back! There's a cliff below you there!" Very faintly, a distance below us, we could just make out the shimmering outline of the cliffs, but on the south side of the mountain. It would have been accursed bad luck to have survived the North Side, only to plummet over the South Side because we had missed the summit!

At half past three the summit was reached.

Anderl Heckmair (born 1906) led his companions Ludwig "Wiggerl" Vörg, Heinrich Harrer, and Fritz Kasparek up the North Face of the Eiger from 22 to 24 September 1938, a feat that brought the mountain guide and ski instructor immediate fame. Yet even before this climb, Heckmair had done the hardest routes around (first ascent of the North Face Direct on the Grand Charmoz, North Face of the Cima Grande, Northwest Face of the Civetta). He also made the eighth ascent of the Walker Spur on the Grandes Jorasses, a route he had attempted at the beginning of the 1930s. Later, expeditions to many of the mountain regions of the world followed. For fifteen years, Heckmair was a trainer for mountain guides with the German Alpine Club. He was instrumental in founding a professional society for German mountain guides, an organization which was inaugurated in 1968. He is a freeman of the town of Oberstdorf and bearer of the Bundesverdienstkreuz (Federal Service Cross).

Problems With the Texts

"I have never written a 'true original text' or a diary," wrote Anderl Heckmair in a letter dated 2 January 1998 to the publisher of the mountain monography you have before you. "Back then, I gave my report in to the publishers and did not concern myself further with it." This is why, at the end of his report "The Ascent of 1938," there is the foolish sentence "The Führer is right when he says that the word 'impossible' is only for cowards." According to Heckmair, this sentence was added by the publishers. The book *Um die Eiger-Nordwand,* in which Heckmair's account of the first ascent of the North Face of the Eiger was printed for the first time, was published by the Central Publications Office of the National Socialist German Worker's Party (NSDAP). In it, the first ascentionists describe the "Battles and Victims of the North Face" (Kasparek), "The Attempts" (Vörg), and "The Ascent of 1938" (Heckmair). Under the title "Ausklang" ("The Final Chorus"), Heinrich Harrer reported on the triumphal reception for the climbers in Germany and the honors bestowed upon them by Adolf Hitler. Heckmair transcribed his 1938 account (reproduced here) in his classic book, first published in 1949 as *Die drei letzten Probleme der Alpen (The Three Last Great Problems of the Alps).* The text, now under the title *Die Lösung des Problems (The Solution to the Problem)* is more or less identical. The language is the same, even if individual words have been substituted, sections left out, or additions made. The sentence about the Führer has, of course, been struck out. There is one thing, however, which is represented differently in the pre- and postwar editions. This is the second meeting of the two—originally separate—parties, Heckmair/Vörg and Kasparek/Harrer.

The first encounter took place on 21 July 1938 above the Shattered Pillar. At that moment, the Germans and the Austrians were merely competitors. And since a third party suddenly

Political crux: What really happened between Kasparek/Harrer and Heckmair/Vörg on the Second Ice Field?

turned up (the Viennese team of Leo Brankowsky and Rudi Fraissl), Heckmair and Vörg decided to descend. However, Brankowsky and Fraissl also had to beat a retreat after an injury due to stonefall. Since the field was now clear, Heckmair and Vörg went back onto the Face in the early morning of 22 July and caught the Austrian party up at the Second Ice Field (they were making only slow progress, since Harrer did not have any crampons!). And here the problems with the texts begin.

"We yodelled a happy greeting and at 11:30 A.M. we had reached them." Up to this point, both versions are in word-for-word agreement. But then, in the 1938 version, which of course came out only a few months after the forceful annexation of Austria by the Third Reich, we read: "We will now climb together and nothing can afford to go wrong! Was this not Providence? Once, two Munich men climbed to their deaths with two Austrians. Now, two Austrians climb to victory with two Munich men." The two last sentences also reappear in Heckmair's account "Die Bezwingung der Eiger-Nordwand" ("The Conquest of the Eigerwand") in the magazine *Der Bergsteiger* of 1938 (and in translation in the

respected French periodical *Alpinisme*); otherwise, this text is at variance with the one in Heckmair's books.

In his 1949 book, Heckmair portrayed the encounter with the Austrians Kasparek and Harrer in a totally different light. "I pointed out to them that at this speed we had little chance of finishing the route and advised them to retreat immediately. Kasparek, however, also had his stubborn streak. 'We'll do it, even if we do need a bit longer!' he reckoned. It was an awkward moment and our decision was not taken lightly. Should we climb through and storm on up to the top, leaving our comrades to their Fate? It was Vörg, by far the most good-natured of the pair of us, who said the magic words: 'It is probably better that we join up and climb as one rope!'" In his book *Mein Leben als Bergsteiger,* published in 1972, Heckmair adds the following, "I did not wish to start an argument, but my agreement was rather reluctant."

The Nazi newspaper *Völkische Beobachter* reported the events quite differently. On 29 July 1938—only five days after the successful ascent—the newspaper published the following piece about the meeting of the two teams on the Second Ice Field: "We stand next to each other, the Viennese and us. And there is only one thing to do—to climb on together, to see it through, to fight through to victory! (…) We have become a single unit." Heckmair is said to have written this himself. In fact, the title of this article (whose second part appeared on 31 July) read: "This is how the Eigerwand was conquered. Special report for the *Völkische Beobachter* by Andreas Heckmaier." Yet we also have the following comment by Heckmair in the letter mentioned at the start of this piece: "I certainly did not write the special report in the *Völkische Beobachter.* It contains so many errors and inaccuracies (not even my name was spelled correctly) that it is not possible for me to set the record straight in a letter."

Corti Bivouac

As if awaking from a nightmare, I slowly grasp the situation: Angelo will not be able to climb this crack. As strong as he was, he would have hauled himself hand over hand up the rope, despite his broken leg. But even I could only manage to pull myself up a few meters with the utmost difficulty.

I held the rope in my hand; I looked at it, knelt down on the little terrace (this was meant to be the so-called Corti Bivouac) that would be my resting place, dead or alive, tied the rope off to a carabiner and began to sob, because I was incapable of doing anything to help. Snow, tears, blood, and snot mixed with each other while I shouted, and I heard his shouts too but because of the howling of the wind I could understand nothing. I knew, and he knew too, what was waiting for us.

How long it all lasted, I will never know. I only know that the morning was beautiful, that morning of Friday, the 17th of August. I shouted one last time and was answered with silence. I was alone; my friend Angelo was climbing on those mountains where the weather never turns bad, and where one cannot fall.

Sergio De Infanti, *Tragico Eiger,* 1973.
Eigerwand in 1970.

(facing page) Ancient rusted pitons and the remains of old rotting ropes: Everywhere on the Heckmair Route one encounters the traces of successful—and not-so-successful—predecessors.

The Survivor Is Right

In 1957, Claudio Corti was rescued from the Wall after nine days. His companion, Stefano Longhi, remained hanging there for a further two years—a macabre tourist attraction. It was only in 1961, when the bodies of the accompanying German climbers Günter Nothdurft and Franz Mayer were found on the West Flank, that poor Corti was freed of suspicion.

Three climbers lost their lives in the Eiger Tragedy of 1957. One of the mountaineers could be rescued, thanks to the actions of an international team of helpers. The story has been written many times. Horst Höfler focuses on the unlucky figure of Claudio Corti himself.

In the early morning of 3 August 1957, Italians Claudio Corti (29) and Stefano Longhi (44) had set out to climb the 1800-meter-high North Face of the Eiger. It was to have been the fourteenth ascent—and the first by an Italian rope. The two men did not, however, follow the usual route, but, like Max Sedlmayr and Karl Mehringer

in 1935, climbed directly up the lower part of the Face. By the time Corti and Longhi had realized their mistake, abseiled and climbed back down, and regained the original route, it was Sunday, perhaps even Monday (5 August). It is certain that the German team of Günter Nothdurft (24) and Franz Mayer (24) joined the Italians at the Hinterstoisser Traverse.

Claudio Corti's Report

What subsequently happened between 4 or 5 and 11 August up on the Eigerwand was written down by Claudio Corti—the sole survivor of the drama—in the form a report for the Club Alpino Italiano. We learn from this report that the Germans had dropped a rucksack containing provisions down the Face, that Nothdurft had fallen sick, and that for this reason the two pairs had joined together and climbed as a rope of four from the Second Ice Field onward. We also read that the four men mistakenly traversed across to the Spider 100 meters higher than the Traverse of the Gods (the Waschak-Forstenlechner Variant); that Longhi fell on this traverse and had to be left on a ledge, equipped with Corti's bivouac bag, after three hours of rescue attempts had failed; that Corti was hit by a rock above the Quartz Crack (in the Exit Cracks), causing him to fall 30 meters (!); that Franz Mayer held the fall, but that Corti was now unable to continue climbing. And finally, that the Germans left Corti their bivi bag and started to struggle on toward the summit.

This last event occurred on 9 August, at about 3 P.M. "From this moment on, until Sunday, 11 August, and the arrival of the German mountain rescue man Hellepart, I experienced moments of both hope and despair. I thought of Stefano and also of the two Germans. The weather remained ugly; rain followed high winds and snowfall. I was lucky that good weather on the Saturday (10 August) and Sunday (11 August) allowed my rescue to proceed. My Stefano did not have the same luck, for just as his rescue was about to begin the weather worsened and it was not possible for my rescuers to get him to safety." (Corti)

The Four Climbers

Who were the four climbers? The two men from Württemberg were known to be among the best around. Some even said Nothdurft was better on rock than the great Hermann Buhl.

With Mayer, Nothdurft had done the first winter ascent of the "Peters-Eidenschink" on the West Face of the Totenkirchl. Together, they made a well-qualified team. Why, if Nothdurft was really as sick as Corti described, they had not climbed back down, will always remain a mystery.

To make a judgment about the abilities of the Italians, both of them members of the legendary "Ragni di Lecco," proves rather more difficult. Renata Rossi, a mountain guide living in Chiavenna, writes and speaks about Bergell pioneer Corti with some respect. "He is a . . . " and instead of finishing her sentence, Rossi's expression takes on a determined look and she punches the air energetically. Reinhold Messner, too, rates Corti as a "steady climber."

Longhi, who left a wife and two children, was without question a tough second. The fact that he possessed great stamina and that he fought a desperate

Due to the bad weather conditions, the official rescue station at Grindelwald at first refused to mount a rescue attempt for the four men up on the North Face. Mountaineers from many countries therefore started their own rescue bid.

battle for survival, is well documented. On 11 August, after Corti had been successfully rescued, the famous French climber Lionel Terray was lowered down the Wall. The lower had to be halted due to a technical hitch and when Terray, out of boredom, shouted across to a team of climbers on the West Ridge, he received an answer. The answer came not from the West Ridge, however, but "other shouts came from far down the precipice; it was old Longhi, refusing to die, still hoping." (Terray had to give up his attempt to locate Longhi as a result of the technical defect—radio contact between the Frenchman and the summit was no

Stefano Longhi fell from above the Traverse of the Gods onto a ledge; his companions were unable to haul him back up. Later, he waved to a passing airplane.

longer possible—and was winched back up.) In the afternoon, when the rescue team was bringing Corti down the West Flank, they again shouted down the Face to Longhi to tell him they would be back to get him off another day. He answered one last time, shouting back just two words, "Fame, freddo." Hungry, cold.

Irresponsible Speculation

Poor Stefano Longhi died during the night of 11 August 1957. His body remained hanging there as a macabre attraction for the telescope tourists at Kleine Scheidegg for almost two years, until July 1959, when Grindelwald mountain guides, working under difficult conditions, were able to recover the completely preserved body. I would have liked to speak to Corti himself, the main figure in the 1957 Eiger drama, but this was not possible.

When Nothdurft and Mayer could not be found, speculation about Corti grew, with certain people even suggesting that "Corti had seized their equipment, cut the Germans' rope, and committed them to the void. Although Corti had always contested such claims, over the next four years (until the bodies of Nothdurft and Mayer were discovered on the West Flank of the Eiger) he remained unable to free himself of suspicion. This was compounded by the many interviews he gave, in which he contradicted himself and presented his arguments in an odd way. However, with the discovery came his complete exoneration—all suspicions turned out to be without substance." (Gramminger/Steinbichler, 1986)

Honor Is Restored

It was to Toni Hiebeler's credit that he spoke up for Corti in his book *Eigerwand* (1976): "The disappearance of the Germans weighed heavily upon a man who was very much alive, and who was fighting desperately for his honor . . . . In the Italian magazine *Epoca*, he [Corti] wrote, "I am not a criminal.'" In 1961, quite by chance, Günter Nothdurft and Franz Mayer were found, still linked by their rope and lying side by side on the Eiger's West Flank—well away from the normal route, and "thirty minutes, at the most an hour, from the safety of the Eiger-gletscher Station." (Hiebeler)

Hermann Huber, who were not only highly regarded as extreme rock climbers, but had also proven themselves to be excellent on ice on their 1955 Andes expedition. It was such men that Wiggerl believed he needed on the Eiger, and rightly so. There were others, too: the Swiss IKAR delegate and rescue expert Erich Friedli with his men from Thun, Max Eiselin, Lothar Brandler, the top Italian Alpinists Ricardo Cassin and Carlo Mauri, Lionel Terray and his Dutch guest, the highly talented Tom de Booy who, thanks to his excellent linguistic abilities, helped to keep everything in perspective. They were joined by eight Polish climbers, and by Robert Seiler, who had made the fifth ascent of the North Face.

Seiler, who had climbed the Eigerwand from 25 to 27 July 1950 as a twenty-one-year-old, with Marcel Hamel, Raymond Monney, and Jean Fuchs, and had as a result come within a hair's breadth of being blackballed by the Swiss Alpine Club, following allegations leveled by his home group of the SAC that he had "contravened the ethics of mountaineering," had founded a rescue group of "guideless extremists" who called themselves "The Steinböcke." "For the Eiger rescue, Seiler brought in two of his people from as far away as Chamonix and Marseilles! Within the group, there was an unwritten rule that whenever one was called on to help one

Longhi's rescue with the cable winch did not work, due to a radio defect. Before the bad weather finally closed in, the rescue team heard his last words: "Fame, freddo" (hungry, cold).

However exhausted Nothdurft may have been, the two Württemburg men had in fact reached the summit, lost their way in poor visibility on the descent, and had fallen asleep for ever in their bivouac.

Corti had thus always spoken the truth! How horrible it must have been for him to have to live with such terrible insinuations.

Hellepart's Big Day

More than forty years on, what really is worthy of celebration is the dedication and solidarity of the international team of rescuers and helpers. More than fifty men had converged on the Eiger, putting to shame the "official" local rescue services. Among the many present were Wiggerl Gramminger, with his invaluable steel cable winch apparatus, and the rescue team members Franz Fellerer, Martin Weixler, Emil Proksch, Alfred Hellepart, and Hubert Bail. They were supported by Alfred Koch and

Hard work for the rescuer: Alfred Hellepart is lowered on the steel cable, 370 meters down the North Face. He finds Corti on a ledge and slings him across his back. This was the first time a climber had been rescued from the Wall.

191

Lionel Terray, one of the party that made the second ascent of the North Face, carries Corti in a fireman's lift (also known as the "Gramminger seat") up the summit ridge of the Eiger. The date is 11 August 1957. On 9 and 10 August, Mayer and Nothdurft had been the same way, hoping to reach safety and get help for the Italians—in vain.

was involved in the haul; the two men were brought up relatively quickly, and Corti was no lightweight. "After we had gone up an ice gully, I experienced a moment of immeasurable happiness, as I saw my comrades again on the summit ridge. The Italian had let his head drop through sheer exhaustion; the lads on the top mistakenly assumed he had become unconscious and speeded up the haul. I needed all the strength I had just to keep up. With the last ounce of strength, and totally drained, I reached the summit. I was just able to call to Friedl and get rid of my load before measuring my own length in the snow . . . . Corti was seen to as well as the circumstances permitted. When I walked over to him he had already smoked a cigarette and had a drink of hot tea; he smiled weakly at me and said, 'Grazie.' I felt a warm feeling going through me, and I knew that the fear I had felt on that hellish wall had not been for nothing." (Hellepart)

Dantean Conditions on the Carry-down

Corti was carried down the Summit Ridge and then manhandled down the West Flank on the short stretcher, which could also be used as a sledge. "The carry was adventurous, down steep ice slopes, accompanied by windblown showers of snow. Progress was painfully slow . . . . We soon realized there was going to be a second bivouac." (Herman Huber) The realization was shocking, the more so when, at half past seven, a thunderstorm broke, with rain and snow showers soaking everyone to the skin. The next hours it was like an inferno, "blazing forks of lightning hissed around us continually, one after the other . . . it fizzed and hummed, wailed and whistled; you could say it was like some hellish symphony . . . . Corti was probably the most afraid, calling to his friends again and again." (Hellepart) It was this terrible Eiger night that proved to be the last test for the tough Longhi.

Claudio Corti, however, was brought down safely. A splendid success, for in

went, with no ifs and buts, whatever else was happening workwise or otherwise." (Hermann Huber)

But for a few hours on Sunday, 11 August 1957, it was Alfred Hellepart who was the hero. Belayed by Gramminger, he "traveled" 370 meters down onto the Eigerwand, found Corti, hoisted him onto his back, and brought him back, alive. It must all have been incredibly strenuous. The whole team

A difficult carry. Two members of the fifty-strong international team of rescuers and helpers carry Corti down the West Flank on a rescue sledge, belayed from above.

reality it had only been possible to rescue the one man. "There's no way you just do nothing at all," Gramminger had said, back in Munich. He was right. And the willingness to help literally knew no bounds. Alfred Koch is of the opinion that the international group of rescuers was less affected by the grimness of the tragedy than by the inspiring thought that together they might be able to achieve something.

Horst Höfler (born 1948), from Munich, is the author of numerous books about climbing and for many years was the "chief reader" at a specialist mountaineering publishing house. He has also been an advertising manager for a mountaineering equipment company and the editor of two renowned mountaineering magazines. For ten years he was a member of the governing body of the German Alpine Club. Since summer 1996 he has been busy with a number of publishing projects about mountaineering. Höfler never got around to trying the North Face of the Eiger, although he maintains that, especially in the mid-1980s, he would have been "up to it" both technically and from the point of view of fitness.

(above, upper) The first cigarette, the first smile. Corti with Italian workmen at Eigergletscher station.

(above, lower) After the mission, the German mountain rescue men at Kleine Scheidegg: from left, Wiggerl Gramminger, Herman Huber, Lothar Brandler, Hubert Bail, Alfred Koch, and Emil Proksch.

Summit Ice Field

At last we were free from the oppressive mass of black wall above our heads and we could see more sky. We had escaped from the "Ogre," from the "man-eater"! It was a pleasure to be able to climb, to relax, to move and to warm up a little. Our hands began to throb painfully in the woolen gloves, which were beginning to get softer, and the ropes, too, were gradually losing their cablelike stiffness; in the morning we had had to push the ropes through the carabiners as if they were heating pipes and bend them every 2 to 3 meters.

We were all concerned about our feet, which remained more or less without feeling. After the terrible icy cracks we had to overcome the last overhangs and set foot on the ice and neve fields which lead up to the Summit Ridge. Guido had lost a crampon, so we had to cut every second step for him. It looked like a giant's trail in the white snow.

Pierre Leroux, *Guide*, 1989.
Eigerwand in 1952.

(facing page) Oswald Oelz tops out on the Exit Cracks and climbs the Summit Ice Field. Mist and light snowfall prevent him getting the breathtaking view down to the green Alpine pastures.

On the Significance of the Eiger in Grindelwald and in Japan

Samuel Brawand, Yuko Maki, Fritz Steuri, and Fritz Amatter (left to right) after the first ascent of the Mittellegi Ridge. The passengers on the Wengernalp Railway look on, fascinated.

Apart from his effective gags with rock fragments from the Eigerwand and bits of "Eiger ice," the long-serving Grindelwald resort director Joe Luggen has really always tried to avoid using the Eiger as the basis for all of Grindelwald's tourist advertisements. It is true that Grindelwald is an invaluable branded article, he says, but they have refrained from trying to market it any further. Walter Däpp visited the village at the foot of the world's most famous wall.

For a long time the Eiger with its imposing North Wall has no longer been all that it once was. It is missing a few fragments of rock—they have been broken off from the wall as they were needed for PR souvenir plaques for Japanese journalists and tour operators.

Eiger Ice

It is not only lumps of Eiger rock, but also lumps of Eiger ice that for years have been used to entice Japanese tourists to Switzerland. A real lump has even been pinched from the Eiger's icy crown so that enterprising Swiss resort directors could mount a marketing campaign right in the middle of Tokyo. And very successful it was, too, as Josef "Joe" Luggen, resort director for almost thirty years, says, with hindsight. Twenty percent of Grindelwald hotel guests are Japanese; in 1997 the Japanese spent a respectable 91,569 nights in the hotels there.

Yet it is not only the gags with rock and ice that have attracted this large number of Japanese tourists. For many years the Eiger has been to the Japanese what the Matterhorn is to the Americans. Luggen: "For many Japanese people the Eiger has almost become a holy mountain."

When Eiger fever broke out in Japan, a certain Yuko Maki was responsible. On 10 September 1921, together with Grindelwald mountain guides Samuel Brawand, Fritz Amatter, and Fritz Steuri, Maki was the first to climb the Eiger via the spectacularly exposed Mittellegi Ridge. These mountaineering achievements, and the visits by Japanese crowned heads of state that followed, paved the way to Grindelwald for many Japanese people. From there they were able to ride the Jungfrau Railway "right through the Eiger North Wall" up to the Jungfraujoch.

Eiger Headlines

"Certainly," says Luggen, "Grindelwald has profited enormously over the years from the Eiger North Wall commotion and from all the tragedies on the Wall. But we have until now consciously avoided bringing the Eiger to the forefront of tourist advertising—firstly because is not necessary, and secondly because it would leave a rather bitter aftertaste. The mountain has claimed too many lives."

Nor, for Luggen, does the mountain stand in isolation, but "as a part of the world-famous three peaks, Eiger, Mönch, and Jungfrau," which—if an action group formed by the Wengen hotelier Andrea Cova and the geography professor Bruno Messerli get its way—will be included in UNESCO's prestigious World Heritage List. Luggen: "The green fields on the one side and the mountains and glaciers on the other, this combination of Alpine might and pleasant countryside is most attractive."

In Grindelwald's tourist advertising this has long since found literary expression. "The world-famous mountain setting of the Wetterhorn, Eiger, Mönch, and Jungfrau crowned in ice," as it was once stirringly described for a glossy brochure, "forms the stage set in Grindelwald."

Eiger Chocolate

Surprisingly, in Grindelwald itself you encounter Eiger as a brand name far less frequently than the image of the Matterhorn in Zermatt, for example. However, Eiger is there in all kinds of places: on pens and walking sticks, on stickers and cloth badges, on T-shirts and sweaters, on penknives and cigarette lighters. There is a Hotel Eiger, an Eigerblick Hotel, an Eiger Travel Agent, an Eiger Garage, and an Eiger Chemist. In the Burgener Bakery you can buy an Eiger Chocolate for 15.50 Swiss Francs.

Walter Däpp (born 1946) is a journalist and editor for the Bern daily newspaper *Der Bund*. He has written many reports about mountaineering topics, but himself prefers to have "rather more solid ground under his feet" on mountaineering and skiing trips.

Prince Chichibu and his princess at the foot of the Eiger, summer 1937.

Yuko Maki and the Consequences

"It may only be a small thing, but when I think about how I was responsible for Japan being eternally linked with the Eiger, I can't help my young blood from becoming heated," the then twenty-seven-year-old Yuko Maki wrote on 10 September 1921 in Japanese script in the guides' book, after the first ascent of the Mittellegi Ridge.

After his return, mountaineering became fashionable, as the leader of the then Japanese government thought that, although it was only a leisure pursuit, mountaineering would raise the prestige of Japan.

The second son of the then Japanese Emperor, Prince Chichibu, visited Grindelwald and went on tours into the Alps. Up until the Second World War young representatives from Japan came to Grindelwald—and also to Zermatt—during their summer holidays, since almost all of them were studying in England, France, or Germany. Many were mountaineers and had climbed in Japan, but they got to know about real mountaineering from Maki's work *SANKO* (1923).

And then they did their own new routes. On 6 August 1927, Samitaro Uramatsu and Saburo Matsukata

undertook the first successful climb of the Hörnli Ridge of the Matterhorn with Grindelwald guides. Uramatsu also did the first successful climb of the West Ridge of the Wetterhorn on 24 August 1928. On 25 August 1938 the Taguchi brothers did the first ascent of the North Face of the Schreckhorn (4078 m) with Samuel Brawand and Christian Kaufmann. In 1961, Mituhiko Yoshino and Daihachi Ohkura attempted the first Japanese ascent of the Heckmair Route, but they were forced to turn back at the Swallow's Nest. Tsuneaki Watabe and Hattori Yoshino were also unlucky the following summer.

In 1965, Watabe tried again, this time with Mitsumasa Takada. Watabe fell in the Exit Cracks and broke his leg. Takada climbed to the summit alone and descended through the night to fetch help. The rescue operation was delayed for a day due to bad weather, and before he could be rescued, Watabe was found smashed against the rocks at the foot of the Wall. He had not been able to cope with his hopeless situation any longer and had undone the knot on his safety rope.

Positive headlines appeared in the summer of 1969, when a Japanese team (five men and a woman) established a new direct route known as the Japanese Direttissima, which has become a classic route.

Further Japanese exploits followed: in 1970 the second winter ascent of both the Harlin Direttissima and the Heckmair Route, and in 1978 the first solo of the Heckmair Route in winter, by Tsuneo Hasegawa.

Suke Okazawa (born 1933) was from 1980 to 1989 chief editor of the Japanese Alpine Club's journal and is the author of the book *On the Trail of the Japanese Guides: Mountaineers with a Japanese Spirit—from the Mountain Guides' Books of Switzerland*.

Mittellegi Ridge

We kept on stopping to rest. Our hearts and lungs were refusing to do their work any more. At long last we reached the final rocks, and there for the first time in two days felt the warm comfort of the sun's blessed rays. Through gaps in the mist we looked down on the Lilliputian roofs of Grindelwald, while we waited for the others at a point some 100 meters below the Summit Ridge. Little by little we revived; life began to reawaken in us with the sight of the top so near at hand. The French party unroped now, wishing to follow a little later. There was smooth ice here, in spite of the fresh fall of snow. One last effort from ankles and stiff muscles driven unwillingly to a final output of energy; then we were standing on the sharp crest of the Mittellegi Ridge.

Hermann Buhl, *Achttausend drüber und drunter (Nanga Parbat Pilgrimage)*, 1954.
Eigerwand in 1952.

(facing page) Just a few more steps along the knife-edged Mittellegi Ridge and the two climbers will stand right on the summit of the 3970-meter-high Eiger. In the background, the three Wetterhörner.

The First Ascent of the North East Ridge of the Eiger

(above) Yuko Maki looks down upon visitors from the wall of the Mittellegi Hut he had endowed.

(facing page) The old question: Are the fixed ropes on the Mittellegi Ridge necessary or superfluous, useful or annoying, for the climber or against the mountain? In their day, Yuko Maki and his guides also employed artificial aids.

On 21 September 1921, four mountaineers set up camp out in the open on the airy and exposed Mittellegi Ridge of the Eiger. They were Fritz Amatter, who had already descended the ridge; Fritz Steuri, the first Swiss ski champion; Samuel Brawand, later to become a Social Democrat government official for the Canton of Bern; and the three Grindelwald guides' client, Yuko Maki. Sport, tourism, and politics mixed. In the book *SANKO (Mountaineering)* published in 1923, Yuko Maki wrote twenty-three pages about the first ascent of the North East Ridge of the Eiger.

The high rock face of the Eiger rises up absurdly proud and steep, wearing a thin layer of new snow and colored red by the evening sun. My wish had almost been extinguished from the outset, since I had heard that the snowy East Ridge was too dangerous and could not be climbed at all. Notwithstanding this, I said to myself, "You should try it anyway, do not be intimidated. It is of no import whether you climb it or not. The main thing is to carry out the plan you have nursed for so long." I immediately called Brawand to me and admitted my desires to him. His father, a world-famous mountaineer, had been struck by lightning on the Wetterhorn and died. Samuel Brawand was a teacher at the village school and a mountain guide. At first, he was astonished at my scheme. "School or mountain? The danger is certainly very great, yet if we manage it we will have pleasure in our achievement which will last for the rest of our lives!" In this way, I pressed him for an answer. And he nodded in agreement. The second man was Fritz Steuri, with whom I had done several climbs in the Zermatt area. He had made over 400 ascents of the four-thousanders, and his name was known to mountaineers everywhere. The third man was called Fritz Amatter and was said to be a first-class mountain guide. Amatter had the first ascent of the Finsteraarhorn and several other remarkable mountaineering achievements under his belt. Furthermore, the man had, with his companion Gustav Hasler, twice taken up the challenge of the North East Ridge of the Eiger—both times without success—and the desire to try his luck on the Ridge again still burned bright within him.

New-fangled Equipment

On 7 September these three men and I discussed our plan thoroughly in

the courtyard in front of the Hotel Adler. And the very next evening all the necessary things were there, among them some newly acquired pieces of equipment:

A 6-meter-long wooden pole, with a hook at the uppermost end and three metal spikes at the bottom, one of which was equipped with a hole and could turn freely, so that when climbing on steep rock walls all of the spikes would make contact with the wall simultaneously.

4 types of piton, some 30 in all.

1 iron hammer. Wooden wedges. The special pitons had been specially made for us by the old ice-axe master Schenk, a job he completed within twenty-four hours!

3 mountain ropes: 2 30-meter ropes and 1 60-meter rope. All were guaranteed by the English Alpine Club.

Bivouac equipment: 2 woolen blankets, large woolen overshoes. No tents, since there could be no thoughts of finding sufficient room to pitch tents on such a narrow ridge and they would in any case have been too heavy to carry.

Cooking apparatus and 3 liters of alcohol.

2 lamps.

Provisions: 2 dozen (raw) eggs. 1 roast chicken. Sausages. Biscuits. Lemons. Butter. Jam. Bread. Brandy. Sugar.

"The East Ridge had repulsed many climbers and was in those days one of the most difficult unclimbed lines in the Alps. After two attempts on the Ridge, Amatter—one of the best Swiss mountain guides—considered it his lifetime ambition to climb it." Text and photo by Yuko Maki

On 8 September the four of us went to Schenk's to fetch the pitons. The three wonderful guides, born to be Alpinists, could not contain their inner excitement and remained quite silent on the way. [The following morning, Maki, Brawand, and Amatter took the 8:15 train up from Grindelwald, meeting up at Eismeer Station with Steuri, who had arrived by an earlier train; after a short rest, the four-man rope set off on their adventure.]

From the Eismeer stop on the Jungfrau Railway we abseiled directly down the South East Face of the Eiger to the Eismeer. Heading in a north-easterly direction—Amatter was leading the rope, while I brought up the rear—we climbed up, crossed the neve field and eventually arrived at the foot of the southern rock face of the East Ridge. The chalky, smooth rocks that comprise the Eiger are extremely difficult to climb and at this point the angle is more than 60 degrees steep. Brawand, now climbing as last man on the rope, suddenly lost his footing. The long wooden pole, which he was carrying on his shoulder, flew through the air. Straightaway, Brawand threw himself upon the pole and slid downhill with it a short distance further. But at the same time we belayed him on the rope to prevent him falling any further. The whole of his left arm was bleeding from abrasion wounds. The entire incident lasted just moments. Without the wooden pole, our undertaking would no longer have been possible. At some considerable danger to himself, Brawand had kept all our hopes alive.

A Cold Night in a Rocky Crevice

Gradually, the wall grew steeper and the climbing correspondingly more severe. Loose stones held together by the ice broke away suddenly beneath our feet. At the steep or even overhanging sections, one of us had to climb on the shoulders of another in order to reach the handholds. Toward 5:00 P.M., after such long and toilsome work, we found a little crack on the southern side of the ridge. Right away, we decided to

use it as a bivouac site. With our axes, we cleared away the little stones, piling them up in front of the crevice to fashion a seat. We could not all lie down at the same time. To begin with, Steuri and I lay down inside the crevice, while Amatter and Brawand sat outside on the little pile of stones. During the night, the mountain guides exchanged places every two hours and warmed themselves with hot drinks. They let me lie in the crevice for the entire icy-cold night, and I was able to sleep for a relatively long time (four hours or so).

At 6 A.M. we roped up and started climbing up again, leaving the woolen blankets and all the other bivouac equipment behind in the crack. In the Alps, one normally sets off early, well before sunrise, by the light of the lamps. But the upper part of the East Ridge had never been climbed by anyone before us, and it would thus have been unusually dangerous to start up it in the dark. Soon, the ridge increased in steepness.

From time to time, we scrambled over the crest of the ridge, sharp as a knife, and could look down onto the huge precipices on both sides. Here and there, we overcame blocks of rock several meters high; to do so, one of us would stand on the head or shoulders of another and search for the right holds. After we had climbed a 30-meter-high rock tower we reached a saddle (3500 m above sea level) at the foot of a steeper section known as a gendarme. The climbers who had tried their luck on the ridge before us had climbed as far as here. Before us, the huge rock wall soared above that had refused to allow our predecessors to continue. We rested at the saddle. Three jackdaws flew by, as if sailing a ship of clouds across the Sea of Ice, and their sharp cawing merely heightened the sense of terror we all had about the rock wall ahead. It is about 80 degrees steep, and the strata run diagonally downward. The wind rose, whipping up flurries of snow.

(above) What a ridge! The proud Eiger with the western boundary of the North Face on the right and the North East Ridge on the left. The great upsweep above the steep ice shield can be clearly seen. To the left, the Mönch.

(following pages) While two climbers press on toward the summit along the narrow ridge, the sun casts the shadow of the Eiger into the Grindelwald Valley.

203

The Wooden Pole Is Pressed into Service

We composed ourselves again. In the meantime, we had readied ourselves for the last battle. In rearranged order (Amatter—Steuri—Brawand—and I) we started the hardest part of the job. The shelving strata of the rock offered neither hand- nor footholds. Finally, the time came to use the wooden pole. Amatter, the lead climber, leaned against the rock face. Steuri, the second man, slotted the lower end into a little crack and, putting his whole weight behind it, levered it securely into place. Amatter took a length of rope, fashioned it into a loop, and hung it from the upper hook on the wooden pole. By such means, we thought to limit the force of any possible fall. Belaying himself in this way, Amatter began to hack out tiny little footholds in the rock with his axe. With every blow of the axe, stone poured like raindrops onto the other companions who stood motionless on a small ledge, their hands and faces cut and battered by the falling rocks.

In the cold and the wind, Amatter and Steuri took turns at this work, searching for possible hand- and footholds. As last man, I had to climb with the pole. With only one free hand it was obviously impossible to climb, so I tied in to an extra rope and was hauled up bodily by the other men. Swinging about in midair, I saw beneath me only the 2000-meter precipice, strewn with clouds and wisps of mist. I had long since lost any notion of time. All feelings of fear had similarly long passed.

At the same speed, and with the same hard work, we conquered the 150-meter stretch. But then there stood before us a much steeper, almost vertical rock wall roughly 50 meters in height. And suddenly, Amatter's rucksack whistled through the air and disappeared into the clouds below. Catastrophe! The word ran like a lightning strike through my mind and I tugged on the rope with all my might. "What is wrong, Amatter?" I shouted up. "Nothing wrong, sir. My sack fell. That

is all. And how are you?" He continued his work as if nothing in particular had happened.

Eventually, the ridge gradually decreased in steepness. We now had the most difficult part of the climb behind us. To climb just 200 meters we had taken eight hours, from nine o'clock until five o'clock, yet it seemed to all of us as if these hours had lasted no longer than one short hour at the most. The physical and mental strain had removed any thought of time. "We have won!" Yet no one among us shouted "Bravo!"—we simply shook hands. Silently, Steuri carved the date on a flat slab of rock: "10. 9. 1921." Then he broke the wooden pole in two and tied a neckerchief to one of the sections. Amatter stuck the pole in a little cairn of stones he had been busy building.

Night Descent

We continued climbing and reached the neve of the Summit Ridge. This, too, was very steep and we climbed on without a break, our progress governed by the laws of inertia. It was not quite quarter past seven when we finally stood atop the summit of the Eiger.

We could not remain standing there for longer than five minutes, it was so cold. In new order (Amatter—me—Steuri—Brawand) we began to climb down the icy slope to the west. During the day the sun had melted the snow and now the evening chill had frozen it again, making the rocks as slippery as enamel. Amatter went first, lamp in hand, but the weak light did nothing to illuminate the feet of Steuri and Brawand, who had to take extra care. After some time we realized that we had selected the wrong route. To the left was a cliff measuring some 300 meters, poised above the Eigergletscher; to the right the precipice above the village of Grindelwald; above us a rock wall of 200 meters. For more than one and a half hours, we climbed up and down, without really making any forward progress. There was hardly any-

"We had no tents, since the ridge was too narrow for a tent, and in any case the tents would have been too heavy to carry. Instead, we took along two woolen blankets. To protect us from the cold, we also had a kind of overshoe fashioned from wool. This looked so grotesquely thick that we dubbed it 'the elephant's foot.'"
—Yuko Maki photographs his three guides at the bivouac in 1921 and recalls the scene in his 1968 book *My Climbs*.

thing left to eat in the rucksacks, only brandy, and nothing else to drink. We had lost nearly everything with Amatter's rucksack. I was uncommonly thirsty. Steuri advised me to suck butter and for the first time I learned that butter can also quench one's thirst. Meanwhile, it had become dark. It was even hailing. With only mental strength remaining, we continued our descent and reached the moraines at the lower end of the Eigergletscher. It was 3 A.M. on 11 September when we finally got to Eigergletscher Station. Presumably, the people there had been waiting for us—half awake, half dozing—for without us shouting anything they came running out of the restaurant to congratulate us on our success.

Yuko Maki (1894–1989) was responsible for introducing modern mountaineering techniques in Japan. A lawyer and graduate of the Keio University of Tokyo, he helped write international mountaineering history: 1921, first ascent of the North East Ridge of the Eiger; 1925, first ascent of Mount Alberta (3619 m) in the Canadian Rocky Mountains; 1956, leader of the third Japanese Manaslu Expedition, which made the first ascent of Manaslu (8163 m). In 1923 his book *SANKO (Mountaineering)* was published, in which he writes at length about the first ascent of the North East Ridge of the Eiger. Maki often philosophizes about the spiritual value of climbing the Mittellegi Ridge and relates many of his personal thoughts. In his 1968 book *WATASHI-NO-YAMATABI (My Climbs)* Yuko Maki recalls his most important mountain routes. A brief and rather sobering account of the first ascent of the Mittellegi Ridge also appears in this book.

The Jacob's Ladder of the North East Ridge

The North East Ridge, rising from Ostegg above the gorge of the glacier to the summit of the Eiger, was and remains on the wish-list of many an Alpinist. Such a prominent knife-edged ridge positioned directly above the most famous of the Bernese Oberland's tourist resorts was never going to remain unclimbed. Yet forty-seven years were to elapse between the first attempt and the final successful ascent.

As early as 1874 the Harley brothers from England, with local guides Peter Rubi and Peter Kaufmann, had tried their luck on the Mittellegi Ridge. Eleven years later it was Alexander Burgener, in those days probably the best of the Swiss guides, accompanied by two of his Valais colleagues, Joseph Maria Biner and Anton Kalbermatten, and the Austrian client Moritz von Kuffner. Their party did not get past the Great Tower. Two days later, on 3 July 1885, they nonetheless met with success, albeit from the top down. The first descent party left more than 150 meters of rope behind on the abseils; Burgener even left his axe, to which the rope was tied.

1894 saw an attempt on the Ridge by Claude A. MacDonald, Christian Jossi, and Peter Bernet. Failing on their ascent at about 3500 meters, they did not climb back down the Ridge but descended the North East Face directly, thus making the first descent, so to speak, of the lower section of the Lauper Route. In 1904 three Bernese mountaineers, among them the Grindelwald guide Fritz Amatter, repeated the descent of the Mittellegi Ridge. But still no one could climb it, not even the top German Alpinist Hans Pfann, who tried it in July 1921 and already had the traverse of Uschba (4710 m)—"the Eiger of the Caucasus"—to his name. Every party failed at the steep section beyond the Great Tower.

Since 1926 this and other sections of the Ridge have been equipped with fixed ropes (some 200 meters in all nowadays), making the exposed scramble between heaven and earth a much easier proposition. It was in the same year, too, that Yuko Maki and Fritz Amatter climbed "their" ridge for a second time together. On 12 February 1934, Amatter, then sixty years old, led his mountain guide colleague Fritz Kaufmann on the first winter ascent of the Mittellegi Ridge.

Summit

In less than an hour it would be pitch dark. While the others were packing up their gear, Wolfi and I went on up the narrow, almost level crest of the final ridge, till a hummock of snow loomed up at our feet.

We were on the summit of the Eiger.

It was the first time we had fully grasped the implication of what we had done. We stopped and shook hands again. Our Eiger! Wolfi, we have done it. You and I.

Kurt Diemberger, *Gipfel und Geheimnusse (Summits and Secrets),* 1970.
Eigerwand in 1958.

(facing page) Stephan Siegrist and Ueli Bula shiver and wait for the first rays of sun. They have climbed the North Face in a single day, preferring a cold bivouac to a night descent of the West Flank.

"Try the Eiger or the Matterhorn"

He came, he saw, he conquered—and disappeared forever from the mountains, back to Ireland, to pursue his passion for horse racing. Irishman Charles Barrington appeared in Grindelwald in the summer of 1858 and hired two of the village's best guides, Christian Almer and Peter Bohren, known as Peterli the Glacier Wolf. With them, he traversed the Bernese Alps, across to the Valais and back. And since Barrington still wanted to do something special, he immediately engaged the services of the same two guides for the Eiger (3970 m), which had been unsuccessfully attempted one year before by the Viennese Sigismund Porges, the first ascentionist of the Mönch. Twenty-four years after the first ascent of the Eiger on 11 August 1858 by the West Flank (one of the normal routes still used nowadays), Charles Barrington wrote a letter to his younger brother Richard, which was printed in the English *Alpine Journal*.

"Of the thousands who each year pass beneath the shadows of this grandiose wall, . . . each is deeply impressed by its savage precipices."
—Adolphus Warburton Moore, *The Alps,* 1864.

(above and facing page, upper) H. Fischer: *Das Hochgebirg von Grindelwald.* Viewed from the Bachalp (left to right: Wetterhorn, Schreckhorn, Eiger), 1865, lithograph, 17 x 52 cm.

(facing page, lower) Karl Giradet (1813–1871): *Touristen in den Berner Alpen.* In the background, the Eiger, oil on canvas, 51 x 70.5 cm.

My dear D—,

You will bear with me for not writing a description of my ascent of the Eiger. I have been looking over my papers, without success, for an account I wrote shortly after. But the facts are these:

On Thursday, August 5, 1858, I left Grindelwald about 4 P.M. and walked up the glacier to a small hut, in which we spent the night. It was occupied by a goat keeper. I was eaten up with fleas. Next morning I started with my two guides, Almer and Bohren, and a French gentleman, and crossed the Strahlegg to the Grimsel, where we arrived on Friday evening, the 6th.

On the 7th I started with the same two guides, and walked to the Rhone Valley and up to the Eggischhorn Hotel. On Sunday, the 8th, I slept at the hotel, and in the evening started with Almer and Bohren, and two men to carry the provisions. Had about four and a half hours' walk to the Faulberg, and slept in a small cave. Started early Monday, and got to the top of the Jungfrau, and walked to Grindelwald, where I put up at the Bär-Hof. Here I met some Alpine men whose footsteps I had tracked down the glacier. Talking about climbing, I said to them I did not think much of the work I had done, and was answered, "Try the Eiger or the Matterhorn." "All right," I said. Slept with a beefsteak on my face. In the evening of the next day, the 10th, I made a bargain with the same guides for the Eiger, and walked up to the hotel on the Wengern Alp, stopping to play cards for an hour on the way, and found it quite full at midnight. Threw myself on a sofa, and started at 3:30 A.M. on Aug. 11 for the Eiger. We took a flag from the hotel.

When we came to a point where one descends into a small hollow I looked well with my glass over the face of the Eiger next us, and made up my mind to try the rocks in front instead of going up the other side, which had been tried twice before unsuccessfully. Almer and Bohren said it was no use, and declined to come the way I wished. "All right," I said; "you may stay; I will try." So off I went for about 300 or 400 yards over some smooth rocks to the part which was almost perpendicular. I then shouted and waved the flag for them to come on, and after five minutes they followed and came up to me. They said it was impossible; I said, "I will try." So, with the rope coiled over my shoulders, I scrambled up, sticking like a cat to the rocks, which cut my fingers, and at last got up say 50 to 60 feet. I then lowered the rope and the guides followed with its assistance. We then had to mark our way with chalk and small bits of stone, fearing we might not be able to find it on our return. We went up very close to the edge, looking down on Grindelwald, sometimes throwing over large stones to hear them crash down beneath the clouds. We got to the top—the two guides kindly gave me the place of first man up—at twelve o'clock, stayed about ten minutes, fearing the weather, and came down in four hours, avoiding the very steep place, as, looking down from above, we found out a couloir, down which we came, and just saved ourselves by a few seconds from an avalanche.

I was met at the bottom by about thirty visitors, and we went up to the hotel. They doubted if we had been on the top until the telescope disclosed the flag there. The hotel proprietor had a large gun fired off, and I seemed for the evening to be a "lion."

Thus ended my first and only visit to Switzerland. Not having money enough with me to try the Matterhorn, I went home. Nothing could exceed the kindness of Almer and Bohren. I am sorry to hear the latter has passed away. Both were splendid mountaineers, and had I not been as fit as my old horse "Sir Robert Peel" when I won the "Irish Grand National" with him, I would not have seen half the course. I may add that when leaving Grindelwald for the Eiger I was surprised to see the families of the guides in a state of distraction at their departure for the ascent, and two elderly ladies came out and abused me for taking the guides to risk their lives.

Your affectionate brother,
Charles Barrington

Little is known about Charles Barrington apart from his first ascent of the Eiger. The letter to his brother appeared in the *Alpine Journal* of 1882. In a footnote published in the same journal, his brother, Richard M. Barrington, relates the following anecdote: When, in 1876, he, too, climbed the Eiger with Peter Bohren, the latter showed him the feature known as the "Känzeli," a rock tower protruding from the North Face that stood some 3 meters apart from the West Ridge. According to Bohren, Charles had jumped across the gap, the only one who had dared to do so. Richard completes his footnote with the remark that his brother remembered the rock tower well but was no longer certain if he had jumped across. Today, standing on the rim of the North Face and looking at the tower—nowadays known as the "Pilz" (mushroom)—it is hard to imagine making that Alpine longjump.

Trips and Tips

The Ascent of the Eiger

Even by the Normal Route, the Eiger is a serious undertaking. Those who, when climbing its loftier yet more easily accessible neighbors the Mönch (4107 m) and the Jungfrau (4158 m), realize that there is actually not much more left in reserve, should leave the world-famous three-thousander to the Mittellegi Ridge acrobats and the North Face challengers. In the past, the West Flank, starting from Eigergletscher Station, was the only Normal Route on the Eiger. Nowadays, it shares the claim with the South Ridge, the continuation ridge between the Eigerjochs and the easy continuation via the Mönchsjoch Hut to the Jungfraujoch.

The correct route along the West Flank is not easy to follow, particularly on the descent. The height gain from Eigergletscher Station to the summit is a hard 1650 meters. The West Flank is best ascended when free of snow and ice (there may still be a small ice field high up), in dry weather and on dry rock, following the same route back down again. In mist, the situation can rapidly become hopeless. Beware of stonefall! The routefinding on the way over the Eigerjoch is simpler but it does require some grade II and III scrambling along the narrow rocky ridge.

The Grindelwald guides use neither of these routes when guiding clients but tend to stick to the more exposed, yet safer, Mittellegi Ridge, descending via the Eigerjoch to the Jungfraujoch.

Northern Eigerjoch Ski Tour

In late spring, after a winter of heavy snow, and when the Eiger Glacier is well snowed up, the tour from the Eigergletscher Station (2320 m) up to the Northern Eigerjoch (3614 m) is recommended for adventurous ski-mountaineers. The trip is not without dangers, however, due to the threat of ice avalanches coming down off the Mönch. In normal conditions there are no sections steeper than 40 degrees. The continuation route to the summit should only be attempted by experienced skiers, in good conditions, and with sufficient time to spare.

Rotstock Via Ferrata

The route requires rock climbing experience and the ability to deal with loose rock. Climbers wishing to get to know the "real" Rotstock via ferrata (or what remains of the original) should start at Eigergletscher Station (2320 m) and follow the lower section of the West Flank route (well trodden, cairns) up into the col between the Rotstock and the West Flank. From here, a little searching reveals the ladders, iron rungs and chiselled steps, that mark the descent to Rotstock (2520 m), the former railway station. Then, climb back by the col and finish the ascent up the summit of Rotstock (2663 m). These are plans to extend the Via Ferrata to the foot of the North Face.

Information

A guided ascent of the Eiger, done almost exclusively now via the Mittellegi Ridge, can be booked daily from July to September at the Bergsteiger-Zentrum Grindelwald. The cost for one person is 890 Francs, including everything (accommodation, half board, etc.) except for the client's transport costs (1998 prices). Tel. (033) 853-5200; fax (033) 853-1222.

Travel

The Bernese Oberland is reached easily by rail, with excellent connections to Interlaken from Zürich, Geneva, and elsewhere. From Interlaken's East Station, the Berner Oberland Bahn runs to Grindelwald (1034 m); from here a rack railway goes on up to Kleine Scheidegg (2061 m) and further, with stops at Eigergletscher (2320 m), Eigerwand (2865 m), and Eismeer (3159 m), terminating at the highest station in Europe at Jungfraujoch (3454 m). Kleine Scheidegg can also be reached from Interlaken Ost via Lauterbrunnen (change) and car-free Wengen (1275 m).

Huts and Hotels

Mittellegi Hut (3355 m) Room for 16 in the hut, with 14 additional places in the bivouac shelter below. Always open. Custodian in high season. Two hours from Eismeer Station. Can also be reached from Grindelwald (969) in 8 hours. No phone.

Eiger-Ostegg Hut (2320 m). Sleeps 12, normally closed, information at the Bergsteiger-Zentrum Grindelwald. Situated on the most north-easterly spur of the Mittellegi Ridge. From Alpiglen Station, follow a marked, often exposed path; 3½ hours, the most difficult steps are cable-protected. Climbers only!

Mönchsjoch Hut (3657 m). Privately run hut, sleeps 120. Open all year, serviced April/May and July to September, tel. (033) 971-3472. Reached in about 1 hour by an easy uphill walk from the top station at the Jungfraujoch (3454 m); situated above the Oberes Mönchsjoch.

Bergli Hut (3299 m). SAC Bern, sleeps 20, open all year, no permanent custodian; firewood available. No phone. From the Jungfraujoch, via the Oberes and the Unteres Mönchsjoch (3529 m), then down the steep neve slope and along a snow and rock ridge to the hut; 2–2½ hours. Only suitable for experienced and well-equipped climbers.

Kleine Scheidegg (2061 m). Bahnhofbuffet Röstizzeria, tel. (033) 855-1151.

Eigergletscher (2320 m). Guesthouse, tel. (079) 456-3639.

Alpiglen (1616 m). Hotel des Alpes, tel. (033) 853-1130.

Walks

In Sandals: Männlichen to Kleine Scheidegg High Trail

One of the most popular walks in the Alps. Starting point: top station at Männlichen, reachable from Grindelwald or Wengen. Be sure to make the very worthwhile detour to the summit of the Männlichen (2342 m). One and a half hours.

In Walking Boots: Eiger Trail

Start at Eigergletscher Station (2320 m) and follow the path below the Rotstock and the western part of the Eigerwand (good views of the "Wall of Walls"). Continue across meadows, boulder fields and mountain streams down to restaurant at Alpiglen (1616 m). Two hours.

In Mountain Boots: Challi Route

Newly marked path (colored paint). Crosses the lower Challi terrace. Rope and ice axe needed for the route up to the Mittellegi Hut (3355 m), but as far as the Challi sheep pastures, high-alpine hiking experience should suffice. Easy walking from Grindelwald (969 m) or the Pfingstegg Station (1392 m) to Stierregg (1650 m). Follow the path to the Schreckhorn Hut to 1700 meters, go straight on for a short distance, and drop down steeply through alder groves to the scree-covered Lower Grindelwald Glacier. Traverse the glacier at about 1550 meters. Climb a wide scree gully to a cairn. Follow a well-trodden path to the grassy slopes of the Challi. A zigzag path leads up to a ridge at approximately 2300 meters; 3½–4½ hours. A tough walk with difficult routefinding; not for those of a nervous disposition.

Tourist Information

Berner Oberland Tourismus, Jungfraustrasse 38, CH-3800 Interlaken. Tel. (033) 823-0303. Fax (033) 823-0330. Website: www.berneroberland.com.
Grindelwald Tourist Information: CH-3818 Grindelwald. Tel. (033) 854-1212. Fax (033) 854-3088. Website: www.grindelwald.ch.
Wengen Tourist Information: CH-3823 Wengen. Tel. (033) 855-1414. Fax (033) 855-3060. Website: www.wengen.com.
Automated snow and weather reports: Kleine Scheidegg-Männlichen: (033) 855-4433.

Maps and Topo Guides

Landeskarte der Schweiz/Cartes nationales suisses 1:50,000 scale, sheets 254 Interlaken, 264 Jungfrau. Special edition with the symbols T for walks and S for ski tours. 1:25,000 scale, sheets 1229 Grindelwald, 1249 Finsteraarhorn.
Clubführer Berner Alpen, Band (volume) 4, Tschingelhorn bis Finsteraarhorn. Swiss Alpine Club, Bern, 1997 (in German).
Bernese Oberland, Selected Climbs, Les Swindin, Alpine Club Guide Books, London, 1993.
Ski touren Berner Alpen Ost, Ralph Schnegg and Daniel Anker, Swiss Alpine Club, Bern, 1999 (in German).
Berner Oberland Ost, Daniel Anker, Rother Wanderführer, Munich 1998 (in German).
Hiking Guide Jungfrau Region, Kümmerly and Frey.

Chronology

1858

On 11 August, the occasional mountaineer, Irishman Charles Barrington, accompanied by Grindelwald guides Christian Almer and Peter Bohren, makes the first ascent of the Eiger (3970 m) via the West Flank.

1864

The English woman Lucy Walker is the first woman on the summit of the Eiger.

1871

First ascent of the South West Ridge on 14 July by Englishman (and later Grindelwald resident) W. A. B. Coolidge, with his aunt Meta Brevoort and the local guides Christian Bohren and Christian and Ulrich Almer.

1874

On 6 July, J. W. and F. C. Hartley from England, with the two Grindelwald Peter Rubi und Peter Kaufmann, make the first attempt on the knife-edged North East Ridge, better known as the Mittellegi Ridge.

1876

First ascent of the South Ridge on 31 July by British climber George Edward Foster with local guides Hans Baumann and Ulrich Rubi.

1885

First descent of the Mittellegi Ridge by Valais mountain guides Alexander Burgener, Joseph Maria Biner, and Anton Kalbermatten, with their Austrian client Moritz von Kuffner.

1890

First winter ascent of the Eiger on 7 January by Englishmen Mead and Woodroffe with local guides Ulrich Kaufmann and Christian Jossi.

1894

On 8 August the British climber Claude A. MacDonald, with Grindelwald mountain guides Christian Jossi and Peter Bernet, attempt the Mittellegi Ridge. Their attempt fails at about 3500 meters; however, they do not climb back down the Ridge, but descend straight down the North East Face, thereby making the first descent, as it were, of the lower section of what will come to be the Lauper-Route.

1898

Opening of the Eigergletscher Station (2320 m). Over the next ten years the workers, mainly Italians, drill their way through the Eiger. A total of seven tunnels are created in the Eiger, including the Gallery Window, famous in mountaineering circles, and the two stations, Eigerwand and Eismeer.

1921

On 10 September, the Japanese mountaineer Yuko Maki (the first professional mountaineer in Japan) makes the first ascent of the Mittellegi Ridge with Fritz Amatter, Fritz Steuri, and Samuel Brawand (who celebrated his 100th birthday in 1998).

1924

First ascent on skis on 18 May by the Englishman Arnold Lunn and the Swiss trio of Fritz Amacher, Walter Amstutz, and Willy Richardet; ascent and descent by the Eigergletscher; from the Northern Eigerjoch (3614 m) the four men continue on foot up the South Ridge to the summit.

1927

First ascent of the Hörnli Ridge of the Eiger (the lower part of the North East Ridge from the Ostegg to the Mittellegi Hut) on 6 August, by the Japanese Samitaro Uramatsu and Saburo Matsukata with Grindelwald guides Emil Steuri and Samuel Brawand.

1932

20 August. Swiss climbers Hans Lauper and Alfred Zürcher, with mountain guides Alexander Graven and Joseph Knubel, make the first ascent of the 1700-meter-high North East Face ("Lauper Route").

1934

On 12 February, Grindelwald mountain guides Fritz Amatter and Fritz Kaufmann make the first winter ascent of the Mittellegi Ridge.

In July, on their first attempt, Germans Willy Beck and Kurt and Georg Löwinger reach over 2900 meters on the North Face; they escape through the Gallery Window of the Jungfrau Railway.

1935

First serious attempt to climb the whole of the 1800-meter-high North Face. Munich men Max Sedlmayr and Karl Mehringer set off on 21 August on a direct route. After several days of bad weather, they freeze to death on 25 August at 3300 meters, at a point since known as Death Bivouac.

1936

The German team of Andreas Hinterstoisser and Toni Kurz, and Austrians Willi Angerer and Edi Rainer set off up the Face independently of each other on 18 July. Joining forces, they pull the ropes on the Traverse (thus cutting off their retreat) but are forced by bad weather to turn back. Fate then cruelly intervenes: On 21 July three of the men perish within earshot of the line manager of the Jungfrau Railway, while Toni Kurz dies the following morning, hanging on the end of the rope but unreachable, before the very eyes of his would-be rescuers, who had attempted to rescue him from the Gallery Window of the railway. His merciless end is, together with the death of the four climbers during the first ascent of the Matterhorn in 1865, the most famous tragedy in the history of Alpinism. "Ich kann nicht mehr" ("I can't go on") or "Es geht nicht" ("It's impossible") are his last words.

In July, the State of Bern issues a ban on climbing the North Face of the Eiger; which is repealed only four months later as it has no basis in law.

1937

First woman on the North Face: Genevan Loulou Boulaz, climbing with fellow countryman Pierre Bonnant. Retreat from 2700 meters on 21 July.

First ascent of the 800-meter-high, pure rock route of the South East Face on 11 and 12 August by Germans Otto Eidenschink and Ernst Moeller.

On 11 to 14 August, Austrian Matthias Rebitsch and German Ludwig Vörg embark on their third (and highest) attempt on the North Face, reaching a point a few pitches higher than Death Bivouac. A break in the weather forces them to retreat, the first team to get down alive from the central section of the Wall.

1938

On 21 June, Italians Bartolo Sandri and Mario Menti fall to their deaths from a point level with the Difficult Crack.

First ascent of the North Face of the Eiger by Germans Anderl Heckmair and Ludwig Vörg and Austrians Fritz Kasparek and Heinrich Harrer, accomplished from 22 (21) to 24 July. Heckmair is the leader of the party and the North Face route is thus named after him.

1947

Second ascent of the North Face, 14 to 16 July, by the French pair Lionel Terray and Louis Lachenal.

Third ascent 4 and 5 August by Swiss mountain guides Hans and Karl Schlunegger with their client Gottfried Jermann.

1950

On 26 July, Austrians Leo Forstenlechner and Erich Waschak become the first team to climb the Face in a day: Eighteen hours from the foot of the Wall to the summit. It is also the fourth ascent.

1957

In July, Günther Nothdurft solos up as far as the Second Ice Field in a day.

First successful rescue from the Face. On 11 August, after nine days on the Face, Italian climber Claudio Corti is hauled from the Exit Cracks on a steel cable by a rescue team composed entirely of volunteers from many different countries. The attempts to rescue his companion, Stefano Longhi, fail; from their position on the West Ridge, his would-be rescuers hear his last words; "Fame, freddo!" His corpse is to remain hanging on the Eiger for a further two years, a macabre sensation. And it is only in 1961, with the discovery of the bodies of his German companions Günther Nothdurft and Franz Mayer on the West Flank, that poor Corti is freed of the suspicion of guilt surrounding their disappearance.

1958

The White Spider is published. Written by first ascentionist Heinrich Harrer, it is translated into several languages.

1959

A Dutch publisher sponsors the retrieval of Longhi's body by local guides but insists on the exclusive rights to the story and even tries to ban other reporters from flying the air space around the Eiger.

Between 1959 and 1961 events on the Eiger are cited in a court case concerning defamation of character. German Hans Grünleitner accuses Toni Hiebeler, who (rightly) expresses doubts as to the veracity of Grünleitner's claim to have climbed the Face with Swiss companion Robert Stieger; the pair attempt to prove their claim using fake photgraphs.

1961

First winter ascent of the North Face at the end of February and from 6 to 12 March by Austrian Walter Almberger and Germans Toni Kinshofer, Anderl Mannhardt and Toni Hiebeler. It becomes known that the first winter ascent team did not climb the Face in one push from the bottom up, as Toni Hiebeler maintained, but climbed as far as the Gallery Window on their first attempt and, after a week of bad weather, resumed and completed the climb from that point.

On 28 August Austrian Adi Mayr falls to his death from the Waterfall Chimney during a solo attempt on the Face.

At the end of August, a reporters' plane crashes with its three passengers.

1962

John Harlin becomes the first American to climb the North Face (19 to 22 August); his partner is the German Konrad Kirch.

First British ascent of the North Face (30/31 August) by Chris Bonington and Ian Clough.

At the beginning of September the body of Karl Mehringer is found at the edge of the Second Ice Field.

1963

First solo ascent (and the forty-first overall) of the Heckmair Route on 2 and 3 August by Valais mountain guide Michel Darbellay.

During operations to recover the bodies of Spanish climbers Alberto Rabadà and Roberto Navarro from the Spider, Swiss Paul Etter, Ueli Gantenbein and Sepp Henkl climb and abseil down the whole Face from 27 to 31 Decemberthe first team to do so.

1964

First winter ascent of the Lauper Route from 10 to 12 February by Bernese Oberland men Hanspeter Trachsel and Gerd Siedhoff.

Munchich woman Daisy Voog, accompanied by German Werner Bittner, becomes the first woman to climb the Eigerwand. It is also the fifty-first ascent of the Heckmair Route. The Swiss tabloid newspaper Blick runs the story under the title "Blond Munich Secretary Daisy Breaks Wall of Death Taboo."

1966

The first new route on the North Face of the Eiger. From 23 Febuary to 25 March an Anglo-American and a German team put up the first Direttissima (The "John Harlin Route") in expedition style using fixed ropes. John Harlin falls to his death from just below the Spider when a rope breaks; after this the two competing teams finally join forces to complete the route. On 25

March Dougal Haston, Siegfried Hupfauer, Jörg Lehne, Günther Strobel, and Roland Votteler top out. The names of the other climbers: Chris Bonington, Layton Kor, Don Whillans; Karl Golikow, Peter Haag, Rolf Rosenzopf, and Günther Schnaidt.

First female ascent of the Lauper Route by Daisy Voog and companion.

1968

Two new routes on the North Pillar (it separates the North East Face from the North Face) by the Poles Krzysztof Cielecki, Tadeusz Laukajtys, Ryszard Szafirski and Adam Zysak (set off on 28 July) and a team comprising South Tyrol brothers Reinhold and Günther Messner with Germans Toni Hiebeler and Fritz Maschke (set off on 3 July).

1969

Between 5 July and 15 August, a Japanese team with Mrs. Michiko Imai and Takio Kato, Yasuo Kato, Satoru Negishi, Amano Hirofumi and Susumu Kubo climb the second Direttissima, taking a direct line up the 300-meter-high partially overhanging Rote Fluh. Climbing in expedition style, they haul 1000 kilograms of equipment (including 250 bolts, 200 rock pitons, and 2400 meters of rope). The Japanese Route also becomes known as the Summer Direttissima.

1970

On 20 to 25 January, the Swiss Otto von Almen, Max Dörfliger, Peter Jungen, Hans Müller, and Hanspeter Trachsel make the second (and first winter) ascent of Japanese Direttissima.

January also sees the first winter rescue from the Face as Japanese climber Kenji Kimura is winched out of the Exit Cracks to the summit on a steel cable. Rescue personnel and equipment are ferried to the summit by helicopter.

First ski descent of the 50-degree-steep (in places) West Flank on 9 March by Swiss skier Sylvain Saudan. Nowadays a classic extreme ski trip.

Direct North Buttress, by Scotsmen I. MacEacheran, A. McKeith and K. Spence, from 28 to 31 July.

The British team of Leo Dickinson, Eric Jones, Pete Minks, and Cliff Philipps climb the Heckmair Route; Dickinson films the ascenta world first.

1971

On 12 September from the Second Ice Field, pilot Günther Amann, with climbers Martin Biock and Peter Siegert from Germany, make the first successful direct helicopter rescue from the North Face.

1972

First winter ascent of the South East Face, from 21 to 23 December, by a Swiss team comprising Walter Müller, Ernst Ott, and Markus Wacker.

1973

The second ascent of the Messner-Hiebeler Route on the North Buttress, accomplished in three days in September by a Polish women's team of Wanda Rutkiewicz,

Danuta Wach, and Stefania Egierszdorff. They are the first women to climb the North Face without male accompaniment.

1974

During the filming of the Hollywood thriller The Eiger Sanction, American Dave Knowles is killed by stonefall on 13 August. On viewing the Face for the first time, leading actor Clint Eastwood exclaims, "Oh shit! Let's get the hell out of here!"

On 24 August the Swiss Karl Moser and Walter Müller climb a new direct route on the South East Face.

1976

First summer ascent of the Winter Direttissima (John Harlin Route), from 3 to 9 August by Czech climbers Petr Bednařík, Jindřich Sochor, Pavel Cicàrek, and Pavel Ševčik.

The last greeting from the dead heroes: "Bivouac on 21/8/35 Max Sedelmajr, Karl Mehringer. München H.T.G. Sekt. Oberland." H.T.G. means Hochtouristengruppe (High Mountain Climbing Group). The note was probably written by Mehringer, since the name of his climbing companion is misspelled. A Czech party of four finds the cigarette packet with the mildewed note on 21 June.

A Czech party Jiří Smíd, Sylva Kysilková, Petr Plachecký, and Josef Rybičkaestablish a new line to the right (west) of the Japanese Direttissima. The Czech Pillar, whose lower section takes a line up the right-hand side of the Rote Fluh, is the first North Face climb not to finish at the summit, but at about 3700 meters on the West Ridge.

1977

September sees he first hang glider flight from the summit of the Eiger by Swiss pilot Jürg Frey.

1978

Czech Route II is established up the left-hand (east) part of the Wall by Jiří Smíd, Josef Rybičkaz, Miroslav Smíd, and Jaroslav Flejberk, between 16 January and 23 February.

Frenchman Yvano Ghirardini becomes the first man to do all three big North Faces (Eiger, Matterhorn and Grandes Jorasses) in one (winter) season.

From 3 to 9 March, Japanese climber Tsuneo Hasegawa makes the first solo ascent of the Heckmair Route.

1979

Genevans Michel Piola and Gérard Hopfgartner establish the first free climbing route in the modern idiom (and the tenth route on the North Face) with the Geneva Pillar ("Les portes du chaos"). The route finishes 900 meters below the summit and is to become a modern classic.

1980

First winter ascent of the Heckmair Route by a woman: Claudia Heissenberger with four companions, from 12 to 15 February.

Eiger West Ridge direct: On 3 July the Swiss Michel Piola and Vincent Sprungli make the first ascent of the lowest section of the West Ridge of the Eiger, on the western edge of the North Face.

1981

First winter ascent of the Geneva Pillar, 12 to 16 February, by Swiss climbers Norbert Joos and Kaspar Ochsner.

Swiss climber Ueli Bühler does the Heckmair Route in eight and a half hours on 25 August.

First ascent of the North Corner on the right-hand section of the Face, 26 and 27 August, by the Swiss Christel and Hans Howald and Marcel Rüedi.

1982

Two new free routes on the western section of the Face, right of the Geneva Pillar. On 15 July by Slovenian Franček Knez, solo, and on 13 August by the Swiss Kaspar Ochsner and Urs Brunner: "Schlupfloch Route."

1983

First winter ascent of the North Buttress (Messner Route) on 1 January by the Swiss Norbert Joos and Kaspar Ochsner, Martin Grossen and Bernhard Misteli.

From 2 March to 2 April, Slovakian Pavel Pochylý climbs the Ideal Direttissima, following the direct fall line from the summit.

On 16 and on 19 May, Italians Toni Valeruz and Bruno Pederiva make the first ski descent of the North East Face (up to 60 degrees steep).

The Swiss team of Pierre-Alain Steiner and Paul Maillefer climb "Spit verdonesque édenté" on 3 June and from 9 to 12 July, a pure 300-meter-long sport climb on the West Ridge Pillar; the foot of the route is accessed by abseil from the West Ridge.

On 27 July Austrian Thomas Bubendorfer establishes the still current speed record for the classic North Face route, climbing it in just four hours fifty minutes; a few days earlier he had done the route with Peter Rohrmoser to familiarise himself with the line.

Piola-Ghilini Direttissima, established between 26 and 30 July by Genevan Michel Piola and Frenchman René Ghilini. The 1400-meter-long route takes a line up a continually slightly overhanging pillar; to date it has seen only six ascents; a first winter ascent has been attempted but still remains to be done.

1985

On 10 to 27 March,. Jiří Smíd, with exiled Czechs Michal Pitelka and Čestmír Lukeš, establishes his third Eigerwand route, the "Toni Hiebeler Memorial Route."

On 25 July Frenchman Christophe Profit climbs the three North Faces of the Matterhorn, Eiger, and Grandes Jorasses in only twenty-two and a half hours; in the 1930s these routes were described by their first ascentionists as the "last great problems of the Alps." He does the Eigerwand in nine hours.

New direct route on the left part of the Wall, climbed on 27 and 28 July by Slovenians Franček Knez, Mayan Freser, and Dani Tic.

First solo ascent of the North Corner on 11 and 12 September by Daniel Anker.

First paraglider flight from the summit of the Eiger on 23 September, by Frenchman Pierre Gevaux.

1987

On 11 and 12 March Christophe Profit repeats his Trilogie, but this time in winter conditions and in forty-two hours. He starts the Heckmair Route at 4 P.M. and tops out at 9:30. Then it's off to the Matterhorn.

Frenchman Bruno Gouvy snowboards down the West Flank on 21 April.

1988

Two new and extremely difficult free routes are added on the western section of the Face. From 5 to 7 August, Swiss climbers Daniel Anker and Michel Piola put up "Eigersanction." From 6 to 11 August, the Czech brothers Miroslav and Michal Coubal contribute "Gelber Engel," up the ill-defined pillar between the North Corner and the Piola Ghilini Direttissima; is is the twentieth route on the North Face of the Eiger (including the Lauper Route).

New sport climb on the extreme western edge of the Wall, climbed on 17 August by the Swiss Daniel Anker and Michael Gruber and christened "Löcherspiel."

An Indonesian team climbs a line up alongside the North Corner, in expedition style and over one month. The route is identical in parts to the Howald-Rüedi Route. The Indonesian route is not recognized as an independent new route.

1990

Slovenian Slavko Sveticic soloes the Harlin Direttissima in twenty-seven hours in January.

1991

Climbing solo and without bolts, American Jeff Lowe works his way up his own new route during the period 19 February to 4 March (with one day off); he takes a line somewhere between the Japanese Direttissima and the Pochylý Route, heading directly for the upper West Ridge.

A Yugoslavian climber is swept away by an avalanche on 1 or 2 June at the First Pillar. He is one of the latest victims of the North Face. To date there have been about fifty-five deaths.

Completion of the third, and most difficult, route on the South East Face: "Panoramaweg" is the work of Werner Burgener and Hannes and Ueli Stähli; it was started in 1987.

1992

On 1 March 1992, Frenchwoman Catherine Destivelle makes the first female solo ascent of the classic North Face Route in seventeen hours climbing time. This is also the first female winter ascent and the first

female-only ascent of the Heckmair Route.

On 17 and 18 July, Swiss climbers Daniel Anker and Michel Piola complete their route "Le Chant du Cygne" in the fall line of the Geneva Pillar. The most modern of the Eiger routes, it becomes a classic after only a few summer seasons.

1994

First rescue using the longline technique. On 26 July two Dutch climbersone of them with a badly broken leg sustained during a fallare hauled out of the upper overhanging section of the Geneva Pillar.

1996

First nighttime rescue from the Face, on 31 January. An exhausted, and poorly equipped, pair of Swiss climbers radio for the helicopter from the Traverse of the Gods. In spite of the dark and the difficult winter conditions the rescue team manage to fly the two climbers off the Face.

1997

Austrian journalist Gerald Lehner reveals Heinrich Harrer's Nazi past in an expose published in the German Stern magazine. The revelations come shortly before the release of the film Seven Years in Tibet, which glorifies in typical Hollywood fashion the life of the former member of the SA, SS, and NSDAP.

Italian Benedetto Salaroli (72 years old) becomes the oldest person to have climbed the North Face. On 5 October he steps onto the Face from the Gallery Window and climbs the Heckmair Route to the summit, guided by Ueli Bühler II and Köbi Reichen.

1998

Italians Andrea Forlini and Gianni Faggiana establish the new extreme route "Yeti," which takes a line between the North Corner and the "Eigersanction."

Swiss pair Daniel Anker and Stephan Siegrist start working the twenty-fifth and most difficult free route on the Eigerwand. It goes from the Gallery Window up the highest and most overhanging part of the Rote Fluh and then follows the Direct Czech Pillar to the West Ridge. It should be complete sometime in 200.

1999

In August, Germans Daniela Jasper-Klindt and Robert Jasper free climb a few hard link pitches to connect the lower half of "Le Chant du Cygne" to "Spit verdonesque édenté." The completed route is called "Symphonie du liberté"; it is accepted as an independent new route.

On 9 and 1 September the Swiss television company SF DRS, in collaboration with the German Südwestfunk, broadcasts "Eiger-Nordwand live": With cameras running, two ropes of mountain guides (the Swiss Evelyne Binsack, Stephan Siegrist, and Hansruedi Gertsch and the German Ralf Dujmovits) climb the Heckmair Route on the North Face.

Bibliography

Amstädter, Rainer, *Der Alpinismus. Kultur–Organisation–Politik,* WUV-Universitätsverlag, Vienna, 1996.

Amstutz, Walter, *Eiger, 3974 m. Erste Begehung mit Ski,* in 19. Jahresbericht des Akademischen Alpenklub Bern 1, November 1923 bis 31, Oktober 1924, Berne, 1925, p. 16–17.

Anker, Daniel, *Oben statt unten. Der Schweizer Alpen-Club und die Politik, die Gesellschaft und die Ideologie der Berge,* Lizentiatsarbeit, Berne, 1986.

Barrington, Charles, *The First Ascent of the Eiger,* in *Alpine Journal* Vol. XI, 1882, p. 172–174.

Birkett, Bill, and Peascod, W., *Women Climbing: 200 Years of Achievement,* A&C Black, London, 1989; The Mountaineers, Seattle, 1990.

Bonatti, Walter, *The Great Days,* Gollancz, London, 1974.

Bonington, Chris, *I Chose to Climb,* Gollancz, London, 1975.

Boulaz, Loulou, *La seconde ascension de la face Nord des Grandes Jorasses,* in *La Montagne.* Revue du Club Alpin Français (Paris) No. 272, novembre 1935, p. 329–334.

Bracher, Hans, *Das Verbot der Besteigung der Eiger-Nordwand,* in *Die Alpen. Chronik des SAC,* 1936, p. 223 and following pages.

Brawand, Samuel, *Erinnerungen an Yuko Maki,* Sutter Druck AG, Grindelwald, 1989.

Breuer, Thomas M., *Eiger im Detail,* Edité par l'auteur, Sumiswald, 1983.

Bubendorfer, Thomas, *Der Alleingänger. Leben und Aufstieg eines ungewöhnlichen Bergsteigers,* Pinguin-Verlag, Innsbruck, 1984.

Buhl, Hermann, *From the Tyrol to Nanga Parbat,* Hoëbeke, Paris, 1998.

Burns, Christopher, *The Condition of Ice,* Sceptre, London, 1991.

Capus, Alex, *Eigermönchjungfrau. Geschichten,* Diogenes Verlag, Zürich, 1998.

Crockett, Samuel Rutherford, *Lone March,* Hodder, London, 1899; Dodd Mead, New York 1900.

De Infanti, Sergio, *Tragico Eiger,* in Ursella, Angelo, *Il ragazzo di Buia. Appunti di un alpinista,* Vivalda Editori, Turin, 1994.

Desmaison, Simone, *La face de l'ogre,* Flammarion, Paris 1985.

Devies, Lucien, *Eiger et Walker,* in *La Montagne,* 1939, pages 129 and following pages.

Dickinson, Leo, *Filming the Impossible,* Jonathan Cape, London, 1982.

Die Jungfrau und die Jungfraubahn, Verlag A. Spühler, Neuchâtel, 1903.

Diemberger, Kurt, *De zéro à huit mille mètres,* Albin Michel, Paris, 1974.

Duino, Michel, *Les vainqueurs de l'Eiger,* collection marabout junior, Editions Gérard & Cie, Verviers, 1957.

Egger, Carl, *Pioniere der Alpen. 30 Lebensbilder der grossen Schweizer Bergführer,* Verlag Amstutz, Herdeg & Co., Zürich, 1946.

Eiger 1252–1988, *Eine Chronik und Berichte von Besteigungen,* Herausgegeben vom Bergführerverein Grindelwald, Grindelwald, 1988.

Etter, Paul, *Gipfelwärts. Ein junger Bergführer erzählt,* Verlag Huber, Frauenfeld und Stuttgart, 1968.

Falke, Konrad, *Alpiner Totentanz,* Bücher der Heimat, 4. Bändchen, Verlag K. J. Wyss Erben, Interlaken, 1928.

Frey, Oswald, *Im Schatten der grossen Wand,* Gute Schriften, Bâle, 1963.

Friedli, Erich, *Rettung aus der Eigernordwand 1957–1970,* in *Die Alpen.* Monatsbulletin des SAC 1970, p. 158 and following pages.

Frison-Roche; Jouty, Sylvain, *Histoire de l'alpinisme,* Arthaud, Paris, 1996.

Gillman, Peter; Haston, Dougal, *Eiger Direct,* Collins, London; Harper, New York, 1966.

Gramminger, Ludwig, *Das gerettete Leben,* herausgegeben von Hans Steinbichler, Bergverlag Rudolf Rother, Munich, 1986.

Gramminger, Ludwig, *We recover the bodies of our comrades. Eiger North Wall, 1935–36,* in MacInnes, Hamish, *High Drama, Mountain Rescue Stories from Four Continents.* Hodder & Stoughton, London, 1980; The Mountaineers, Seattle, 1981.

Gruner, Dorothea, *Hesch e Kiosk a der Eigernordwand? Schülersprache, dargestellt am Beispiel Berns,* Viktoria Verlag, Ostermundigen, 1977.

Gurtner, Othmar, *EntgPotzung der Eigerwand,* in *Berge der Welt,* 1958/59, Zürich, pages 21–43.

Hargreaves, Alison, *A Hard Day's Summer, Six classic North Faces Solo,* Coronet Books, Hodder & Stoughton, London, 1994.

Harlin, John, *The Eigerwand,* in *American Alpine Journal,* vol. 13, 1963, pages 362–374.

Harrer, Carina; Heinrich Harrer, *Alle Träume beginnen in der Jugend,* Pinguin-Verlag Innsbruck; Umschau-Verlag, Frankfurt a. M., s. d.

Harrer, Heinrich, *Das Buch vom Eiger,* Pinguin-Verlag, Innsbruck, 1989.

Harrer, Heinrich, *The White Spider,* Granada, London, 1983 (rev. ed.); Dutton, New York, 1960.

Haston, Dougal, *In High Places,* Hutchinson, London, 1974; Macmillan, New York, 1973.

Haston, Dougal, *The Eiger,* Cassell, London, 1974.

Heckmair, Anderl, (traduit par Loulou Boulaz) *Les trois derniers problèmes des Alpes,* Arthaud, Paris 1996.

Heckmair, Anderl, *Alpiniste,* Editions Guérin, Chamonix, 1997.

Heckmair, Anderl, *La conquête de la face nord de l'Eiger,* in *Alpinisme GHM* 1939, p. 1–7.

Heckmair, Anderl; Vörg, Ludwig; Kasparek, Fritz; Harrer, Heinrich, *Um die Eigernordwand,* Zentralverlag der NSDAP, Franz Eher Nachfolger, Munich, 1938.

Hiebeler, Toni, *Abenteuer Eiger,* Albert Müller Verlag, Zürich, 1973.

Hiebeler, Toni, *Combats pour l'Eiger,* Arthaud, Paris, 1966.

Hiebeler, Toni, *Die Retter. Geschichte und Abenteuer der Rettung aus der Luft.* Schweizer Verlagshaus, Zürich, 1978.

Hiebeler, Toni, *Eigerwand. Von der Erstbesteigung bis heute,* Goldmann Taschenbuch, 1978.

Hiebeler, Toni, *North Face in Winter,* Barrie & Rockcliff, London, 1962; Lippincott, Philadelphia, 1963.

Hiebeler, Toni, *Première hivernale de la face nord de l'Eiger,* in *La Montagne,* revue du CAF, 1961–1962, p. 61 and following pages.

Hiebeler, Toni, *SOS roc et glace,* Ed. Arthaud, Grenoble, 1976.

Hiebeler, Toni, *Swischen Himmel und Hölle: Aus dem Leben eines Bergsteigers,* Wilhelm Limpert Verlag, Frankfurt, 1965.

Jegerlehner, Johannes, *Bergführer Melchior. Ein Jungfrau-Roman,* G. Grote'sche Verlagsbuchhandlung, Berlin, 1929.

Jemelin Erika, *Die Wand. Tagebuch eines jungen Bergsteigers,* Orell Füssli Verlag, Zürich, 1936.

Jourdan, Frank, *Im Lot. Grenzgänge in Fels und Eis,* Panico Alpinverlag, Köngen, 1995.

Jungen, Peter, *Winterbegehung der Japaner-Directissima an der Aigernordwand,* in *Die Alpen,* 1971, pages 135–142.

Karl, Reinhard, *Erlebnis Berg, Zeit zum Atmen.* Alpinen Klassiker, Verlag J. Berg, Munich, 1993.

Kasparek, Fritz, *Vom Peilstein zur Eiger-Nordwand. Erlebnisse eines Bergsteigers,* Verlag "Das Bergland-Buch," Salzburg/Stuttgart, s.d.

Krakauer, Jon, *Eiger Dreams. Ventures Among Men and Mountains.* Lyons & Burford 1990; Anchor Book, New York, 1990.

Kuchar, Radovan, *Deset Velkych Sten. Prag 1967. Allemand, Zehn grosse Wände,* Orell Füssli Verlag, Zürich, 1968.

Lachenal, Louis, *Carnets du Vertige,* Editions Guérin, Chamonix, 1996.

Lachenal, Louis, *Eigerwand,* in *Alpinisme*

GHM (Paris), 1948, p. 39 and following pages.

Langley, Bob, *Traverse of the Gods,* Michael Joseph, London 1980.

Lauper, Hans, *L'Eiger,* in *Alpinisme GHM* (Paris) 1933, p. 287.

Lehne, Jörg; Haag, Peter, *Eiger, 30 jours de combat pour la "Directissime,"* Hatier, Paris, 1967.

Leroux, Pierre, *Guide,* Arthaud, Paris, 1989.

Lunn, Arnold, *The Mountains of Youth,* Eyre & Spottiswoode, London, 1943.

Lütolf, Theo, *Das Drama am Eiger,* Verein für kulturellen Aufbau, Zürich, 1936.

Machardy, Charles, *The Ice Mirror,* Fontana, London, 1973.

MacInnes, Hamish, *The Eigerwand 1957–62,* in MacInnes, *High Drama, Mountain Rescue Stories from Four Continents,* Hodder & Stoughton, London, 1980; The Mountaineers, Seattle, 1981.

Masterson, Whit, *Man on a Nylon String,* W. H. Allen, London; New York, Dodd Mead, 1963.

Messner, Reinhold, *The Big Walls,* Kaye & Ward, London, Oxford, New York, 1978.

Nobs, Ernst, *Die Wand,* in Nobs, *Breitlauinen. Oberländer Novellen,* Morgarten Verlag, Zürich, 1956, p. 7–55.

Olsen, John Edward, *The Climb up to Hell,* Gollancz, London, 1962; Harper & Row, New York, 1963.

Patey, Tom, *A Short Walk with Whillans; Two Tiny Figures, The John Harlin Song (Two Ballads),* in Patey, *One Man's Mountains,* Canongate; Edinburgh; The Mountaineers, Seattle, 1998.

Piola, Michel, *La face nord de l'Eiger,* in *Annales du GHM,* 1988.

Rapp, Christian, *Höhenrausch. Der deutsche Bergfilm,* Sonderzahl, Vienna, 1997.

Raymond, Diana, *The Climb,* Cassell, London, 1962.

Rébuffat, Gaston, *Starlight and Storm,* Kaye & Ward, London; Oxford, New York, 1968.

Reinisch, Gertrude, *Wanda Rutkiewicz–Karawane der Träume,* Bergverlag Rother, Munich, 1998.

Renker, Gustav, *L'épopée de la paroi nord,* Jeheber, Genève, 1952.

Roberts, David, *A Mountain of Trouble,* in Roberts, *Escape Routes,* The Mountaineers, Seattle, 1997.

Roeper, Malte, *Auf Abwegen. Bergsteigen und andere Zwischenfälle,* Rother Verlag, Munich, 1995.

Roth, Arthur, *Eiger, Wall of Death,* Norton, New York; Gollancz, London, 1982.

Rubi, Rudolf, *Der Eiger, Berner Heimatbuch 74,* Verlag Paul Haupt, Berne, 1979.

Sayer, Peter, *Der tragische Tod des Bergsteigers Toni Kurz. Tragödie in drei Akten mit Erzähler,* Ludwigshafen, 1987.

Schlömmer, Leo, *Meine Welt die Berge. Vom Dachstein zum Mount Everest,* Verlag Styria, Graz, 1973.

Schwanda, Hans, *Heldentum und Tragik im Alpinismus,* in Barobek, Hans, *Weg ins Licht,* Wiener Verlag, 1943, p. 141–143.

Schwendener, Kurt, *Rettungen und Leichenbergungen aus der Eigernordwand 1935–1987,* Grindelwald, 1987.

Simpson, Joe, *This Game of Ghosts,* Jonathan Cape Random House, London, 1993; The Mountaineers, Seattle, 1994.

Somers, Dermot, *Nightfall,* in Somers, *Mountains and Other Ghosts,* Diadem Books, London, 1990.

Sonnier, Georges, *Eiger* (roman), Albin Michel, Paris, 1977.

Stangier, Siegfried, *Les secours qui tombent du ciel, un pionnier du sauvetage aérien raconte ses missions dramatiques,* Arthaud, Paris, 1982.

Steiner, Max, *Guschti, der Eiger-Flieger,* Bergroman. Frieling, Berlin 1994.

Strutt, Edward L., *Valedictory Address,* in *Alpine Journal,* vol. L, 1938, p. 9. (Page 311, the following judgment is made on the North face: "The Eigerwand may be said to possess little or no 'mountaineering' value."

Terray, Lionel, *Le sauvetage de l'Eiger,* in *La Montagne,* revue du CAF, 1957–58, p. 164 and following pages.

Terray, Lionel, *Conquistadors of the Useless,* Gollancz, London, 1963; *Borders of the Impossible,* Doubleday, New York, 1964

Thomas, D. M., *Lying Together,* London, 1990.

Townend, Paul, *The Man on the End of the Rope,* Fontana, London, 1962; Dutton, New York, 1960.

Trevanian, *Eiger Sanction,* Crown, New York, 1972; Heinemann, London, 1973.

Unsworth, Walt, *North Face,* Hutchinson, London, 1969.

Vanis, Erich, *Im steilen Eis. 50 Eiswände in den Alpen,* BLV Verlagsgesellschaft, Munich, 1964.

Widmann, Joseph Victor, *Der Held des Eiger,* in Widmann, *Touristennovellen,* Verlag der J. G. Cotta'schen Buchhandlung, Stuttgart, 1892.

Zebhauser, Helmuth, *Alpinismus im Hitlerstaat,* Rother Verlag, Munich, 1998.

Zinniker, Otto, *Die Nordwand,* Walter Loepthien AG, Meiringen, 1960.

Zwahlen, Otto, *Der Kampf um die Eiger-Nordwand, Illustrierter Bericht über die Tragödie 1935 und 1936 in der Eiger-Nordwand,* Buchdruckerei zum Basler Berichtshaus AG, Bâle, 1936.

Photo credits

Christoph Aeby, Edmund von Fellenberg, Rudolph Gerwer, *Das Hochgebirge von Grindelwald*, Coblenz, 1865 : 212-213.
Jost von Allmen: 6, 11, 13,15, 38-39, 59, 216-217.
Die Alpen/Revue du Club alpin suisse: 18 (1938), 52 (1936).
Walter Amstutz, *Der Schneehase*. Annuaire du Ski club académique suisse 1981–1983: 94.
Daniel Anker: 37, 41, 54.
Collection Daniel Anker: 136 (b), 165, 167 (t,b), 197.
Daniel H. Anker: 163.
Ascent, San Francisco, 1976: 113 (t).
Berge No. 5, Berne, 1984: 148.
Archives Bergfalken: 2, 75, 78, 79, 80-81, 82 (t).
Marco Bomio: 51, 71 (t,b), 99 (t), 105, 199, 200, 201.
Chris Bonington, *I Chose to Climb*, London, 1966: 20 (b), 139 (t).
Robert Bösch: B. Cover, 9, 49, 57, 89, 101, 103, 117 (b), 127, 143, 169, 195.
Ueli Bühler: 155 (b).
Compagnie des guides de Grindelwald: 73.
Bruno Cormier/Agence Vertical: 93, 95, 130, 131(t,b).
Filmbild Fundus Robert Fischer: 113 (b).
Roland Flück: 33.
Andrea Forlini: 86, 121, 164.
Martin Funk/VAW: 99 (m).
Collection Yvano Ghirardini: 129 (t).
Peter Gillman, Dougal Haston, *Eiger Direct*, New York, 1966: 77.

Collection Heinz Glaser-Gertsch: 32, 92.
Ludwig Gramminger/Archives Hans Steinbichler: 12, 20 (t), 58, 63, 189, 190, 191 (t,b), 192 (b), 193 (t,b).
Archives Josef Gloger: 67, 112.
Michael Gruber/Collection Kaspar Ochsner: 83, 85.
Markus Gyger: 16–17.
Roland Hammann: 69, 84.
Heinrich Harrer, *White Spider*, New York, 1960: 133.
Anderl Heckmair, *Alpiniste*, Chamonix, 1997: 138 (b), 176.
Toni Hiebeler, *Abenteuer Eiger*, Zürich, 1973: 88.
Toni Hiebeler: *Combats pour l'Eiger*, Paris, 1966: 140 (m).
Archives Jungfraubahn: 31, 36, 42, 43, 44 (t,b), 45, 46, 47, 98, 158.
Keystone: 141 (l).
Klubhüttenalbum des Schweizer Alpen-Club, 1911: 72.
Stefan König, Florian Trenker, *Bera Luis. Das Phänomen Luis Trenker*, Munich, 1992: 117 (t).
Edwin Krähenbühl/Collection Terray: 155 (t).
Jon Krakauer: 150.
Peter Krebs: 99 (b).
Yuko Maki/collection Rudolf Rubi: 202, 206.
La Montagne, revue du Club Alpin Français, 1935: 55.
Ernst Moeller/*Alpine Journal* Vol. 49, 1937: 160.

Xavier Murillo: 129 (b), 134.
Kaspar Ochsner: 4, 27, 76, 82 (b), 133.
John E. Olsen, *The Climb up to Hell*, New York, 1963: 188, 192 (t).
Michel Piola: 149.
Gaston Rébuffat, *Starlight and Storm*, New York, 1968: 128.
Ringier Dokumentation Bild + Text: 145.
René Robert: 144, 146-147, 179.
Collection Rudolf Rubi: 10, 14 (t,b), 22 (t,b), 24, 50, 70, 98, 120, 122, 123, 125 (b), 136 (t), 137, 140 (t), 196.
Rudolf Rubi, *Der Eiger*, 1979: 102.
Ernst Schudel: 203.
Musée alpin suisse: 139 (b), 141 (t), 154.
Schweizerische Bankgesellschaft: 53.
Archives fédérales suisses: 29, 30, 45 (t).
Schweizerisches Institut für Kunstwissenschaft: 211, 213 (b).
Markus Schwyn/Musée alpin suisse: 23 (r).
Hannes Stähli: 97, 106, 107, 109, 111, 116 (t,b), 159, 161.
Collection Hannes Stähli: 124 (b), 125 (t).
Thomas Ulrich: 19, 35, 91, 110, 114-115, 119, 153, 157, 187, 204-205, 209.
Um die Eiger-Nordwand, Munich, 1938: 5, 23 (l), 25, 61, 66, 124 (t) , 138 (t), 170, 171, 172, 173, 181, 184, 185.
Vertical No. 1, 1985: 140 (b), 151.
Ludwig Vörg, *Um die Eiger-Nordwand*, Munich, 1938: 180, 182, 183 (t,b).
Christoph Wyss: 33.
Sammlung Elsbeth et Niklaus Wyss: 210, 215 (t,b).

© 2000 by The Mountaineers Books, 1001 SW Klickitat Way, Suite 201, Seattle, Washington 98134

All rights reserved. No part of this book may be reproduced in any form, or by any electronic, mechanical, or other means without written permission from the publisher.

Printed February 2000; Printed in the European Union by Pollina s.a. - n° 79550.B

© by AS Verlag & Buchkonzept AG, Zurich, 1998
Title of the edition in German: *Eiger—Die Vertikale Arena*

Cover: *Eiger Peak, Grindelwald, Switzerland* (photo: © Jack Olson).

Library of Congress Cataloging-in-Publication Data
Eiger, die vertikale Arena. English.
Eiger, the vertical arena / edited by Daniel Anker—1st English language ed.
    p. cm.
    Includes bibliographical references.
    ISBN 0-89886-679-0 (hardcover)
    1. Mountaineering—Switzerland—Eiger—History. 2. Eiger (Switzerland)—Description and travel. I. Title: Eiger. II. Anker, Daniel. III. Title.
GV199.44.S92 E35213 2000
796.52'2'0949454--dc21
                                            99-050425